Unwin Education Books: 4

THE BACKGROUND OF IMMIGRANT CHI

Books by Ivor Morrish

Disciplines of Education
Education Since 1800
The Background of Immigrant Children

Unwin Education Books
Series Editor: Ivor Morrish, B.D., B.A., Dip.Ed. (London), B.A. (Bristol).

1. Education Since 1800 IVOR MORRISH
2. Moral Development WILLIAM KAY
3. Physical Education for Teaching BARBARA CHURCHER
4. The Background of Immigrant Children IVOR MORRISH
5. Organising and Integrating the Infant Day JOY TAYLOR

Unwin Education Books: 4
Series Editor: Ivor Morrish

The Background of Immigrant Children

IVOR MORRISH
Principal Lecturer in Education
La Sainte Union College of Education
Southampton

London
GEORGE ALLEN AND UNWIN LTD
RUSKIN HOUSE MUSEUM STREET

First published in 1971

ISBN 0 04 301034 2 (Cloth)
ISBN 0 04 301035 0 (Paper)

Printed in Great Britain
in 10 point Times Roman
by Cox & Wyman Ltd
London, Fakenham and Reading

To My Mother and Father

Contents

Illustrations

ACKNOWLEDGEMENTS

The author and publishers are grateful to the following
for supplying the photographs numbered below, and for
permitting their use:
Paul Popper Ltd: Nos 1 (top), 9–12
J. Allan Cash: (Nos 1 (bottom), 2, 3, 4 (top)
Jamaican High Commission: No. 4 (bottom)
Information Service of India: India House, London: Nos 5–8.

Author's Preface

The purpose of this book is not primarily to provide glimpses of the village life of the Punjabi Sikh, the religious festivals of the Gujarati Hindu, the food tabus of the Muslim, or the communal activities of the West Indian 'yard' society – although the writer fully recognizes the importance of a knowledge of all these things. My main aim has been to convince the student that, in order to understand the problems of the 'immigrant' child, he must have more than a smattering of knowledge of odd marriage customs, exotic foods, and national dress. We must regard these things as the mere external trappings of something far more vital and basic if we are to tackle the fundamental problems of colour, culture and race differences.

If there is to be not merely tolerance but also deep understanding in our multi-cultural society, we must make the effort to get inside the very minds of the members of other cultural groups. This is why I have, for example, used so much space on the discussion of the religious thoughts and ideas of these societies, not (I hope) at too superficial a level. But I have attempted also to take cognizance of the fact that many books on the background of immigrants leave one with the impression that nothing has developed in their countries since they acquired self-government. I have tried, to some extent at least, to redress the balance by showing how the three societies that I have selected for consideration in this book are attempting to meet their own serious and growing social, educational and economic problems. All this is, to me, an essential feature of the 'immigrant' background and culture.

I obviously owe a great debt to all the authors I have referred to and quoted; but I am particularly grateful for all the generous help afforded me by the High Commissions for India, Pakistan and Jamaica. It also gives me great pleasure to thank my many students for the way in which they have always willingly shared their knowledge, experience and literature. Finally, without my wife's constant encouragement and her patient reading and typing of my manuscript, I would certainly never have completed it.

Southampton   IVOR MORRISH
Hants

Common Ground

In any discussion of the development of a multi-racial society and in the consideration of any immigrant problems, it is commonplace to begin with some reference to the stark differences of background and culture, and to proceed with a delineation of the culture-shocks and culture contacts that arise. It is, naturally, my purpose to deal with these latter; no serious writer could hope to avoid them; but what I hope to do throughout is to indicate that there are innumerable possibilities of 'common ground' between the various races and cultures that are meeting and evolving within our society.

Of course there are geographical differences that have produced a variety of racial distinctions; of course there are socio-economic factors that have led to vastly heterogeneous social developments; and of course there are rich diversities of religious belief and concept which have led to whole structures of philosophical and theological doctrines and their accompanying forms of activity and worship. No one could ignore these things. But if we are to get to grips with those who join our society with vastly different social formats, *mores* and ideals we must seek those things which are common as well as those which are at variance. We must remember that our differences have arisen largely through geographical distance during long periods of historical time. We are now being brought together in the same area in present time, and our future lies together. It is, therefore, as important to elicit our common ground, and to build upon that together, as to delineate in great detail our multitudinous differences, which can emphasize only the barriers to co-operative action.

To elicit common ground is to go deeper than tacitly to accept our differences, each of us invariably with a sense of his own superior knowledge of truth and reality. A 'liberal' acceptance of our dissimilarities can almost as easily lead to the formation of ghettos and disparate culture groups as an 'illiberal' rejection of diversities regarded as incommensurable. To 'live together' is not the same as living side by side in segregation or in some form of cultural apartheid. It means not merely to share the economy of a society and its social amenities: it signifies a mutual acceptance at certain human, mental and spiritual levels. This is not simply a question of allowing the other man 'his point of view', nor even of knowing what that point of view is. It is a question of reaching out for the other in dialogue in order to find some level of identity with the other.

In an essay entitled 'Towards a Multi-Racial Society' (1), Dipak Nandy makes the point that as a result of perpetually thinking in terms of the immigrant as a 'problem' we tend to regard him as a deviant or as a member of some sub-standard group. In consequence there is a considerable emphasis upon the problems of educating the immigrant. But *we* are as much a problem as the immigrant. We can no longer think of ourselves as the highly generous benefactors who shelter the world's refugees, and who can then withdraw from all further responsibility except, of course, that of providing them with the necessities envisaged by a welfare state, including a minimum of education. The introduction of other races into our society can no longer be regarded as an isolated, self-contained problem; this introduction has already changed *us* and our relationships within our society. It is as much a problem of educating ourselves as of educating immigrants.

There is a very real sense in which the inroads into our society by immigrants from all over the world, and our general move towards a multiracial society, should lead to fundamental changes within the whole of our school curricula. And these should be changes, not in order to accommodate and educate a million or so immigrants, but in order to make us fully aware of the richness of their cultures, and of the immense varieties and possibilities that they bring with them for our own social, personal and spiritual expansion.

Our knowledge of the history of India, for example, should extend to something far deeper, and perhaps more elevating, than the expansion in one particular area of the British Empire. For many English people India connotes little more than snake-charmers, yogis, fakirs, maharajahs and the rope-trick, with perhaps a dash of Kipling. But a close examination of the prehistory of India has revealed, since the early 1920s, the existence of a fascinating pre-Aryan civilization in the Indus Valley, centred upon Mohenjo-Daro and Harappa (2). The Harappa culture existed from about 3000 B C to 1500 B C. Could we really expect to 'educate' such a people as the Indians in the sophisticated and technological developments of our own culture without being sensitively aware of theirs?

Our former imperial contacts with the outposts of our world still linger with us as the method of our present attitudes towards our immigrants. We conquered them, did our best (as we thought) to convert them from savagery and paganism to civilization and Christianity; and too often they bring with them reminders, such as their religion, their customs, and their dress, not of our success but of our failure. But even a cursory look at their religions and cultures will reveal something of that 'perennial philosophy' to which Aldous Huxley (3) and many other thinkers have referred. They always had something to give us if only we had been ready to listen and not quite so anxious to proselytize. Just consider the Vedic verse (4):

> Prajapatir vai idam agre asit;
> Tasya vag divitiya asit;
> Vag vai Paramam Brahma.
>
> (In the beginning was Prajapati, or Brahman;
> With whom was the word;
> And the word was verily the Supreme Brahman.)

Hindu philosophy and religious mysticism are certainly much older than Christian thought; and, although the minutiae of theological exegesis may reveal a multitude of incompatible differences, there is a wealth of common ground to be revealed between Eastern and Western thought. There may certainly be no literary connection between Johannine thought and the quotation from the Vedas above, but it is equally certain that there is a spiritual and intuitive connection. The insights of the deeply religious are not the prerogative of any particular country or of any individual generation; they belong to every race and every age. If we would take the trouble to examine them more closely we would inevitably find that commitment to truth will lead us to an identity with men of every shade of thought and belief. It is commitment to some peculiar and obscurantist interpretation of truth that divides men, not truth itself. As E. W. F. Tomlin has remarked:

'The Western World, having afforded the Orient some dubious specimens of its own wisdom, may well profit from deeper acquaintance with this great oriental tradition, thereby calling to mind the source of wisdom from which its own faith is derived' (15).

In seeking a common ground there is no suggestion that we should also seek to elide all differences. The proposition is, quite simply, that the differences are frequently more patent and obtrusive, and therefore divisive. We should become more intellectually and factually aware of them, it is true, so that we are less influenced by ignorant prejudice and partiality. But if we were equally more conscious of the common ground, the differences would soon find their proper level and be accepted for what they really are. Tolerance, real tolerance, is born of knowledge, understanding, sympathetic awareness, and a sense of unity – not of a generalized, ignorant and aphoristic attitude of 'live and let live'.

In the evolution of a multi-racial society we are not just doing something to the immigrants to make them more acceptable to our own white community. Nor are we, for our part, absorbing a few incidental facts about *purdah*, curry, *gurdwara* or *shalwar* – important though these may be.

B

Integration implies more than the learning of English on their part and a bit of background material on ours. We are not concerned simply with group or individual survival; we are concerned with both total community and the quality of life. An evolving multi-racial society is implicated not in the 'integration of the immigrant', but in the elicitation of community through the absorption by both host and immigrant of each other's culture. In the words of Dipak Nandy:

'Each age and each generation has to re-define for itself what it means to be human, and perhaps, if we are wise, we will allow the coloured communities to help us shape our idea of humanity' (6).

REFERENCES

1 Nandy, Dipak, 'Towards a Multi-Racial Society', pp. 32–4 in N.C.C.I. publication, *Towards a Multi-Racial Society* (National Committee for Commonwealth Immigrants, n.d.).
2 *Vide* Thapar, Romila, *A History of India*, Vol. I (Penguin, 1966).
3 Huxley, Aldous, *The Perennial Philosophy* (Collins, Fontana Books, 1946).
4 Isherwood, C. (ed.), *Vedanta for the Western World* (Allen & Unwin, 1948), pp. 150–1. Quoted from the Vedas.
5 Tomlin, E. W. F., *The Eastern Philosophers: an Introduction* (Hutchinson, 1968), p. 313.
6 Op. cit., p. 33.

Part One
The West Indians

Chapter 1

General Background
of the West Indies

A THE WEST INDIAN REGION
In his book entitled *The West Indian Scene*, G. Etzel Pearcy discusses some
of the complexities involved in the terminology used to identify the area
with which we are here concerned (1). The situation becomes even more
complicated when one is talking not merely of islands but also of parts of
the mainland of Central and Southern America, and when an island such
as Dominica is listed variously as belonging now to the Leeward Islands,
and then elsewhere to the Windward Islands. In 1957 the name 'The West
Indies' was adopted to describe the federation of ten British colonies in the
Caribbean. The federation, however, broke up in 1962 so that the term 'The
West Indies' is something of a misnomer and at best misleading. Pearcy
argues that

'reference to the West Indian *islands*, *region* or *realm* avoids the difficulty of
distinguishing the more limited political from the broad geographic
connotation, though in some instances the context makes the meaning
clear' (2).

There are objections also to the term 'Caribbean islands' as a synonym
for the West Indian islands since, as Pearcy points out, the archipelago
forms only the eastern and northern limits of the sea.
    In an area such as this, where geographical and political terms are some-
times identical but have differing connotations, it is not always easy to be
clear and accurate. Despite, therefore, the adoption of somewhat popular
usage the terms 'West Indian' and 'Caribbean' will here be used interchangeably; and 'Caribbean islands' will be synonymous with 'West
Indian islands'. In a consideration of the problems of emigration from this
area we are obviously more involved with some islands than with others,
and in this part of the book we are particularly concerned with Jamaica,
Trinidad, Tobago, Barbados; the Windward Islands including Dominica,
St Lucia, St Vincent and Grenada; the Leeward Islands including Anguilla,
Sombrero, Barbuda, St Kitts, Antigua and Montserrat; and the Virgin
Islands of Tortola and Anegada.
    In addition to the West Indian or Caribbean islands mentioned above we

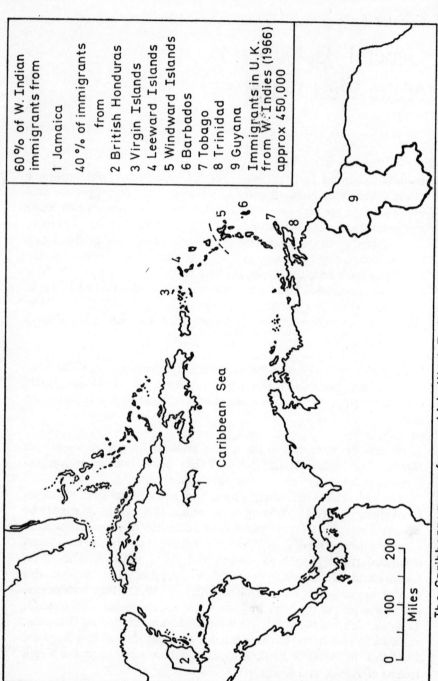

60% of W. Indian immigrants from

1 Jamaica

40% of immigrants from

2 British Honduras
3 Virgin Islands
4 Leeward Islands
5 Windward Islands
6 Barbados
7 Tobago
8 Trinidad
9 Guyana

Immigrants in U.K. from W. Indies (1966) approx 450,000

Caribbean Sea

0   100   200
Miles

The Caribbean: areas from which West Indians have emigrated to the U.K.

are also concerned with certain areas on the mainland of Central America, namely British Honduras; and on the mainland of South America, namely Guyana, formerly British Guiana. But whether the Isla de Margarita is considered to be West Indian, or the Bahamas to be included in the term Caribbean are matters of little more than academic interest. Certainly they are included in annual statistical lists concerned with the British West Indies, but these are not areas from which our West Indian immigrants come (3).

Certain geographical and environmental facts are very important when we are considering the background of such immigrants. One such fact is that by no stretch of imagination can one think of 'The West Indies' as a single unit, either in terms of land mass or in terms of a homogeneous people. To a limited extent there are parallels here with East and West Pakistan. The Caribbean arc is some 1,500 miles long, and no point on any of the islands is more than fifty-five miles from the sea. Sir Learie Constantine, speaking of the fact that the various branches of West Indian people were virtually strangers to one another, has said that

'now we are in Britain, we have perhaps for the first time in our lives seen so many of our countrymen from other islands. That to us is not strange, for water divides us, the sea divides us all, and Barbados and Montserrat may be less familiar to a Jamaican than Bermondsey or Liverpool' (4).

There is, of course, nothing particularly surprising about this since there are many Londoners who have seen more of France and Spain than they have of England. But it is a warning to all members of the host society that one can no more generalize about a 'West Indian' than one can about an Englishman.

The climate of the West Indian region generally is tropical – in fact, the whole of the area with which we are concerned lies between the Tropic of Cancer and the Equator, from British Honduras and the Virgin Islands in the north to Guyana in the south. The temperatures are high, there is plentiful rainfall, and there are cooling breezes. The annual range of temperature, however, for any part of the archipelago rarely exceeds 10 degrees F. (5). It is hardly surprising that West Indians who emigrate to this country feel both the cold and the changes in temperature a real problem to cope with, at least for some time after their arrival.

Every year the Caribbean suffers from the destructive effect of the hurricane. Throughout the whole region there may be from four to six of them each year, whilst in a particular island such as Jamaica the incidence is about one in every four years. But the most serious effects of the hurricanes are not simply the physical devastation and havoc they cause; they have a certain debilitating psychological effect upon the islanders. There does not seem to be much point in erecting solid constructions if they can all be destroyed in a matter of minutes. And when plantations can disappear with equal ease it is perhaps not surprising that many adopt an attitude of *dolce far niente*.

In thinking in terms of the natural resources of the Caribbean it must be remembered that what was for many years one of its most prolific productions, namely sugar, was first introduced by the Spaniards and then developed by the British, French and Dutch. In many islands, or parts of islands, the fertility of the soil is perhaps the greatest natural resource available, with its consequent production of lush fruit and vegetation. Indeed, Professor Fernando Henriques has suggested that this is not always an unmixed blessing; and he refers to the parish of Portland in the north-eastern corner of Jamaica where the land is particularly productive and requires no artificial fertilization. Henriques quotes the owner of a plantation who said, pointing to a field lying just outside the window of his house,

'You see that field. There is every conceivable fruit and vegetable in the West Indies growing there, and do I have to do anything to them? No, I just stick them in the ground and they grow. That's what's the matter with the people of Portland, the soil is too good for them. They're all lazy. Look, I import labour from a hard parish like St Elizabeth where they have to fight the soil to grow anything, and they work marvellously until the Portlanders corrupt them' (6).

In addition to the luxuriant growth of fruit and vegetation there are some natural mineral resources in the area we are considering. For example, in Jamaica there are deposits of bauxite which were first discovered during the Second World War. The deposits are estimated as having a potential in the region of 300 million tons, or about one-fifth of the world's total discovered supply. On the island of Trinidad there are deposits of pitch or asphalt which, it is claimed, are unequalled in the world. These deposits have now been mined for almost a century and, according to Pearcy, the continued removal of asphalt during that period has barely reduced the level 'thanks to replacement by seepage from underground sources of oil near by'(7). There are also in Trinidad some regular petroleum deposits and some offshore findings; these are now estimated at 500 million barrels.

B THE EARLY PEOPLES AND THEIR ORIGINS

The aboriginal inhabitants of the West Indian islands are usually referred to as Amerindians, or the 'Indians of America'. These Indians participated in very simple forms of agriculture such as growing roots and gathering berries. One of the earliest groups of Amerindians to exist in the Antilles were a people called the Ciboney who, according to some authorities, migrated originally from Florida. They lived by hunting and fishing.

Eventually another group of Indians displaced the Ciboney – these were the Arawaks who, some believe, came from South America. They quickly dispersed throughout the islands, including the Virgin Islands, Jamaica, the Bahamas and Cuba. The Arawaks lived in thatched villages containing sometimes as many as a thousand houses, and they used cotton fibres to make clothes and to construct sleeping hammocks. In fact, compared with the Ciboney, the Arawaks were quite skilled in agriculture and they developed a large variety of fruits, roots and plants which included cassava, avocados, papayas, maize, manioc, and peanuts.

Each village had its chief, or *cacique* who was responsible for law and order and who also made the necessary contacts with other *caciques* in other villages, and even on other islands. Although the actual means of communication may have been different, there was something in its organization which was similar to the amazing communication system of the Incas throughout their empire. Among the Arawak groups it was customary to trade surplus goods by barter, although on some of the islands they certainly had gold, which they used for ornaments, masks and ceremonial dress generally. They were also skilled in fishing and sailing, and they apparently built long, narrow canoes for seventy or more men (8). They were skilled, too, in the production of artefacts both for domestic and ceremonial use as well as for purposes of barter; they made pots, wooden bowls, bows and poisoned arrows, as well as spears tipped with fishbone.

Just as the Arawaks had replaced the aboriginal Ciboney, so the Arawaks were gradually destroyed by another group of Indians called the Caribs. These latter were a cannibalistic people who came originally from South America, and raided the islands in their long-boats. They captured many of the Arawak women whom they took as their wives, and carried out cannibalistic rites upon the men. Thus they established themselves in the place of the Arawaks, particularly in some of the smaller islands of the Lesser Antilles. From these vantage points the Caribs began to raid in the Western Caribbean as far as Jamaica.

Like the Arawaks, the Caribs were skilled in sailing, and they developed their economy by cultivating a large number of fruits and vegetables, and by fishing. Although they were obviously in many ways a progressive, vigorous and certainly warlike race, the Carib men appear to have done very little themselves in the actual work of agriculture. As in many other simple societies, the really hard work in the fields was left mainly to the wives, who not only reared their children and looked after their homes but were regarded somewhat as chattels and directed labour.

When the Spanish conquistadores descended upon the Caribbean scene, during the last decade of the fifteenth century, these two main aboriginal groups began to disappear. This was one of the many examples of the way in which sudden, violent culture contact can destroy rather than enrich an existing simpler society. During the next 150 years after the arrival of the Spanish in the Caribbean, both the Amerindian culture and the Amerindian peoples were virtually eliminated. Apart from a very few Caribs living on a reservation in the island of Dominica, there are practically no aborigines left on the islands (9). Many of these brave people resisted with the aid of their primitive arms, but were no match for European armoury; others were killed off by the incidence of European diseases against which they had no resistance; and still others died after spells of various types of forced labour for their conquerors.

C FROM SLAVERY TO SELF-GOVERNMENT

African natives were first introduced into the West Indies as slaves by the Portuguese and Spanish during the early days of colonization. From that time until the abolition of the English slave trade in 1807, and the French slave trade in 1830, it has been estimated that something like twenty million African natives were sold out of Africa. How many of these survived to work in the West Indies it is not possible to say, although some estimates suggest that nearly two million slaves arrived in the English islands between 1651 and 1807, over one and a half millions in the French islands between 1664 and 1830, and about 900,000 in the Guianas and the Dutch West Indies (10).

These figures may be exaggerated, but one thing is clear: the black immigrants into the islands began to swell the population through the encouraged promiscuity between slaves. The disintegration of culture was inevitable since nothing was done to retain even the semblance of tribal *mores* or social structure; whilst the sole relief provided from the boredom and tyranny of forced labour was the complete lack of sexual tabu within the slave community. Slaves were bought and sold like cattle in order to meet the rapidly growing demands of the expanding sugar-cane industry.

Most of the slaves were shipped from the west coast of Africa where the trade centred on such areas as Angola and Senegal, although most of the slaves themselves came from the Congo and Nigeria. At first blush the attitude of the traders towards their cargo seems almost uneconomic as well as callous in view of the large number of deaths before a ship reached the West Indies from Africa. But, in fact, it proves to be sound economics as well since the demand, certainly for some time, exceeded the supply and in consequence better prices were received for slaves.

It has been emphasized by a number of writers, including Cahnman, Tannenbaum, Hoetink and Etzel Pearcy (11), that the treatment of slaves by the Spanish and by the British was fundamentally different. The Spaniards regarded the slaves as individuals, as persons, even if they were also pieces of property; and no master had absolute rights over his slaves.

Indeed, there were courts in which a master could be brought to task, and even lose his ownership, if there were sound evidence of maltreatment. There was also a practice during Spanish rule of what was known as *coartación*, whereby a slave paid for his freedom by instalments, and when the last payment had been made he was set free.

But, as Pearcy points out, although they were free under the law, manumitted slaves were never regarded as better than second-rate citizens (12). No Negro was allowed to carry firearms of any description, and there was a variety of restrictions regarding dress and behaviour in public and towards their European masters. In fact, the very word *coartación* (from the verb *coartar*, to limit) implies a 'restraint' or 'limitation' upon both ownership and freedom.

Slavery is always slavery, but it is possible to see how slavery under a democratic regime could be more inhumane than under a despotic rule. Despotism always sets limits to property ownership; democracy has tended to grant greater freedom to the individual over his personal property. Thus, under British rule, the slave-master had practically absolute power of life and death over his human slave property. The laws relating to slavery were almost all to the advantage of the white owners and to the detriment of the slaves. It took a considerable amount of political, social and religious propaganda to arouse any sort of public conscience in this country in relation to the plight of the slaves. A great deal was said and written about the problem, and such poets as William Cowper made their sympathetic and social comment in emotional verse:

> Still in thought as free as ever,
>   What are England's rights, I ask,
> Me from my delights to sever,
>   Me to torture, me to task?
> Fleecy locks, and black complexion
>   Cannot forfeit nature's claim;
> Skins may differ, but affection
>   Dwells in white and black the same (13).

Slave trade in the British Caribbean was abolished in 1807, and in 1833 the Emancipation of Slaves Act was passed through Parliament. The compulsory apprenticeship of slaves was a scheme which, it was hoped, would gradually acclimatize the slaves to their newly-won freedom and would help them to appreciate some of the responsibilities that went with wage-earning. But the apprenticeship scheme had little real support from either the former masters or the emancipated slaves. The associations of the previous years of slavery were all against the success of such a plan, and it was generally abandoned within about five years.

When the apprenticeship scheme finally failed, it became clear that both more plentiful and cheaper sources of labour than that of the emancipated slaves had to be sought. Labour markets were soon found in Europe, China and, in particular, India. The labour from China and India was indentured, usually for a period of five years, after which time the labourer was free to return home if he wished or to change his employer. During the period of indentured labour, which eventually ended in 1917, over half a million East Indians went to the West Indies under official immigration and indenture schemes.

Whilst emancipation certainly freed the Negro from the virtually legalized brutality of the slave-masters, it really meant for many that they were now free to work as hard as before for a minimum wage, or else to escape to the hills and live in disgusting conditions of squalor and poverty. Emancipation was a big word for a big ideal, with sometimes quite frightening and desolating consequences in actuality. As Pearcy puts it:

'Some began to scratch out a miserable existence on the mountainsides or other deserted areas because they were afraid to stay with the former master, and others stayed because they were afraid to go' (14).

There has been a considerable increase in population in the West Indies as a whole during the last 150 years. In 1960 it was estimated at about 19 millions, and by 1975 it is expected to reach at least 27 millions. These figures include, of course, the United States areas, the Dutch and French islands, and the independent states of Haiti, Cuba and the Dominican Republic. The population, in 1960, of the British islands (including Jamaica, Trinidad and Tobago) was in the region of 3,300,000; and with British Honduras and British Guiana it was nearly 4 millions. The largest increase has been that of Trinidad, whose population between the years 1844 and 1960 expanded eleven-fold (15).

With many of the islands becoming over-populated and lacking in employment, the only solution was a policy of migration, in particular to the United Kingdom. Immigrants have arrived in this country from all over the West Indian region. In 1966 the total figure was approximately half a million, of whom 60 per cent came from Jamaica and the remainder from British Honduras, Guyana and the islands from Trinidad in the south to the Virgin Islands in the north. The wheel has, in fact, come full circle. The lands which Europe peopled with Portuguese, Spanish, French, British and Dutch, as well as black Africans, Indians and Chinese, are sending back to Britain their own white descendants, Creoles, coloureds and blacks. And some of the problems that we have created through culture contact in the past are now being recreated in our own society in the present.

REFERENCES

1 Pearcy, G. Etzel, *The West Indian Scene* (Van Nostrand, 1965), pp. 17–22.
2 Ibid., pp. 17–18.
3 *Vide* Richmond, A. H., *The Colour Problem* (Penguin, revised edition 1961), p. 217.
4 Hooper, R. (ed.), *Colour in Britain* (B.B.C., 1965); Sir Learie Constantine is quoted on p. 27.
5 Pearcy, G. Etzel, op. cit., p. 33.
6 Henriques, F., *Family and Colour in Jamaica* (MacGibbon & Kee, 2nd edition 1968), p. 73.
7 Pearcy, G. Etzel, op. cit., p. 36.
8 *Vide* Augier, F. R. *et al.*, *The Making of the West Indies* (Longmans, 1960), Chapter 1.
9 Pearcy, G. Etzel, op. cit., p. 41.
10 Augier, F. R. *et al.*, op. cit., Chapter 7.
11 *Vide* Hoetink, H., *The Two Variants in Caribbean Race Relations* (O.U.P., 1967); Tannenbaum, F., *Slave and Citizen* (Knopf, N.Y., 1947); Pearcy, G. Etzel, op. cit.
12 Pearcy, G. Etzel, op. cit., p. 44.
13 Cowper, William, 'The Negro's Complaint'.
14 Pearcy, G. Etzel, op. cit., pp. 49–50.
15 Ibid., p. 51.

BIBLIOGRAPHY

Augier, F. R. *et al.*, *The Making of the West Indies* (Longmans, 1960).
Ayearst, M., *The British West Indies: the Search for Self-Government* (Allen & Unwin, 1960).
Bent, R. M. *et al.*, *A Complete Geography of Jamaica* (Collins, 1966).
Black, C. V., *History of Jamaica* (Collins, 1958).
Black, C. V., *The Story of Jamaica* (Collins, 1965).
Bryans, R., *Trinidad and Tobago* (Faber, 1967).
Burn, W. L., *The British West Indies* (Hutchinson's Univ. Lib., 1951).
Burns, A., *History of the British West Indies* (Allen & Unwin, 2nd edition 1965).
Caiger, S. L., *British Honduras: Past and Present* (Allen & Unwin, 1951).
Carley, M. M., *Jamaica: The Old and the New* (Allen & Unwin, 1963).
Central Office of Information, *Barbados* (H.M.S.O., 1966).
Central Office of Information, *Guyana* (H.M.S.O., 1966).
Chapman, E., *Pleasure Island: the Book of Jamaica* (Aberdeen Univ. Press, 6th edition 1965).
Francis, O. C., *The People of Modern Jamaica* (Dept. of Statistics, Kingston, Jamaica, 1963).
Guerin, D., *The British West Indies and their Future* (D. Dobson, 1961).
Henfrey, C., *The Gentle People: A Journey Among the Indian Tribes of Guiana* (Hutchinson, 1964).
Herskovits, J. M. and F., *Trinidad Village* (A. A. Knopf, 1947).
Hoetink, H., *The Two Variants in Caribbean Race Relations* (O.U.P., 1967).
Klass, M., *East Indians in Trinidad: A Study of Cultural Persistence* (Columbia Univ. Press, 1961).

Lowenthal, D. (ed.), *The West Indies Federation* (Columbia Univ. Press, 1961).
Macpherson, J., *Caribbean Lands: A Geography of the West Indies* (Longmans, 1963).
Naipaul, V. S., *The Middle Passage* (Deutsch, 1962).
Newman, P., *British Guiana: Problems of Cohesion in an Immigrant Society* (O.U.P., 1964).
Nicole, C., *The West Indies: Their People and History* (Hutchinson, 1965).
Norris, K., *Jamaica: The Search for an Identity* (O.U.P., 1962).
Parry, J. H. and Sherlock, P. M., *A Short History of the West Indies* (Macmillan, 2nd edition 1963).
Pearcy, G. Etzel, *The West Indian Scene* (Van Nostrand, 1965).
Sherlock, P. M., *West Indian Story* (Longmans, 1960).
Sherlock, P. M., *Jamaica Way* (Longmans, 1962).
Sherlock, P. M., *Caribbean Citizen* (Longmans, 2nd edition 1963).
Sherlock, P. M., *The West Indies* (Thames & Hudson, 1966).
Smith, M. G., *The Plural Society in the British West Indies* (Univ. of California Press, Berkeley, 1965).
Smith R. T., *British Guiana* (O.U.P., 1962).
Starkey, P. O., *The Economic Geography of Barbados* (Columbia Univ. Press, 1939).
Suze, J. A. de, *The New Trinidad and Tobago* (Collins, 14th edition 1965).
Waddell, D. A. G., *British Honduras: A Historical and Contemporary Survey* (O.U.P., 1961).
Williams, E., *History of the People of Trinidad and Tobago* (Deutsch, 1964).

Chapter 2

Religion in the
West Indies

A GENERAL INTRODUCTION

It is as difficult to be specific about religion in the West Indies as it is to be about religion in the USA or, for that matter, in any country which is multi-racial and multi-cultural. The West Indies, quite naturally, present their own particular problems historically and socially; historically, because they have experienced the invasion and regimes of a number of European countries; socially, because each island or group of islands, as well as countries on the mainland such as British Honduras and Guyana, have all their own individual background as well as a more general one.

We have already made reference to the great distances between the islands of the Caribbean and the comments made by Sir Learie Constantine with regard to this particular point (1). These physical distances have led to a variegated development with a resultant unfamiliarity and lack of contact between the various islands and West Indian societies. Indeed, it has been said that before the Second World War a letter which was sent direct from Barbados to Jamaica could take up to three months to arrive.

And this unfamiliarity is not simply a physical one: it relates also to the great variety of religious beliefs and customs to be found among the countries of the West Indies. Of course, in some, such as Jamaica, the whole spectrum of religious sects and cults is to be seen; in others there may be a greater unity of idea and purpose as expressed in a few denominations. Even a superficial study of the Caribbean culture, however, soon reveals some of the basic reasons for the difficulties experienced in integrating a people with such a varied culture.

Statistics on religion are notoriously inaccurate and misleading, but there have been some interesting figures published for Jamaica as a result of a census held in 1943 and another in 1960. The figures for 1943 are those provided by Professor Fernando Henriques (2), and those for 1960 are the present author's attempt to reduce to percentages the actual numbers, provided by the Jamaica Information Service, of adherents to the various churches and religions (3). The reader will note that Professor Henriques included a number of categories which do not appear in the 1960 figures, so that the percentages are not strictly comparable. At best they can only reflect trends, the most general being: an apparent move away from the more orthodox and traditional Protestant sects, such as the Anglican, Baptist, Methodist, Moravian and Presbyterian; an increase in the number of Roman Catholics, Adventists, Pentecostalists and devotees of the Church of God; a decrease in followers of the cult of Pocomania; and a considerable increase in those who either had no religion or would not specify any – a total of nearly 17 per cent as compared with 4·3 per cent in 1943.

Some of the reasons for these changes will be discussed later, but it is important first to trace the history of the rise of the various religious groups and sects in the development of the West Indies generally. It must be remembered also that something like 60 per cent of the West Indian immigrants to Britain come from Jamaica, so that much of the general discussion will centre upon that island. But the reader must also be aware that, whilst some areas appear to be diffuse and diverse in their religious development, other areas (such as Trinidad) have become predominantly Roman Catholic, whilst others (such as Barbados) have become mainly Protestant and Anglican. The reasons for these differences are chiefly of a historical nature. In general, the statistics quoted indicate that something like 60 per cent of the population of Jamaica are adherents of one of the more orthodox and established of the Christian denominations, whilst another 18 per cent belong to the Seventh Day Adventists, Church of God, Pentecostalists and so forth.

B THE RELIGION OF THE ABORIGINES

In discussing the religion of Jamaica and of the other islands of the West Indies, it is important to remember that neither the Negro nor the white man represents in any sense the indigenous element of this area. The aboriginal element of the Caribbean islands was, in the Greater Antilles, made up mostly of the Arawak Indians, who, it is believed, in all probability reached their new habitat from South America. In the Lesser Antilles the Caribs, who were skilled navigators of long ships holding up to fifty or more people, had by the end of the fifteenth century occupied most of the smaller islands, and even began raiding some of the larger islands including Jamaica.

The religion of the Arawaks was certainly animistic. Their stories and myths were largely of an aetiological character, invented to explain the causes of natural phenomena; and in this respect they differed very little from other simple, Amerindian societies. They worshipped two main gods, one male and one female; and this pair were responsible for the creation of all life and for natural fertility. But, like all primitive peoples, the Arawaks believed that all things had life and were inhabited by, or infused with, spiritual entities. These spirits, or *zemes*, could converse with them, pass on messages to them from the gods, and guide their public and private lives.

All the evils of man's experience, including sickness and bereavement, were caused through the anger of the *zemes*, which in turn had been aroused by man's foolish activity. It was therefore highly important to placate the *zemes* at all times, but particularly on certain public and ritualistic occasions. Festivals were held in their honour, and these were organized and conducted by a priestly or shamanistic hierarchy, who were held responsible for the health, happiness and fertility of the whole society. During the festivals the Indians dressed in all their finery, including feathers and shells, and painted themselves in specific symbolic and ritualistic ways.

Throughout the festival the worshippers used to sing and dance, and they would offer gifts of bread and meat to the *zemes*. After the gifts of food, other offerings of natural objects were made, and these were duly blessed by the priests. It was always assumed that the *zemes* were pleased with the presents offered to them and that the acceptance implied health and prosperity for the future. Once the ceremonies and festivities were all over, the priests would distribute the gifts to the people and these would be used during the ensuing year against the assaults of nature, such as hurricanes, fire, accidents and disease. The priests acted throughout as intermediaries between the *zemes* and the people, and upon them lay the responsibility for healing the diseases of people, animals and crops.

The religious ideas and beliefs of the Caribs, and of the Amerindians of Guyana (formerly British Guiana), were very similar to those of the Arawaks and to the native peoples of British Honduras: namely, animism and magic with a sense of the urgent necessity of placating evil and harmful spirits.

C THE ADVENT AND DEVELOPMENT OF CHRISTIANITY

When the first Spanish settlers arrived in Jamaica in 1509 they began an immediate campaign to convert the native population to Christianity. They built simple churches of straw and wood, which were gradually replaced by larger and more solid structures of stone, the first one being built at St Ann's Bay, then known as Sevilla Nueva. Abbeys were also constructed and abbots soon appointed. The Amerindian Arawaks, however, were not particularly impressed by the new religion preached to them, since they associated it very closely with the heavy work they were forced to do for their conquerors. Moreover, the Arawaks were unable physically to survive the harsh treatment they received at the hands of the conquistadores, and within a little over a century their population had declined from something in the region of 60,000 to 74 (4). It is interesting to note that at the census made in 1946 of the population of the British West Indies there were over 16,000 Amerindians in British Guiana and over 14,000 in British Honduras; but a mere handful remained in Trinidad and about 400 in the Windward Islands.

c

As the native population of Jamaica declined, the Spanish had to depend increasingly upon the use of Negro slaves who had been imported from Africa since the beginning of the sixteenth century. The colony, however, remained poverty-stricken and very open to the attacks of pirateers and runaway slaves, who ganged up in order to sack churches, pillage homes and cause havoc wherever they could. Added to all this the colonists suffered considerable damage and loss from hurricanes. In 1655, as a consequence of the failure of an expedition sent by Oliver Cromwell to attack Haiti, its leaders, Penn and Venables, went on to make an assault upon Jamaica and, after a brief struggle, this island became a British colony. It is not our purpose in this chapter to give the full history of the development of Jamaica into a crown colony, but it is important to note that the established Roman Catholic faith and the Spanish way of life were soon superseded by Protestantism and the current British *ambiance*.

King Charles II (1660–85) received reports from the colony concerning the general lack of religious organization, and the immorality and uncivilized behaviour of a certain proportion of the colonizers in the island. He therefore issued instructions that, in addition to rule by martial law, the Church of England was to become established in the colony in order, as he put it, 'to discourage vice and debauchery'. As an increasing number of settlers arrived, and the population of Negro slaves increased, the whole question of slavery and its morality began to be mooted. The planters made it quite clear that, whatever the Anglican clergy preached and taught, they did not want the slaves to get ideas above their station, which was essentially one of total subservience; nor did they want the slaves to be worried too much about such things as sexual morality. The planters and their white managers lived lives in which gambling, immorality and heavy drinking seemed to be the main forms of leisure activity. Female slaves were simply chattels to be used by their masters in any way they wished. Meanwhile the Anglican clergy took the path of discretion and exhorted the slaves to please their masters by working hard, and to accept with resignation the lot which God had predestined for them.

The number of Anglican clergymen in Jamaica at this time was very small, and there is no doubt that they felt that discretion was the better part of valour. Some of them also considered that they might be able to do more for their coloured parishioners if they did not openly oppose and anger the planters; others, of course, were just cowards. Henry Long, who published his *History of Jamaica* in 1774, considered that some clerics were more qualified to retail salt fish or to act as boatswains to privateers than to be Christian priests. Only twenty clergymen of the Church of England were listed in the Jamaican Almanac for 1812, and it became very clear that if the Anglican Church were to become in any sense a force in Jamaican society, or were to give even the most elementary instruction to its flock, whether white or black, the number of priests had to be increased. During the next ten years only another dozen clerics were appointed, and it was another two years, in 1824, before Jamaica was able to appoint its own bishop who was to be responsible for the selection, character and supervision of the clergy.

Whilst the Anglican Church did little or nothing to alleviate the sad and painful lot of the slave, there were other sects and denominations of Christianity gradually arriving and developing in the West Indies. In the middle of the eighteenth century, the Moravians were somewhat surprisingly invited by two wealthy plantation-owners to send missionaries to their estates in Jamaica. It seems fairly clear that, despite their humanity and good intentions, these owners did not fully understand or appreciate the real situation *vis-à-vis* the planters and the slaves. They were themselves living in England and were employing estate managers on the island to run their plantations for them. Planters on the spot were certainly not in favour of anything that gave the Negro a sense of his own worth, whether in the eyes of God or man. After the Moravians, missionaries of other denominations soon followed, including Wesleyan Methodists, Baptists, Presbyterians and Congregationalists. The Wesleyan Methodists were amongst some of the most enthusiastic in their desire to convert the Negro slaves, but also to improve their physical and material situation; and they quickly aroused the anger and opposition of the planters.

In 1782 there arrived on the Jamaican scene two American slaves who initiated the Native Baptist Movement. The Baptist denomination has always been the home of different and varying levels of thought, belief and faith, and has embraced all types of disciple: from the scholar, the intellectual, the keen Biblical critic to the fundamentalist and literalist, the authoritarian, the evangelist; from the brilliant teacher to the emotional orator; from the lover of freedom of thought and conscience to the superstitious and hidebound moralist. The two American slaves were simple and uneducated Negroes who easily mingled the Christian element of their faith with the superstition and the more pagan ideas of primitive cultures. Before long an invitation was extended by the Government to the Baptist Missionary Society in England to send missionaries to Jamaica. They were invited to go in order to establish what the Baptist message really was, and to assist in the development of the Baptist mission. The Baptist Missionary Society was only too happy to comply and the Jamaican Mission was established in 1814; it was not long before the Presbyterians and Congregationalists followed.

One of the seemingly inevitable tragedies of the spread of the Christian faith has been the incredibly disparate conglomeration of sects and denominations that has always followed the colonization of more primitive societies. Not so many years ago the native population of Papua pleaded that no more 'Christian' missionaries should be sent to their country; not because they were opposed to Christianity *per se* or to some of the wonderful 'mitsinaris' or missionaries who had helped them in their initial development from paganism and primitivity to something more akin to Western civilization. It was because they were becoming inextricably confused by the great variety of presentations of the Christian gospel from Jehovah's Witnesses to Roman Catholicism, to say nothing of the burgeoning of their own cargo and messianic cults. The present multiplicity of Christian sects and denominations in Jamaica and the West Indies generally is but another example of the proselytizing zeal of the many people who believe firmly that they have the only right presentation of the truth.

But, despite this sometimes confusing desire to convert to a particular sect or denomination rather than to some master faith, it should be noted that the nonconformist groups in Jamaica, in particular, worked together in order to improve the condition of the slaves by providing them with a programme of instruction in the whole question of the sanctity of human life and personality, the importance of self-respect and the development of a sense of individual responsibility. It did not take long for the planters to see in all this an attempt to end slavery and at the same time their own economic security, if not personal safety. The hostility which the planters very clearly expressed soon turned to open threats, and when the threats were ignored there followed deliberate and unveiled persecution. Some groups of proselytizers decided to act with discretion and to compromise; others, including the Baptists, stood firm and organized a plan for the abolition of slavery.

The liberty which the Baptists and Moravians in particular taught was blamed for the slave revolts which broke out in 1831, and these two sects were attacked by the established Anglican Church for their responsibility in the affair. A union, called the Colonial Church Union, was founded ostensibly to protect the rights of the Anglican Church. In actuality the union was a somewhat thinly disguised subterfuge designed to destroy the nonconformist missionary effort. The destruction of the latter's churches, mission-huts and property generally, and the hounding, persecution and beating of the missionaries themselves was carried out largely by the planters' tough employees. Leaders of the Moravian and Baptist missionary societies, such as Pfeiffer and William Knibb, were arrested and charged with inciting the slave revolt. The Government, however, saw that both the newly-formed union and the sentiments which inspired it were running counter to the tide of events, and so it disbanded the union. When slavery was finally abolished by the Act of Emancipation of 1833 the slaves gave thanks for their freedom in churches all over the island.

The Christian churches were largely responsible for assisting the released slaves to make the difficult transition from servitude to freedom. The missionaries particularly saw it as a part of their duty to help the new citizens of the colony to purchase plots of land, and small dwellings, in order to settle down as full members of their society. Throughout this period of transition the released slaves were aided specially by the Moravians and Baptists, whilst the Anglicans remained somewhat aloof, in part because they represented essentially the planters who had everything to lose from the increasing self-sufficiency of a formerly slave population. But it is also true to say that the representatives of the Anglican Church found it very difficult to collaborate with missionaries whom, not so long ago, they had violently persecuted and sought to destroy; or to treat as equals coloured peoples whom they had exhorted to obey their masters and be content with their condition.

After the rebellion at Morant Bay in 1865, which resulted from head-on clashes between the rulers and the masses over the social and economic position of the latter, the Government of Jamaica was forced to resign, and the constitution was surrendered, giving place to the establishment of a crown colony government. The new Governor of Jamaica disestablished the Anglican Church in 1870, so that the Church of England became just another Christian denomination in this society. Today it is represented by about one-fifth of the total population, and is still the largest single sect of Christianity in Jamaica, closely rivalled by the Baptists of the more orthodox variety. The Roman Catholics, who had been given freedom to exercise their religion once more in 1792, appear from a comparison of the census figures of 1943 and 1960 to be steadily on the increase.

D HINDUISM AND ISLAM

There seems little doubt that some of the slaves imported into Jamaica from West Africa had already been converted, at some time, to Islam. In his *History of the West Indies*, which was published in the late eighteenth century, Bryan Edwards refers to an African tribe called the Mandingoes who were considered by him to be a link between the Moors and the Negroes; these Mandingoes were unquestionably Muslims. Some of them could read and write, and could also recite passages from Muslim prayers and the *Koran*; moreover, they would insist that Friday demanded respect as the holy day of Islam. So that in the early days of slavery there was to be seen some Muslim influence at work in the religion of groups of Negroes (5).

It is not intended to give a full account here of all the eastern religions represented in Jamaica, or in the West Indies in general; Indian religions will be discussed in some detail in Part Two, and Islam in Part Three. After the Act of Emancipation of 1833, in order to replace the emancipated slave labour the planters had to seek help elsewhere. At first they looked to immigrants from Europe generally and some indentured labour from

RELIGIONS IN JAMAICA

Religious Denomination or Sect	1943 Census Percentage of all religious groups	1960 Census Percentage of all religious groups
All religious groups	100·0	100·0
Anglican	28·3	19·7
Baptist	25·8	19·0
Methodist	8·9	6·8
Presbyterian	7·5	5·1
Roman Catholic	5·7	7·2
Moravian	4·1	3·25
Church of God	3·5	11·9
Seventh Day Adventist	2·2	4·9
Congregationalist	1·7	1·39
Salvation Army	1·1	0·64
Pentecostal	0·4	0·91
Friends	0·3	0·25
Plymouth Brethren	0·3	0·9
Christian Science	*	0·02
Pocomania	0·3	0·05
Christian	0·5	0·05
Brethren	0·4	
Evangelical Association	0·4	
Bible Student	0·1	
Mission	0·1	
Jewish	0·1	0·04
Bedwardite	*	
Hindu	0·3	0·07
Buddhist	*	
Confucian	2·1	
Other religions	1·6	0·92
No religion	4·0	11·4
Not specified	0·3	5·56

* Denotes a very small percentage.

China, but this help proved far from sufficient. Slaves had always been expendable and, moreover, they could be encouraged to multiply since sexual pleasure was virtually the only one left to them. Now that the planters had to pay for every unit of labour it was proving quite a costly business. Eventually cheap indentured labour was obtained from India and the East Indies, and at the same time elements of Hindu, Buddhist and Muslim religion entered the West Indies. Indentures were usually for a period of from three to five years, after which they might be renewed or the labourers could be given assisted passages back to their country of origin. Many inevitably stayed and were integrated, partially at least, into their host society; some who sought to retain their own culture and religion intact met with a great deal of physical and legal opposition. Even today there is no strictly Hindu temple in Jamaica, and those who wish to continue their religious rituals must do so in their own homes, with self-appointed priests performing the ceremonies.

Indian indentured labourers and their descendants were discriminated against until 1959, and were all labelled 'immigrants' in much the same way as we tend to label as immigrants – in our minds, at least, if not in law – all the children born to immigrants in this country. Hindu marriages (until 1959) have always been regarded as non-events, and children born of such marriages have been considered illegitimate, which has further meant that, under Jamaican law, they have had no automatic right of inheritance. Any Hindu who wanted a child to inherit had to make a will specifically stating so, otherwise the money, property or land reverted to the Government. In consequence, many Hindus have in the past married in a Christian Church or at the Registry Office. Today, however, largely through the efforts of the East Indian Progressive Society, all forms of marriage, whether performed by Hindu, Jew, Muslim or Christian, are recognized as legal. This has made it possible for those members of faiths other than Christian to pursue more precisely, if they so wish, their own culture.

From the census figures already quoted, it would appear that the number of Hindus in Jamaica has declined, but Trinidad has a Hindu and Muslim minority of something slightly more than one-third of the population, whilst Guyana has an even larger percentage of Hindus and Muslims. According to figures provided by Professor A. H. Richmond, about 2·3 per cent of the total population of Jamaica in 1946 were Asian – in fact, over 29,000 (6). If this is taken in conjunction with the figures provided by Henriques for the 1943 census it becomes clear that the Asian element, which has remained unassimilated in any way to the main stream of Jamaican culture, is mainly composed of the Confucian or Chinese people, namely 2·1 per cent (7).

E SOME ASPECTS OF AFRICAN RELIGION
Despite the considerable influence and impact of Christianity in its various forms, it must be remembered that the origin of the Negro slaves imported into Jamaica and the West Indies generally was African and that today the black people represent 78·1 per cent of the total population (8). Whilst it is true, as Dr P. C. C. Evans points out (9), that the religious patterns and

beliefs which the slaves brought with them from Africa to the West Indies were discouraged, they nevertheless continued to exist underground and later emerged either as spiritualistic cults or as an Afro-Christianity. In forming any views about the religious attitudes and behaviour of the West Indians who come to this country, we must remember that, whatever religious label they may use, their religious practices are likely to be influenced to some extent at least by their African inheritance.

Many conflicting views have been expressed concerning, for example, the nature of the idea of God in Africa. But Africa is a very large continent with a great variety of groups and tribes, and it would be surprising if one single idea emerged out of the wealth of religious concepts to be found there. G. Parrinder has summed up the situation as follows:

'The study of the idea of God in Africa has been weakened by theorists, some of whom think that there has been an inevitable evolution from fetishism, to animism, to polytheism and finally to monotheism. Others consider that there was an original monotheism from which all Africans fell, in a kind of Fall of Adam. Looking at things as they are today there is a picture of a mixed religion, which is not mere animism, nor a democratic polytheism, nor a pure monotheism. E. B. Idowu calls it "diffused theism"' (10).

Certainly there is to be found in tribal religion a belief in God as a Supreme Being, and Joachim Wach has made the point that much of our depreciation of African religion in terms of animism and totemism has been due to our lack of knowledge and understanding of primitive society. There is, for Wach, a great similarity between Awlawrun, 'Lord of the Sky' or 'Owner of the Sky', and the high gods of the great ancient civilizations such as Babylonia, Greece and Rome (11).

In the main these tribal ideas appear to be, as Wach suggests, cosmo-centric and theocentric, and there is the ever recurring attempt to explain the origins of man, life and the universe through sometimes incredibly naïve myth and symbol. Yet when these myths are analysed and 'demythol-ogized' one finds some essential expression of religious or spiritual truth. Indeed, these myths are in fact no more naïve than the stories to be found in the early chapters of Genesis, or in parts of the Koran, and much of the phallic symbolism in aetiological stories of man's creation and procreation is the same (12).

We are here, however, much more concerned with those elements of African religion which relate to ritual, magic and the plurality of spiritual powers and entities rather than of the gods. The gods and Sky God of the Africans find expression in the multiplicity of spiritual beings which inhabit man, beast and what, at first sight, appear to be inanimate objects.

To the African the latter is really a contradiction in terms: there is, in reality, no inert matter; the whole of nature teems with spirits or spiritual presences which are but a sort of hierarchical emanation of the Supreme Being. In a sense, it is the African's way of making deity safe. He can happily curse the local spirit for having despoiled his crops or destroyed his animals by disease, but he would not direct such blasphemies against the God of the firmament. Many of the spirits around him are able to activate natural objects; among the Ashanti there are stone-throwing spirits called *mmotia* which are represented in Jamaican mythology by 'duppies', which have a variety of activity and function.

Drought and infertility are problems for the primitive society without technical and artificial means to combat them. Hence much of the African ritual has been associated with overcoming the anger of the gods, or the hero-gods, associated with the production of rain and the prolongation of fertility. Schleiermacher maintained that the origin of religion was a feeling of absolute dependence upon God, or gods; and in his efforts to redress the balance of nature the African has always shown his dependence upon the native spirits for his needs. These spirits, of course, can be influenced, placated and cajoled by rituals, sacrifices and the activities of particular types of intermediary such as the rain-maker or the rain-stopper, the sorcerer or the witch-doctor.

Among the Ibo, barren women pray to the Earth Mother, called Ala, who is the spirit of fertility. She will also aid the farmers to increase their animal stock, and will eventually receive the dead into her womb. Rocks, hills and mountains are particularly the habitats of spirits who will vary in importance according to the size of the natural object. Rivers, springs, streams, lakes and wells are indwelt by spirits and are frequently the centres of fertility cults in which ritual bathing in the waters may produce the required effect for a barren woman. A certain amount of sexual licence on these occasions may also assist in the process.

Magic has always been used in Africa in order to protect the group or the individual against disease and evil spirits. Almost any object may be used for magical purposes provided the necessary sympathetic contagion has been effected between the person and the object. Both white and black magic may be employed: white magic in order to bring health, success and food; black magic in order to attract evil, failure, disease and death.

Amongst the spiritual forces appealed to and strongly accredited by the African are his ancestors. Some of these are accepted as gods for whom are performed regular ceremonies at which prayers are said, and offerings of meat, vegetables and blood are made. The ancestors are viewed as beings who, having originally emanated from the great Sky God, have at length returned to their creator, but who in a sense also act as intermediaries who are more accessible to the worshipper because remotely related to him during their earthly existence. Thus the ideas of God's transcendence and immanence find a meeting-place in the persons of the ancestors. Parrinder quotes an Ashanti prayer which a chief offered with a sheep to his ancestors:

'Ancient ones . . . who came from the Sky God, receive this sheep and eat, permit me to have a long reign, let this nation prosper, do not let it act foolishly' (13).

It is important, in considering later the spiritualistic developments in West Indian religion, to note that the African has always appeared to believe in some sort of spirit-possession. This is not something that all are subject to; some individuals appear to have psychic faculties which are more highly developed in them than in others. These powers are believed to come from some familiar spirit which has attached itself to the individual, and which may prophesy through them, or heal, or produce some other form of psi-phenomena or paranormal activity. Some of these 'possessed' individuals go into trance states and appear to be different personalities altogether.

Finally, there is quite prevalent throughout Africa a belief in some form of reincarnation. At first sight this appears to contradict the idea of the continued existence of their ancestors in another dimension with the gods; but the African sees nothing illogical or contradictory in these beliefs. Ancestors can be in the heavens, or in the grave, and yet reincarnated upon earth in one or more bodies. Lévy-Bruhl has referred to this type of thinking amongst primitive groups as 'pre-logical', and the whole concept of absorption in, and identification with, his ancestors as a sort of *participation mystique* (14). But, in fact, there is a certain coherence in the African's view which involves not so much the concept of isolated human souls as a sort of *élan vital* which immortally informs all life. To that extent it is, in a sense, a mystical participation: but it is more than that since the influence of the ancestor is not contingent upon the acts of participation of the worshipper. It is an autonomous influence which, like the Spirit of God, 'bloweth where it listeth'.

F CULTS, OBEAH AND POCOMANIA

'Religious freedom is entrenched in the country's constitution,' says the hand-out of the Jamaica Information Service (15). Certainly there is almost every conceivable sect and denomination of Christianity represented in the West Indies somewhere or other, and also practically every other religion, including Judaism which is briefly mentioned here, not as one of the resurgent cults but as illustrating the rich variety of West Indian culture and the general tolerance towards all religion. When the Spaniards were operating the Inquisition in Spain, Jewish emigrants from Spain and

Portugal fled to Jamaica where the Spanish were already in occupation, and they referred to themselves as 'Portugals'. In this way they were able for some time to conceal the fact that they were Jews who had escaped the Inquisition. When the British occupied the island in 1655 the Jews once more began to practise Judaism openly, and other Jews who were undergoing pressures and pogroms in Germany and central Europe joined them and formed what was finally called the United Congregation of Israelites.

In the late eighteenth century there began a revival of some of the traditional African cults in Jamaica. There appears to be a variety of reasons for this sudden recrudescence of 'primitivity'. The more orthodox forms of Christianity, in particular Anglicanism, offered the Negro slave little consolation in the face of his miserable lot as a chattel of the planter. The most that he was ever offered was 'pie in the sky' when he died, but nothing of any value in this life. Even the more humane missionaries of the nonconformist sects could offer very little here and now, except their own sympathy, comfort, concern and broad humanity. We have already mentioned the slaves who participated in the attempt at revival in 1782, and the way in which this was linked to the Baptist denomination in particular. The official line throughout seems to have been that the most effective way of stopping these native movements was to provide as effectively as possible the official teaching of each particular Christian denomination. Coupled with this was the attempt by the missionaries, particularly noticeable during the uprisings at Morant Bay between about 1840 and 1865, to bar all traditional Negro cults, customs and rituals. Many Negroes must have seen this move as an attempt to restrict the thought, belief and activity of a people who, all too recently, had been at last liberated from their physical enslavement.

A people who have been freed in this way obviously will seek, as soon as possible, to establish some form of identity as a group. Their only real links were not with the now defunct Arawaks, not with the planters, not yet with the somewhat cautious and sometimes theologically forbidding missionaries, but with their ancestors in Africa, their land of origin. In 1861 there spread through Jamaica a movement which attempted to restore and revitalize their natural spiritual inheritance. This movement received the appellation 'The Great Awakening', and it developed into what must have been a frightening return to mass trance states, abandoned dancing, sexual orgies, public confessions and masochistic forms of self-punishment and flagellation (16). This sort of movement was as sporadic as it was spontaneous: it lacked organization and direction as well as any real understanding of its own purpose. Like many other popular movements directed at ignorant people, it depended very much upon the persuasion and eloquence of the few.

Again, a people who have recently acquired freedom after a long period of repression, and who in consequence do not know where they are going and lack leaders at the economic and social levels to provide them with any sense of physical security and direction, frequently look for some temporary messiah who may at least give them some spiritual solace and a sense of divine redemption. Such a man was Alexander Bedward who, in 1920, called himself the Messiah, or Christ, the Son of God. This was no mean claim by a man who was virtually illiterate and a labourer, though no doubt many felt that he compared quite favourably with one who, making similar claims, was the son of a carpenter.

Bedward was a Jamaican who had originally joined the Methodist Church; however he possessed just that eloquence and persuasion which impressed a profoundly inarticulate group who, because of their sheer frustration and desperation, barely noticed the blasphemy involved in Bedward's claims. No doubt he received considerable support from certain elements in his society who were looking for a leader and a prophet. From then on the prophetic mantle of Elijah seemed naturally to fall upon him, and he was emboldened to prophesy that, like Elijah, he would soon be taken up into heaven, after which he would return in power to the earth and would gather together his Elect. After his 'second coming' the earth would be destroyed in an apocalyptic convulsion involving earthquakes, fires and a general devastation. Bedward also claimed to have powers of healing by the process of laying-on of hands, and also by the sprinkling of water. In one unguarded moment he stated that his 'ascension' would take place on December 31, 1920. Sadly, when the day approached and then was past, Bedward failed to fulfil this, his ultimate prophecy. Then, like all prophets who have overreached themselves by being too precise, Bedward attempted to quieten his followers by further predictions. Eventually, after a series of failures in fulfilment, Bedward was arrested and confined in a mental home. There is something very tragic about the charismatic leader who lacks the power to fulfil his promise, and the history of religious revival and messianism is replete with the sad stories of leaders retiring to the homes for the mentally unbalanced, or to their own mansions where they may practise a comfortable and divinely-sanctioned polygamy; or who like the Mahdi or Bab may end their days in violence and ignominy.

One of the interesting features that becomes apparent from the comparison of the Jamaican census of 1943 with that of 1960 is the reduction in the percentage of devotees of Pocomania, namely from 0·3 to 0·05 per cent of the total population. Katrin Norris certainly supports this finding when she remarks that

'Pocomania and Zion are dying out under the influence of American revivalist teaching and the increased opportunities for political and social activity' (17).

In general terms Pocomania is a revival of the magical beliefs of African religion blended naturally, at the more emotional and ecstatic levels, with Christianity. It has been mentioned previously that the Baptist denomination comprises a very wide and rich variety of belief, thought and attitude. At one end of the scale in the West Indies the Baptists may be very orthodox and conventional, at the other end they may border on Pocomania, which is essentially a proletarian movement. Fernando Henriques, who provides a great deal of information on the subject, defines Pocomania as

'a type of Christian revivalism combined with certain specific West African religious devices, such as the use of trance. Its origin can possibly be traced back to the Myal movement of slavery days. Myal was a quasi-religious movement of the slaves which was directed against practitioners of witchcraft, the Obeahmen' (18).

Obeah was, and is, a magical means by which the individual may obtain his personal desires, eradicate ill-health, obtain good fortune in life and business, turn the affections of the object of his love towards himself, evince revenge or retribution upon his enemies, and generally manipulate the spiritual forces of the cosmos in order to obtain his will. It is the function of the obeahman, the expert Jamaican witch-doctor, to provide what the individual desires for a price; for obeah is concerned with the individual and his appetites as opposed to the total good and welfare of society – and to this extent it is antisocial. Strongly linked with the practice of obeah is the belief in, and fear of, ghosts or 'duppies'. Control of the 'duppies', which may be anything from the ghosts of ancestors to mischievous local spirits or demons, is effected mainly by forms of obeah, whilst 'duppy-catching' becomes a major occupation at a wake, when the spirit of the dead has to be protected. Adherents of obeah are to be found in all the social classes in Jamaica and, whilst the practice of obeah is a criminal offence and is strongly condemned by all in public, it is still practised in secret. Pocomania, on the other hand, is condemned by both the middle and upper classes who see in it a lowering of the general tone of their society.

Despite the condemnation of Pocomania, however, it is not something that is practised in secret. Its devotees are concerned with social identification and with combating the evil forces of obeah. Their methods, however, are really the equivalent of the production of a white magic effectively to destroy a black magic. Those who practise Pocomania hold their services either in special meeting halls or in the open air; they usually begin by singing revivalist hymns, accompanied by clapping and stamping, and continue far into the night. The purpose of the singing and physical activity is to produce a rhythm which, in turn, will result in a trance state. In this state various psychic phenomena take place, and it is believed by the devotees that they are taken over by spirits who speak through them and talk in a variety of 'tongues'. This phenomenon is known as glossolalia, or speaking with tongues. Worshippers are convinced that they are being guided by entities referred to as 'Captain', 'Mother' or 'Shepherd', or possibly a plurality of 'captains' and so forth. This whole experience has a great deal in common with the practice of voodoo in Haiti, in which the loa, or 'divine horsemen', possess the worshippers and ride them to a final state of prostration. There is something infectious about the whole proceedings, and even observers (such as the American anthropologist Maya Deren) have been known to become involved in the trance situation, and have participated in the ceremonies (19). The Pocomanians are known also to use herbs and drugs to induce the trance state in which eventually the spirits take over possession.

The Zion cult, which Katrin Norris coupled with Pocomania above (20), is another revivalist cult similar in many respects to Pocomania itself. It involves the same sort of ritual dancing leading to collective possession by the archaic African deities as well as by Biblical characters such as the archangels Michael and Gabriel, the prophets Samuel and Jeremiah, and a strange mixture of other personalities such as Jehovah, Holy Ghost, Jesus Christ, Moses, Solomon, Rachael, Miriam and even Satan. The rite of baptism by immersion is practised as a sort of *rite de passage* similar to African initiation ceremonies.

G THE RAS TAFARIANS

One of the escapist movements in Jamaica is that of the Ras Tafarians which centres in West Kingston, although the sect is found throughout Jamaica and represents the modern crystallization of the general 'back to Africa' movement. The original impetus to this concept was provided by a black Jamaican called Marcus Garvey who established in 1918 the United Negro Improvement Association. Garvey attempted, with a great deal of drive and revivalist oratory, to instil into the black people a pride in their race, colour and country of origin; he was a messiah preaching the possibilities of a new identity from archaic beginnings to a people who lacked unity, purpose and self-esteem. Garvey's movement was a political one inspired and informed by religious emotion and sentiment and reinforced by his own messianic personality. He died, however, in 1926 without having accomplished anything of his main purpose – the return of Negroes to Africa.

It was after the death of Garvey that the Ras Tafari movement began to develop and take shape, and particularly in the 1930s when its inspiration derived largely from the Ethiopian resistance to Mussolini's attacks on their territory. At last they had a specific, oppressed group with whom to identify, for Africa is a large continent with many different groups and peoples. The imagination of the depressed Jamaican Negroes was fired by the similar sufferings of the Africans undergoing enforced colonization.

Although it clearly possesses certain political and territorial aims, the movement is not concerned to use political or military means to achieve its goals. It is strictly a waiting game in which those who are involved – the Brethren (in no way connected with the Plymouth Brethren), Ras Tafarians, or Ras Tafarites – are supported in their hopes by a sense of religious and spiritual community. Nor are they buoyed up by any messianic hopes: they expect no messiah to appear out of the sky to redeem them, nor even any divine revelations or apparitions produced through ecstasy. Indeed, there is very little relief from their present state of depression save their final hope of return to their homeland accompanied by freedom and salvation.

The somewhat mixed and simple beliefs of the Ras Tafarians have been analysed and summarized by Professor Vittorio Lanternari as being essentially as follows. Some of the ancient tribes of Israel were exiled to the West Indies as a punishment for their repeated disobedience to the demands of Yahweh and transgression of his divine Law which he gave through Moses. The present-day Negroes in Jamaica and elsewhere are a reincarnation of those Israelite tribes, and their sufferings are, in effect, an extension of Yahweh's retribution. The white man is inferior to the black man, and Jamaica is the latter's earthly hell. Heaven is Ethiopia, remote and idealized, and both the symbol of Negro freedom as well as the physical goal of that freedom. Haile Selassie, the Emperor of Ethiopia, is the living God, the King of Kings and Lord of Lords, and the conquering Lion of the Tribe of Judah. All the hopes of the Ras Tafarians are placed upon this one man who will somehow make it possible for the black man to be revenged upon the white man, who will become his servant, and all individuals of African descent will then return to Ethiopia (21). For the devotees of this cult there is one God, one aim and one destiny.

The main body of the Ras Tafarians live in the worst slums of Kingston, the 'Back o' Wall' and the 'Dungle' or Dung-hill. They live as squatters in squalid settlements composed of shanty-huts hanging together with bits of board, scrap metal, cardboard, cloth and motor tyres. In the main they are dirty, hairy, out-of-work, and addicted to 'ganga' or marijuana. Professor Henriques believes, however, that despite their appearance and their seeming inertia the Ras Tafarians are, on the whole, sincere and lacking in violence. A research instigated by the University of Jamaica in 1960 reported that the more recent spread of Ras Tafari ideas among the better-educated middle-class youths was due mainly to the generally increasing appeal of marijuana smoking and Marxism. The researchers concluded that such expansion of the movement would continue so long as the youth of the Jamaican society were not provided with 'significant ideals of social justice for which to strive and opportunities for their achievement' (22).

These researches are important since they underline one of the disturbing features in all movements that begin with common aims inspired by equally common beliefs and faith. It has been estimated that by 1953 there were at least twelve different sects of the Ras Tafarians, each with its own organization and leaders, so that it has become as difficult to generalize about the Ras Tafarians in Jamaica as about any other religious or politico-religious groups. The possibilities of 'repatriation' to Ethiopia or elsewhere in Africa were considered by the People's National Party in 1961, when they were governing the country. There were certainly some favourable moves on the side of Ethiopia, but since the Labour Party came to power under the leadership of Bustamante, in 1962, nothing more appears to have been done about the matter.

Those elements of the Ras Tafari movement which are still essentially religious have their own rituals, Biblical readings and interpretations (in which the white man is always identified with evil), hymns, symbols and images (in particular pictures of Haile Selassie), and prayers. G. E. Simpson has recorded one of their concluding prayers as follows:

'Deliver us from the hands of our enemies, that we might prove fruitful for the last days. When our enemies are passed and decayed in the depths of the sea, in the depths of the earth or in the belly of a beast, oh, give us all a place in Thy kingdom forever and ever. Selah!' (23).

H CONCLUSION

It is clearly not easy to assess the religious situation of Jamaica which is but one island in the total number of West Indian communities. Sheila Patterson has emphasized the socially binding force of orthodox Christian churches (such as the Anglican and Roman Catholic) in the West Indies – a social function which is no longer of any great consequence in most of our own urban churches (24). The sense of community experienced by West Indians in this religious society, with all its warmth of feeling and fellowship, and sense of identity, is something which they do not equally experience when they come to this country. The mere ritual of wearing one's finest clothes and of engaging in ceremonies that have in themselves some form of social prestige, such as weddings, christenings and so forth, provides in the West Indies a certain status to the participants. We have been through this somewhat Victorian phase of religio-social identity and have emerged into something which is becoming increasingly classless. At least, what class consciousness there may be is quite unrelated to the

1. *Top:* The Ministry of Education building at Kingston, Jamaica, (*bottom*) Selling fish at Savanna la Mar, Jamaica.

2. Street market scene, St George's, Grenada.

individual's religious orthodoxy; we do not any longer lean upon religious affiliations or practices to provide us with what little social status or prestige we may seek to acquire.

Whilst most of the members of the upper classes in the West Indies belong to the more orthodox churches, the black lower classes are members of the nonconformist Christian sects and the multifarious cults that keep cropping up in a society seeking to establish an identity as well as some outlet for its frustrations and strong emotions. These cults are virtually a form of 'mass catharsis' for the sense of despair and hopelessness that invades the more poverty-stricken people (25).

There is, in the realm of religion, literally something for everybody in West Indian societies. Where the Bible is considered to be the sacred scriptures given by God, the general view is a fundamentalist one accepting belief in verbal inspiration and the literal accuracy and truth of everything written therein. Coupled with this view is usually also an authoritarian attitude towards interpretation and religious practice.

Those who want ecstasy and cultist phenomena can find them in a variety of sects of Christianity, Pocomania, spiritualism, the Church of God and Pentecostalists. It has already been pointed out that the division between many of these sects and cults is not always very sharp, and some of them tend to merge almost imperceptibly into one another. The syncretic elements of Christianity, West African polytheism and obeah or magic, tend to have a great appeal to many groups who, apart from the ecstatic experiences which provide release from the despair or sheer ordinariness of life, have really very little to live for. Children are, from birth, surrounded by spirits, ghosts or duppies; this is their African inheritance, and even some of the names of the spirits of their Ashanti ancestors still remain with them (26). Many also believe that they are themselves possessed of a sort of double, again a duppy, which will remain behind after death, whilst the true soul will return for personal judgement to God. This is the element of reincarnation to be found in African religion, where the ancestors may be viewed as being in heaven with the Supreme God and yet also in the ground, and in addition reincarnated in some living person.

The Pentecostalists have certainly increased in numbers between the years 1943 and 1960, and at the last census they represented about 1 per cent of the population. The Church of God, which is another cult group of a similar nature, represents about 12 per cent of the population. C. S. Hill has pointed out that these Pentecostal groups are rapidly developing all over London, and that the devotees express themselves very loudly through the media of hand-clapping, guitars, tambourines and singing. They are, however, so exclusive that they believe that they alone are true Christians. Hill sees in the development of the Pentecostal movement a real hindrance to the effective creation of a multi-racial and multi-cultural society, since

D

the Church as an institution can be, he suggests, the greatest and most effective organ for racial integration in this country.

'The worst result of the Pentecostal movement amongst the immigrants lies in the barrier it represents to their integration into the community. The very beliefs of the Pentecostals must lead to a "separatist" movement. Their mode of worship is far more likely to appeal to West Indians than to English people. This in turn tends towards a voluntary segregation and the formation of all-coloured churches' (27).

Religion inevitably unites or divides. The great tragedy in culture contacts such as those of the West Indians and the natives of our own society is that the barriers which externally appear to be of colour are, in fact, those of levels of faith, belief and practice even within the same religious sect. Hill is right, of course, in maintaining that religion could be a very great and effective means of racial integration. But, unfortunately, religion is the one area where devotees cannot compromise. They believe what they believe, and what they feel they must believe; the external expression of their belief is very much guided and controlled by their social and cultural inheritance and those incommensurables such as racial character and levels of emotion and physical expression. Compromise is essentially a rational process; within the realm of highly emotive religious expression compromise is unlikely.

REFERENCES

1 Quoted by Geoffrey Gorer in Hooper, R. (ed.), *Colour in Britain* (B.B.C., 1965), p. 27.
2 Henriques, F., *Family and Colour in Jamaica* (MacGibbon & Kee, 2nd edition 1968), p. 83.
3 Jamaica Information Service, *Facts on Jamaica: No. 7 – Religion in Jamaica* (Jamaica Information Service, Kingston, Jamaica, n.d.), p. 5.
4 *Vide* Henriques, F., op. cit., p. 23.
5 *Vide* ibid., p. 32.
6 Richmond, A. H., *The Colour Problem* (Penguin, revised edition 1961), p. 217. The column headed 'TOTAL at Last Census' refers to the Census of 1946, and the figures are quoted from the *Digest of Colonial Statistics*, No. 10, September–October 1953, Tables H, M, and N (Colonial Office, H.M.S.O., 1953).
7 Since the Chinese are an 'integrating' group rather than an 'assimilating' one, they remain largely unaffected by their environment, nor do they pass on their culture to the host society. There is, therefore, no account here of Chinese religion. The student who is interested should refer to Tomlin, E. W. F., *The Eastern Philosophers* (Hutchinson: A Radius Book, 1968) for an authoritative account of Confucianism.
8 Henriques, F., op. cit., p. 50.
9 Evans, P. C. C. and Le Page, R. B., *The Education of West Indian Immigrant Children* (National Committee for Commonwealth Immigrants, n.d.), p. 10.

10 Parrinder, G., *Religion in Africa* (Penguin, 1969), p. 46.
11 Wach, J., *Sociology of Religion* (Univ. of Chicago Press, Phœnix Edition, 11th impression 1967), pp. 23–4, 230–2.
12 Parrinder, G., op. cit., p. 35.
13 Ibid., p. 70.
14 *Vide* Lévy-Bruhl, L., *Primitive Mentality* (Macmillan, 1923).
15 *Facts on Jamaica: No. 7–Religion in Jamaica*, p. 1.
16 *Vide* Simpson, G. E., 'Jamaican Revivalist Cults', *Social and Economic Studies* (Kingston, Jamaica, 1956), pp. 334–6.
17 Norris, K., *Jamaica: The Search for an Identity* (O.U.P., 1962), p. 17.
18 Henriques, F., op. cit., pp. 84–5.
19 *Vide* Deren, Maya, *Divine Horsemen* (Thames & Hudson, 1953).
20 See reference 17 above.
21 *Vide* Lanternari, V., *The Religions of the Oppressed* (New American Lib., 1965), pp. 135–7.
22 *Vide* Henriques, F., op. cit., pp. 180–1.
23 Simpson, G. E., 'Political Cultism in West Kingston, Jamaica', *Social and Economic Studies* (Kingston, Jamaica, 1955), p. 140.
24 Patterson, S., *Dark Strangers* (Penguin, 1965), p. 205.
25 Evans, P. C. C., op. cit., p. 11.
26 *Vide* Rattray, R. S., *Akan-Ashanti Folk Tales* (O.U.P., 1930), p. 73, where Anansi and Ntikuma are referred to. Compare West Indian folk stories with reference to Anansi, the Spider, and Tacooma his son (*vide* Henriques, F., op. cit., pp. 33, 127–8).
27 Hill, C. S., *West Indian Migrants and the London Churches* (O.U.P., 1963), pp. 73–4.

BIBLIOGRAPHY

Beckwith, M., *Black Roadways* (Chapel Hill, 1929).
Calley, M. J. C., *God's People: W. Indian Pentecostalist Sects in England* (O.U.P., 1965).
Evans, P. C. C. and Le Page, R. B., *The Education of West Indian Immigrant Children* (National Committee for Commonwealth Immigrants, n.d.).
Henriques, F., *Family and Colour in Jamaica* (MacGibbon & Kee, 2nd edition 1968).
Hill, C. S., *West Indian Migrants and the London Churches* (O.U.P., 1963).
Lanternari, V., *The Religions of the Oppressed* (New American Lib., 1965).
Norris, K., *Jamaica: The Search for an Identity* (O.U.P., 1962).
Parrinder, G., *Religion in Africa* (Penguin, 1969).
Patterson, Sheila, *Dark Strangers* (Penguin, 1965).
Simpson, G. E., 'Political Cultism in West Kingston, Jamaica', *Social and Economic Studies* (Kingston, Jamaica, 1955), pp. 133–49.
Simpson, G. E., 'Jamaican Revivalist Cults', *Social and Economic Studies* (Kingston, Jamaica, 1956), pp. 321–442.
Smith, M. G., Augier, R., and Nettleford, R., *The Ras Tafari Movement in Kingston, Jamaica* (Jamaica, 1960).
Wach, J., *Sociology of Religion* (Univ. of Chicago Press, Phœnix Edition, 11th impression 1967).

Chapter 3

Social Background
of the West Indies

A THE FAMILY SYSTEM

It is not our purpose here to enter into some of the finer and more detailed questions of precise anthropological argument. The interested reader is referred, in particular, to the works of M. Herskovits (1), T. S. Simey (2), F. Henriques (3) and E. Clarke (4). There is certainly a variety of interpretation concerning family structures, and also concerning the origins of what on the surface may appear to be illegitimacy, polygamy and promiscuity. Professor M. G. Smith, of the University of California at Los Angeles, considers that the studies of T. S. Simey and F. Henriques, although indicative, do not give 'explicit attention to extra-residential mating as a widespread institutional pattern' (5), and they are inadequate as an analysis of the mating and family organization of the West Indies. The studies of the family in three selected communities in Jamaica by Edith Clarke indicate that there is no facile generalization which applies to the whole of a society such as the Jamaican; even less, of course, can one really generalize about the whole of the West Indies. It must, therefore, be remembered that it is necessary, to understand fully the variety of familial formats and problems in the Caribbean, to examine each island society in some detail. This, however, is not possible here.

We shall discuss the typology proposed by Simey and Henriques as being at least one general theory of the classification of the Jamaican family. In stating this theory, similar in many ways to that expressed by R. T. Smith in relation to the Negro family in Guyana (6), one must accept Professor M. G. Smith's caution that the variations in community organization and ethos have a considerable influence upon local patterns of family life. But if, as a typology, it does not represent the whole West Indian, or even Jamaican, familial structure, it nevertheless describes certain discrete elements in that structure. Whether or not each family pattern delineated represents, in reality, a function of economic and social status, and whether or not each indicates a point on the scale of upward social mobility may be questioned. It depends very much upon the particular community under discussion. What is not questionable is that such patterns or modes of family life do exist.

During the long years of slavery the planters refused to allow their slaves to marry under the aegis of Christian ritual. Whilst the slaves were given every encouragement to have promiscuous sex relations and to reproduce as fast as possible, they were not encouraged to develop permanent relationships. A planter could always get more money for slaves who were sold separately than for those put up for auction as man and wife; and, in consequence, 'marriage' of any sort was not encouraged among them. Today *Christian marriage* is more of an ideal than an actuality; it represents the consummation not so much of love or desire as of social ambition. It is, as Katrin FitzHerbert puts it,

'still more important as a statement of economic achievement and class affiliation, than as a context for a sexual relationship, a shared home, or raising children' (7).

In order to fulfil this 'Christian' ideal of marriage it is considered necessary for the prospective bridegroom to have attained a level of social and economic security, which in turn will provide that ethos of respectability which such a marriage demands. In fact, the picture of ideal marriage here envisaged is really a reflection of the planter's home, with its amenities and admirable furnishings and, of course, a servant or even two. Not only is the resultant home in such a marriage expensive, but the wedding occasion itself is an occasion of expansive generosity. It is an opportunity for the whole kin group and in fact the whole village to participate in the church ritual, when the pair to be married will appear in all their finery and, because they have in all probability been living together for many years, when they will be accompanied by their children. Certainly very few of the lowest strata of society are able to get married when they are young because of the formidable expense of such a wedding, and also because of the subsequent standard of living expected. Indeed, the consummation in marriage of a lifetime of cohabitation might eventually occur in old age; but it is still very important, even up to the deathbed, because of its prestige value. It is, in effect, the only form of marriage recognized legally, and it is 'patriarchal' in nature. Christian marriage confers upon the male that legal position and sanction which he appears to lack in society generally. The inability of the lower-class male to support his family in a generous and 'middle-class' manner produces in him a sense of inferiority, and also of subjection to the powerful female elements in the family.

The second pattern of male-female relationships is referred to as *faithful concubinage*. Like Christian marriage this is also mainly patriarchal, at least ostensibly, but it has no legal status or support. Henriques maintains that any distinction between Christian marriage and faithful concubinage, or common-law marriage, is sociologically useless (8). He regards Jamaica as 'the example of a society in which there is a contradiction as regards conjugal unions between what is legally accepted as the norm for the whole society, and what is socially accepted' (9).

Concubinage is the union in cohabitation of a man and woman, lasting indefinitely but without the full sanction of law or religion. Such unions are very often successful throughout the lifetime of the pair concerned; but, at the same time, it is a union which by its very nature is inherently unstable. Having no legal sanction it depends so often upon the character and personal stability of the male partner. The instability of the union is further underlined by the fact that it may be terminated at any time by either partner, and there tends therefore to be something basically impermanent and capricious about it. Edith Clarke, however, is not happy with Henriques' identification of faithful concubinage with 'common-law' marriage. The latter, she maintains, is

'a legal term describing a type of union which at one time was recognized by the law as marriage although it had been entered upon without all the formalities which the law prescribes. It is therefore not appropriate to apply it to unions which are clearly distinguishable from marriage, both by the partners and by the society at large, and, in my experience, it is never used of any type of unions by the Jamaicans who are themselves participants in these forms of union' (10).

It will, therefore, be more satisfactory if we keep to the term 'faithful concubinage' for this second type of relationship.

Whilst it is true that faithful concubinage implies no overt legal or religious sanctions, there are certain sanctions of conscience which enter into the relationship where many of the couples are concerned. It is a relationship of equality which has all the potential of final solemnization in church or at the registry office if all goes well; and there are inbuilt attitudes of pride and endeavour in making a success of the union as the only likely means to this ideal. There is an acceptance by both partners of individual as well as corporate responsibility for the maintenance and improvement of the household. The man is responsible for the provision of a home, however poor it may be, food and social security; the woman looks after the cooking, cleaning and the general chores of the home. She is also largely responsible for the upbringing of the children – and in the event of desertion by the male she will continue to look after them. When, however, this sort of union is successful the male takes a keen interest, as well as pride, in his children's progress and is usually very fond of them. Edith Clarke comments on the high ratio of outside children of the woman who are also included in the faithful concubinage home as compared with those of the man:

'in other words, the marked tendency for women to keep their young children wherever it was possible, and the rejection by the stepmother of her husband's children by another woman' (11).

But, in any case, Miss Clarke's first statement implies that the husband's children by another woman are likely to be retained by the latter anyway if she is now cohabiting with another man – so that 'rejection by the step-mother' is more of a passive than an active thing.

The third type of family structure is variously called a *companionate union* or *keeper family*. This is a consensual cohabitation or temporary union which, of course, may eventually become a faithful concubinage if the two partners are perfectly happy with their relationship. Normally such a union would be of less than about three years' duration, and its chief purpose is to provide companionship and a sexual outlet for the two partners. In return for the home which the man provides for the woman and her children, if any, she will be expected to act as his housekeeper and to look after his physical comfort. This form of union, however, is consider-ably more unstable than faithful concubinage; it is recognized from the start as being of a temporary nature, and in many instances the woman is increasingly imposed upon by the man. She may in consequence frequently go out to work in order to support her mate and the children. Gradually the keeper union breaks up and is replaced by a series of relationships which are merely casual. Henriques maintains that this type of union tends to occur more in the younger age groups during the period of sexual experimentation, although it is by no means confined to such age groups (12).

The fourth form of familial structure is referred to by T. S. Simey as the *disintegrate family*, and by Henriques as the *maternal* or *grandmother family*. In a series of propositions about the family structure in Guyana, R. T. Smith underlines his belief, as a result of detailed and systematic study, that most Negro lower-class householders are 'matrifocal', that is, they are dominated by women in their various roles as grandmother, mother and wife (13). All these terms are open to question, and 'distintegrate' and 'maternal' are not necessarily interchangeable; in fact, it is doubtful whether Simey's term 'disintegrate' can really be applied to all these families in any meaningful sort of way. Many of them are far from disintegrate in the sense that they are lacking in cohesion; this sense of cohesion is, in fact, provided by the matrifocal dimension. Certainly European concepts of the nuclear family cannot be applied to the West Indies, and what would appear as 'disintegrate' in our society is not necessarily so in theirs.

The maternal family may, in fact, originate in a variety of ways; it may be a family from which the adult male has withdrawn at the end of an unsatisfactory temporary union. Quite commonly it is the sort of family in which young daughters have become pregnant, have had their children and have now left them to their mothers or grandmothers to look after whilst they go out to work and earn money to provide for their children. Henriques distinguishes two types of family in this category:

'One where there is no male head of the family and the grandmother or other female relative fulfils the function of both father and mother; and the other where the grandmother may stand in the place of the mother but a man is nominally the head of the household' (14).

Should any of the girls later develop a keeper relationship with some male, or participate in a faithful concubinage, she will probably claim her child, or children, and settle down elsewhere with her newly acquired mate.

According to Henriques 'polygamy' occurs in Jamaica most frequently in the sugar parishes, that is, those areas where the main occupation of the people is labouring on the sugar estates (15). Since this is seasonal work there is a tendency for a man to keep a concubine and a household near the sugar estate, and to run a similar establishment in the town where he works during the off-season. Edith Clarke, however, rejects Henriques' definition of polygamy as unacceptable. For Henriques polygamy 'describes a man or woman cohabiting with more than one of the opposite sex' (16). But what Henriques refers to as 'polygamy' is simply an established form of extra-residential mating; polygamy, in the social anthropological sense of the term, can exist only where the law recognizes it (17).

One wonders, however, whether it is not possible to carry precise terminology too far. From an official anthropological point of view polygamy as such may not exist in Jamaica, but in more popular terms there is an incidence of polygamous behaviour, which to some extent supports the view put forward by M. J. Herskovits that the contemporary West Indian *mores* in relation to sex, marriage and the family are a survival of West African life prior to enslavement (18). It has been forcefully argued that not only is there considerable variety of sexual behaviour and familial structure amongst Negroes in the New World, but that there was also as much variety in the Old World from which the Negro came. The argument goes on to contend that it would be virtually impossible for any one culture to survive in its entirety; but this is by no means here suggested. All that is affirmed is that polygamy has had a long history in Africa, and that even if it were not established as an institution in the West Indies the concept and attitude of 'polygamy' has lingered on. The post-slavery patterns of sex life are undoubtedly in many ways a continuance of the situation under the conditions of slavery, with its permissive promiscuity. And the present family structure, though not exclusively a product of slavery, was certainly hardened by it.

It is a fact that there is a very high illegitimacy rate in the Caribbean area – in most islands it is between about 50 and 70 per cent of all live births. That is to say, from a purely legal point of view, they are illegitimate. In Jamaica the rate of illegitimacy was as high as 72 per cent in 1954, and is still in the region of 70 per cent (19). To Henriques this indicates that the

'so-called deviation from the norm of Christian monogamous marriage appears to be fairly uniform over the whole area. It is suggested, therefore, that a single type of family organization exists throughout the Caribbean' (20).

It is impossible to demonstrate this here by dealing with every single Caribbean community, but the evidence is certainly sufficiently strong to support this generalization. For example, the statements made by R. T. Smith with reference to marriage and family in what is now Guyana (formerly British Guiana) are applicable at least to the Negro element of most Caribbean societies (21). Smith also suggests that for probably between a quarter and a third of East Indian girls in Guyana the early years of adult life may be as unstable as they are for the Negro girl. The only difference is that the parents of Indian girls will constantly attempt to get them settled, and initially they will have been through the experience of a community-recognized ceremony.

The majority of illegitimate births in Guyana result from pregnancies among Negro girls before marriage, from births to women involved in unions similar to the faithful concubinage of the Jamaican society, and from the Indian marriages which have not been formally legalized. In a society in which young people meet very frequently at dances, at wakes, and on many other social occasions, it is perhaps not surprising that pregnancies occur quite early in the life of a young girl. There is a lack of general education and of contraceptive practice; and the male's virility is demonstrated only by his impregnation of the female; and the female's fertility is equally demonstrated by her capacity to become pregnant. At first the pregnant girl will be violently upbraided and rejected by her outraged mother – who will herself have produced a number of illegitimate children. But the only social considerations here are not of a moral nature but of an economic one: the birth of the illegitimate child carries no social stigma in itself; it merely presents a barrier to immediate social advance for its mother. And, whilst the grandmother will gladly look after the child and help to rear it once the initial stage of almost dramatized anger and rejection has been overcome, pressure will almost certainly be brought to bear upon the father to assist financially in the maintenance of his child. If he should prove reluctant to assist, an affiliation order may eventually be applied for at the courts.

B COLOUR AND CLASS SYSTEMS

The black people of Jamaica represent about 78 per cent of the total population, and the majority of them fall within the labourer-peasant or lower class (22). The word 'black' refers to people who are predominantly African in origin; but, unlike the United States of America, which divides its citizens into white and black, Jamaica uses the term 'coloured' for those individuals who are a mixture of white and black. This group is usually referred to by the general term 'mulatto'. Strictly speaking a mulatto is the offspring of a white and a black; a quadroon is the offspring of a white and a mulatto; a mustee is the offspring of a white and a quadroon; a musteffino is the offspring of a white and a mustee; and a sambo is the offspring of a black and a mulatto. But of these the only terms remaining in common use are mulatto and sambo.

Throughout the whole of the West Indies there is a large number of different ethnic groups. The aboriginal peoples of these islands, the Arawak in the Greater Antilles and the Carib in the Lesser Antilles, declined rapidly as the islands were conquered by European adventurers. Any aboriginal biological traits have long ago been absorbed into the European and African elements; the only exceptions appear to be British Honduras, Guyana and the Windward Islands.

European planters included those of Spanish, French, Portuguese and British nationality. Many of these Europeans brought their servants with them; other individuals were kidnapped and pressed into various forms of service; and, finally, criminals who had committed serious crimes were deported to the Caribbean for life. To these elements were added the African slaves from a heterogeneous number of tribes, with varying genetic heredity as well as a variety of languages, dialects, cultures and customs. And, finally, in order to maintain the plantation economy, Chinese and East Indian labour was introduced.

It is true that some of these elements have integrated without any attempts at complete assimilation; they have managed to retain their biological and cultural identity. There are, however, many West Indians who are of mixed descent; Jamaica is reported as having 17 per cent of mixed race; Trinidad 16 per cent; the Windward Islands 12·8 per cent; Guyana 10 per cent and Barbados 6 per cent (23). It must be admitted, however, that such figures are a somewhat unreliable indication of the extent of miscegenation.

The West Indians have developed an almost minutely analytical approach towards the question of colour. It is certainly not as simple as 'black' and 'white' – or even, for that matter, 'black', 'white' and 'coloured'. There is a graduation from very dark to pure white including such categories as 'dark', 'fair', 'red skin', 'bad hair' or kinky, 'good hair' or straight, and so on. The 'fair' group is mainly European in appearance, and some are indistinguishable from Europeans. Indeed, for most 'coloured' as distinct from 'Negro' West Indians, the ideal is identification with the European. This colour consciousness is very strong among the West Indians and although, as Henriques points out (24), the actual value of a particular characteristic may vary from island to island, nearness to European and distance from African characteristics – from skin colour to skin texture and facial configuration – are the main criteria in a consideration of an individual's social position.

In the recent past the processes of hair-straightening and skin-bleaching have been an indication of this racial and colour consciousness. Where, however, African nationalist groups and black power groups have developed, such practices have become anathema and a betrayal of the Negro cause. The fact remains, however, that in the West Indian social hierarchy the upper classes are, in broad terms, represented by the whites and the fair coloureds, the middle classes by a variety of coloureds, and the lower classes mostly by blacks or near blacks. And inevitably those in the professions and executive positions are mainly white or fair coloured, those in jobs involving supervisory ability and clerical competence are mainly in the coloured and black middle classes, whilst the black lower classes are mainly peasant labourers.

But here again it would seem to be impossible to generalize since, for example, a dark-coloured doctor would probably not be regarded as more than middle class. It is clear that social class and economic class are not necessarily identical, since a poor white may, in fact, be higher in the social scale than a rich black man. As Madeline Kerr has remarked,

'class and colour interweave to such an extent that a problem which has its origin in class structure may appear to be a conflict over colour' (25),

and one might add that the reverse is also true, that what might appear at first sight to be a conflict in class structure may have its origin in conflict over colour. Thus the appointment, for instance, of *custos* in Jamaica, which is similar to that of a Lord-Lieutenant in this country, was never until recent years given to a black man. In fact Henriques said in 1953 that it was one of the offices in Jamaica that had 'never been held by a black man' (26). A black man may have greater social status through the fact of being married to a fair wife than because of his personal wealth.

R. T. Smith mentions similar class, colour, social and economic problems in Guyana, and he makes the point that social identification depends upon criteria other than just physical appearance (27). According to Smith, the two factors in every society which *may* remain 'the crucial social attributes' throughout the individual's life are his family and his place of birth. But in some societies such natal criteria may be devalued and greater stress may be placed upon individual achievement. In Guyana the category 'white' implies of European origin – other than Portuguese – and is regarded as possessing a certain superiority and authority. This exclusion of the Portuguese under the category of 'white' or 'European' is interesting. At the 1946 census the number of Europeans, including Portuguese, was given as about 11,000; the figure given by Smith for 1959 was about 5,000 Europeans, excluding Portuguese. Smith suggests that it is the English life-style, including dress, choice of food, and speech patterns, which provides the social image of the 'white' group. Hence the exclusion of the Portuguese element from this highest social stratum is a logical one, if looked at simply from the point of view of the style of life rather than colour or race.

Times are, however, changing. Smith wrote his book in 1961 and many things have happened since then in what was formerly British Guiana. The Portuguese have some of the largest business houses in Guyana; they are basically traders; they are Roman Catholics; and most of them are, in politics, opposed to left-wing movements. Although little effort has been made by many Portuguese to preserve their national identity, or even to speak their mother-tongue, there can be little doubt about the increasing importance of certain Portuguese elements both in politics and in society (28).

Unlike the Chinese in Jamaica, who constitute a separatist group of the middle class, the Chinese in Guyana have assimilated to such an extent that they have intermarried with women of all other ethnic groups. In Jamaica a Chinese man may certainly have a concubine who is black or coloured, but he will invariably marry a Chinese wife and maintain an ethnic and social isolation. But in Guyana he has gradually become absorbed into the major society and, because of his fair skin, straight hair, and his pertinacious ability to progress in his occupation, he has ascended in the social hierarchy. Although there is a Chinese Association still in existence in Georgetown which, from time to time, attempts to resuscitate vestiges of Chinese customs and festivals, there is no organized or institutionalized maintenance of Chinese culture.

The groups which are most numerous in Guyana are the East Indians and the Africans. The latter have intermingled with most of the other races to be found there, and in consequence it is not always easy to view them as an entirely separate ethnic group. Indeed, the 1946 Census showed a classification of 'Mixed' which numbered 37,685, that is, about 10 per cent of the total population. But there must have been many others in the 'African' group, which numbered 143,385, who were certainly not pure Negro. The Negroes as a group, however, were the first to assimilate to English culture. In this steady assimilation many, of course, have passed through the Commonwealth system of education; and this has given them at least the possibility of entering the middle class. Most of them have, however, remained members of the lower classes working in factories in the towns or on sugar plantations, or as farm labourers.

The East Indian element represents about 45 per cent of the peoples of Guyana, and they have been absorbed more recently into the society and represent a more clearly defined racial group. This fact is even more remarkable when one realizes the conditions under which these indentured labourers worked on the plantations after the emancipation of slaves. Because of the incredibly cramped conditions of their quarters the Indians were quite unable to pursue their religious practices, or to maintain their laws of avoidance and ritual purity under the caste system. In fact, the caste system as such practically disappeared quite early on, with the possible exception of the extremes between the high-caste Brahmins at the top of the scale and the Chamar caste of leather-workers at the lowest end of the untouchables. A further modification of Hindu culture and social structure has been effected through the lack of Indian women, at least initially. The traditional Indian family life and kin-group system found it difficult to persist in a society which did little or nothing to help in the maintenance of Hindu culture, and in which Indian women were frequently enticed from their menfolk.

The development of Indians within the Guyanese social system has been a slow one. According to R. T. Smith most of them adopted the prevailing middle-class creole culture despite the discrimination which they frequently experienced when seeking an entrée to particular social clubs, cliques and associations. Smith states that in 1914 there were only five Indians in the legal profession and three in medical practice (29). An East Indian Association was founded in 1916, which later established its headquarters at Georgetown, with the object at its inception of redressing the urgent grievances of Indian workers. As the control of this Association gradually passed over to the merchant group its purpose changed into one concerned mainly with the furtherance of Indian culture and religion.

Gradually, however, the creolization of the East Indian proceeded, so that Indian languages and vernaculars were replaced by one or more dialects of English; and Indian dress, homes, recreations and interests became increasingly modified by the environment. From time to time there has been a recrudescence of Indian culture through such movements as the *Arya Samaj*; but in the long run not only has traditional Hinduism steadily decreased, but attempts at arousing racial identity even for political purposes have never really been a viable proposition. Interests can, however, quickly change; and a highly fertile group such as the East Indians, who already represent 45 per cent of the population, could well present a political as well as a social solidarity.

It was noted earlier that the Arawak Indians have virtually disappeared from the islands of the West Indies, and that very few people of near-pure Carib stock remain in the Lesser Antilles. There are, however, about twenty thousand or so Amerindians still in the interior areas of Guyana, and also nearer the coast, particularly north-west of Georgetown. Any organized attempts to protect the Amerindians from the evils of civilization have been abandoned, and the official policy is now to integrate the aborigines within the Guyanese population. Such a policy is not a particularly easy one in a country where there are very few railways indeed, a limited complex of passable roads, and a steadily increasing number of trails. Before the Amerindians can be fully integrated they must first be reached, and this means considerably improved communications. Through such improvements more and better schools could eventually be established; it must inevitably be a slow business absorbing any indigenous group such as these, although in 1962 R. T. Smith claimed that missionaries

'have been, and are increasingly, active and at least half the Amerindian population is now literate in English. Government and law reaches even the most remote areas though justice has to be tempered with understanding sometimes' (30).

Certainly Guyana may lack railways and roads, but even the most remote areas are ultimately accessible by air. Michael Swan suggests that it is possible that eventually cheap transport on a large scale will make the development of trunk roads unnecessary (31). At first blush it would appear that even the most remote areas ought eventually to be accessible to any really determined group, such as explorers or police, through the innumerable rivers and waterways. But travel on the larger rivers is usually impeded, beyond a certain point, by cataracts and rapids.

In general, in a consideration of the class system and social status in Guyana, it becomes clear that both birth and colour are important; but perhaps equally so are educational levels, manners, dress and speech patterns. There is a great emphasis upon the value of white-collar occupations for which a jacket and a tie must be worn, and which are considered the highest in the hierarchy of jobs. Status is also indicated by speech; lower-class groups will speak a variety of dialects of English, a Creole or local patois, whilst those who belong to the upper class speak an accurate form of English. The Guyanese refer to Creole as 'talkie-talkie', and it is frequently used as a second language for common chatter amongst the young, who will readily lapse into more formal English when talking to the better educated.

The upper class is represented by a small group of Guyanese who are separated from the large lower-class group by an ever-increasing middle class. Many in this class, however, are in reality very little better off than the peasant labourers because, although initially they may be higher paid, in attempting to keep up with the top levels of the middle class, their expenditure is disproportionate to their remuneration.

We have considered colour and class in two of the largest territories in the West Indies, namely Jamaica and Guyana. It is as dangerous to generalize about the islands and mainland countries of the Caribbean as it is concerning any other heterogeneous groups of human beings or societies. But there is a certain pattern which runs through all these societies which have a basically common history and development, involving conquest, subjugation, slavery and colonization. And whilst it is desirable to look at them all individually in order to understand more fully the specific problems of immigrants from, say, Trinidad, British Honduras or the Windward Islands, it is nevertheless true to say that the question of class and colour as experienced in Jamaica and Guyana are fundamentally the same sort of problems as one finds in the rest of the Caribbean. It is said that today no absolute colour bar exists in the West Indies, although some discrimination against the very dark may be found in certain public places. Wealth is still a decisive factor which will open the door to the darkest. However, as Richmond comments,

'The fact remains that the lighter a West Indian's complexion, the more acceptable he is in middle- and upper-class society' (32).

C KINSHIP
There is a very strong sense of kinship among the lower classes of Jamaican society, which is also fairly general throughout the West Indies. The extended family of the Caribbean societies will include father, mother, their own children, their children by other mates, adopted children, aunts and uncles, and other relatives whose connection may be somewhat remote. Edith Clarke made a thorough study of three different cultural areas in Jamaica, and of something like 679 households studied about 14 per cent were of the 'extended' variety. Miss Clarke's study is a highly detailed and sophisticated one, and the categories of household organization which she delineates are the result of a thorough anthropological study. It is impossible, even in outline, to reproduce her classification of household types here without doing her work an injustice. Her research, however, supports the statement made by Sheila Patterson to the effect that

'The West Indian literature emphasizes the relative strength among the lower-class majority of the consanguineous kinship link, particularly on the mother's side. . . . The most important link, not only through childhood, but usually throughout adult life, is that between mother (or mother-substitute) and child' (33).

And in the West Indies the customary mother-substitute is the maternal grandmother.

In the maternal family, with the grandmother in control, there is a greatly accentuated sense of kinship, of family or group identity, which is carried into all of the group's activities. The members of the group may not know precisely what their relationship is to one another; but, despite this vagueness of precise genetic relationship, once kinship is accepted because of the presence of individuals within the home, no one questions what the basis of that kinship is. 'Legitimate', 'illegitimate', 'adopted' – these are not terms used by kin groups themselves; they are the classifications of statisticians and of social anthropologists seeking to establish some sort of pattern of social behaviour.

Henriques tells us that there are three general relationship terms used, which are in themselves vague and which express equally vague relationships, but which nevertheless establish an acceptable and relatively permanent position. One is 'coz', which is really an abbreviation for 'cousin', an archaic survival of sixteenth-century English and certainly found in Shakespeare's plays. The second term is 'uncle', which is used generally for all male relatives of an older generation. This is a quite common usage in many simpler societies and tribal communities in the islands of the Pacific. The third term is 'aunty', which is used for a father's or mother's sisters; and in any discussion of the family fortunes there may be far more numerous references to a particular 'aunty' and her influence in the family group than to the mother or father. 'Coz' has become an appellation for any member of the kin group of any generation, irrespective of age, and irrespective of true genetic connection (34).

In general, it is true that the upper classes experience less of this feeling of kinship than do the lower classes. One obvious reason for this is the palpable willingness of people to extend their sense of equality at impoverished levels, and their reluctance to include others within their affluence – particularly those who are, in reality, in no way related to them by blood. But there is one event which levels everyone even in the West Indies, namely death, which only serves to underline the fact of kinship even among the higher levels of society. Death is a great occasion in the West Indies when sorrow, fear, rejoicing, adulation, confession, storytelling, obscenity, singing, dancing, eating and drinking are all mingled in a long, almost uninterrupted repetition of elemental rituals. Obeah, duppy catching, esoteric rites, formulas – all have their place in the long, seemingly endless wakes which are the inevitable concomitant of the burial, which must take place within twenty-four hours of death for hygienic rather than religious reasons. A wake is an occasion as well as an excuse for a kinship reunion which welcomes at the same time any passing homeless tramp looking for a free meal.

3. A country home and family, Grenada.

4. *Top:* 'Cricket, lovely Cricket' at Woburn, Grenada, (*bottom*) Caribbean ethnic group, Jamaica.

It is, of course, easy to misinterpret the wake and to misconstrue it as a glorified binge, without order and purpose. In fact, however primitive in form it may be, the West Indian wake is a carefully ordered and dramatized ritual. Not only does the kin group adjust to the fact of the loss of a member, it also ensures that the spirit of the lost member can never return. This is done more specifically by sweeping behind the coffin as it is conveyed to the family graveyard, which is usually situated in the kin-group yard which contains a washroom, a tap and a latrine. The body is then buried with an Eastern orientation, and the wake begins. The latter will continue for nine days, and most of the nights as well. Everything leads up to the ninth night – referred to as 'Nint Night' – when the games, food and African folk stories eventually give way to a ritual of rhythmic music and dancing, hymn singing, Bible reading, and a conscienceless flattery of the departed.

At first sight one element appears out of character with the rest of the ritual, namely the singing of obscene songs. Henriques considers that this latter activity 'can be regarded as an outlet for the fear implicit in any situation concerned with the spirits' (35). It is certainly difficult to explain obscenity in the context of the wake in teleological terms: and anything so alien to the general tenor of the ritual, at least in terms of Bible reading and hymn singing, clearly has no theological or philosophical rationale. A psychological explanation, therefore, such as that of Henriques seems the most likely. The obscenity, however, may present not so much a spirit-directed activity as an expression of bravado in the face of the ultimate terror of death itself. It may be a demonstration in the final hours of 'Nint Night' that death has at least no power to claim them, and their obscenities are an expression of superiority over the dead man who has at last succumbed.

Another explanation at the psychological level may be that the wake is an expression, in intensive micro-form, of the totality of the life of the participants. In a period of nine days they manage to cover all their normal activities and functionings, and the multiplexity of the levels of life. The obscene is no exception in this respect. It is a level which, for the most part, may be kept under control and is unconscious. The wake is literally an occasion when the individual, as well as the group, passes through the whole gamut of human emotions which are released in a ritualistic and stylized way. And the permissibility and acceptance of this particular form of expression make it possible to take up levels of thought which normally would be resisted and would be regarded as socially unacceptable. Indeed, collective obscenity on these occasions may simply represent a further expression of social and kinship identity at the lowest and most earthy level, just as the hymns, the Bible readings, the prayers, and the Buchmanite-like confessions represent a social and spiritual solidarity at the highest level. And the secret obeah activity, with the Anansi-Tacooma folklore cycle, together provide a racial and historical identity that makes the 'Nine Days' and the 'Nint Night' a socially, spiritually and psychically integrating experience. Ultimately, the extended family and the kinship group are one at the level of the racial unconscious.

REFERENCES

1 Herskovits, M. J., *The Myth of the Negro Past* (Harpers, 1941).
2 Simey, T. S., *Welfare and Planning in the West Indies* (O.U.P., 1946).
3 Henriques, F., *Family and Colour in Jamaica* (MacGibbon & Kee, 2nd edition 1968).
4 Clarke, Edith, *My Mother Who Fathered Me* (Allen & Unwin, 2nd edition 1966).
5 *Vide* Clarke, E., op. cit., p. x.
6 *Vide* Smith, R. T., *The Negro Family in British Guiana* (Routledge, 1956).
7 FitzHerbert, Katrin, 'The West Indian Background' in Oakley, R. (ed.), *New Backgrounds* (O.U.P., 1968), p. 9.
8 Henriques, F., op. cit., pp. 90 and 110.
9 Ibid., p. 109.
10 Clarke, E., op. cit., pp. 29–30.
11 Ibid., p. 75.
12 Henriques, F., op. cit., p. 114.
13 Smith, R. T., op. cit., pp. 223–4.
14 Henriques, F., op. cit., p. 113.
15 Ibid., pp. 96–7.
16 Ibid., p. 90.
17 *Vide* Clarke, E., op. cit., p. 30.
18 *Vide* Herskovits, M. J., *The Myth of the Negro Past* (Harpers, 1941), pp. 143–206.
19 *Vide* Merton, R. K. (ed.), *Contemporary Social Problems* (Hart-Davis, 1965).
20 Henriques, F., op. cit., p. 108.
21 *Vide* Smith, R. T., *British Guiana* (O.U.P., 1962), pp. 128–34.
22 Henriques, F., op. cit., p. 50.
23 Hooper, R. (ed.), *Colour in Britain* (B.B.C., 1965), p. 31.
24 Henriques, F., op. cit., pp. 54–5.
25 Kerr, Madeline, *Personality and Conflict in Jamaica* (Liverpool Univ. Press, 1952), p. 93.
26 Henriques, F., op. cit., p. 60. Cf. p. 173.
27 Smith, R. T., op. cit., pp. 98–117.
28 *Vide* Swan, M., *British Guiana* (H.M.S.O., 1957), pp. 55–6; and Smith, R. T., op. cit., pp. 102–4.
29 Smith, R. T., op. cit., p. 108.
30 Ibid., p. 113.
31 Swan, M., op. cit., p. 160.
32 Richmond, A. H., *The Colour Problem* (Penguin, revised edition 1961), p. 225.
33 *Vide* Clarke, E., op. cit., p. 123; and Patterson, Sheila, *Dark Strangers* (Penguin, 1965), p. 295.

34 Henriques, F., op. cit., pp. 139–40.
35 Ibid., p. 145.

BIBLIOGRAPHY

A GENERAL
Ayearst, M., *The British West Indies: The Search for Self-Government* (Allen & Unwin, 1960).
Davis, A. *et al.*, *Deep South* (Chicago, 1941).
Guerin, D., *The British West Indies and their Future* (Dennis Dobson, 1961).
Herskovits, M. J., *The Myth of the Negro Past* (Harpers, 1941).
Hoetink, H., *The Two Variants in Caribbean Relations* (O.U.P., 1967).
Naipaul, V. S., *The Middle Passage* (A. Deutsch, 1962).
Nicole, C., *The West Indies* (Hutchinson, 1965).
Oakley, R. (ed.), *New Backgrounds* (O.U.P., 1968); Chapter I, 'The West Indian Background', by Katrin FitzHerbert.
Patterson, Sheila, *Dark Strangers* (Penguin, 1965).
Pearcy, G. E., *The West Indian Scene* (Van Nostrand, 1965).
Rattray, R. S., *Akan-Ashanti Folk-Tales* (O.U.P., 1930).
Richmond, A. H., *The Colour Problem* (Penguin, revised edition 1961), Chapter 4, 'Aftermath of Slavery in the West Indies'.
Rubin, V. (ed.), *Caribbean Studies: A Symposium* (Jamaica, 1957).
Sherlock, P., *West Indies* (Thames & Hudson, 1966).
Simey, T. S., *Welfare and Planning in the West Indies* (O.U.P., 1946).
Smith, M. G., *West Indian Family Structure* (Univ. of Washington Press, 1962).
Smith, M. G., *The Plural Society in the British West Indies* (Univ. of California Press, 1965).

B JAMAICA
Blake, Judith, *Family Structure in Jamaica* (Free Press of Glencoe, 1961).
Clarke, Edith, *My Mother Who Fathered Me* (Allen & Unwin, 2nd edition 1966).
Davenport, W., 'The Family System of Jamaica', *Social and Economic Studies* (Univ. College of West Indies, Jamaica, 1961).
Francis, O. C., *The People of Modern Jamaica* (Jamaica, Dept. of Statistics, 1964).
Henriques, F., *Family and Colour in Jamaica* (MacGibbon & Kee, 2nd edition 1968).
Jamaican High Commission, *Cultural and Educational Background of Jamaican Children* (London, H.C.O., 1967).
Jekyll, W. (ed.), *Jamaican Song and Story* (Dover, 1966).
Kerr, Madeline, *Personality and Conflict in Jamaica* (Liverpool Univ. Press, 1952).
Norris, K., *Jamaica: The Search for an Identity* (O.U.P., 1962).

C TRINIDAD
Herskovits, M. J. and F. S., *Trinidad Village* (Knopf, 1947).
Klass, M., *East Indians in Trinidad: A Study of Cultural Persistence* (Columbia Univ. Press, 1961).
Suze, J. A. de, *The New Trinidad and Tobago* (Collins, 1965).

D GUYANA

Central Office of Information, *Guyana* (H.M.S.O., 1966).

Henfrey, C., *The Gentle People* (Hutchinson, 1964).

Nath, Dwarka, *A History of Indians in British Guiana* (Nelson, 1950).

Newman, P., *British Guiana: Problems of Cohesion in an Immigrant Society* (O.U.P., 1964).

Smith, R. T., *The Negro Family in British Guiana* (Routledge, 1956).

Smith, R. T., *British Guiana* (O.U.P., 1962).

Swan, M., *British Guiana: The Land of Six Peoples* (H.M.S.O., 1957).

Chapter 4

Education in the
West Indies

A SLAVERY AND EMANCIPATION

It is obviously clear that it was never really in the interests of the planters to educate in any way the slaves they owned. Literacy and articulateness inexorably lead to the expression of personal opinion and to the unification of the oppressed in at least some vocal form of opposition and rebellion. The work demanded of slaves in the plantations required a minimum of intelligence and skill; it seemed pointless, therefore, to spend time or money in educating a group which was basically regarded by the slave-owners as virtually a form of animal labour.

Some writers, however, distinguish very definitely the relations between Iberian colonists and the negroids, and those between north-west European colonists and the negroids. Hoetink puts the case fairly in his *The Two Variants in Caribbean Race Relations* (1), where he contrasts the Spanish and the British forms of colonization, and argues that in the Iberian areas the human element was not completely subsumed in slavery, for the slave was a member of the Christian community. This view is also expressed by W. J. Cahnman who

'contrasts the Spanish, Catholic concept of the all-embracing faith which includes racial assimilation and successfully counteracts all tendencies to social and economic fission, with the British tendency to racialism (based on the supposition of the greater ability of their own, "homogeneous", people for large-scale enterprises which depend upon free co-operation), and the related tendency to abstention, non-involvement and segregation' (2).

It is true that the Iberians generally had more experience of colonization and slavery than the British and the Dutch, and perhaps a greater understanding of the problems of personal relations with members of other races. And no doubt there is a great deal of evidence to support the thesis expressed by Cahnman and developed by Hoetink, but this is not just a question of difference in race; it is also a difference in the brand of Christianity represented by each group, and the extent to which that particular brand was mediated to other races. Certainly the Catholics had a considerable missionary and proselytizing zeal which was in no way matched by the Anglican Church. But whilst there was little enthusiasm on the part of the established Protestant church, it would be wrong to suggest that nothing at all was done to assist the slaves to learn something of Christianity and its values, or even in some instances to develop a minimum literacy.

Nonconformist missionaries frequently found themselves in opposition to both planters and Anglican priests in their endeavour to 'Christianize' the slaves and to improve their cultural, social and educational standards. Thus, whilst the *official* British attitude may have been, as Tannenbaum suggests (3), to deny the slaves almost completely the privileges of Christianity, it is not true to imply that this was the total view of Protestantism. In the eighteenth century the Moravians, Baptists, Methodists and Presbyterians began a vigorous campaign to establish schools to teach the slave population; and, in so far as they were permitted, they continued to do this.

Emancipation in 1833 brought freedom, at least technically, to about three-quarters of a million slaves. It soon became clear that men, women and children who once lived in a state of slavery were now in fact citizens, and that citizens required to be socialized and brought to some realization of their need for order, discipline and unity. A people who were palpably ignorant, and who were lacking in any sort of leadership or possibility of development, needed education above all else. In 1835 a grant of £30,000 was made for the education of ex-slaves in the British colonies; and during that and the ensuing year three training colleges were established, one in Jamaica, one in Trinidad, and one in Demerara. Their immediate purpose was to train native teachers to teach in new schools of all denominations as they were built.

There has always been the feeling amongst the West Indians that the only way finally to obtain any real sort of equality with white people and with the ruling classes generally was to become as well educated as possible – in fact, as well educated as those who have in the past ruled them. But the development and expansion of education has been slow. It is of interest to note that whilst the earliest teachers' training college in England, namely Borough Road College, was founded in 1798, the next development of any importance of such colleges was at just about the same time as that of the colleges in the West Indies.

B MORE RECENT DEVELOPMENTS

The years between 1838 and 1938 have been characterized by the Jamaican High Commission in London as 'an era of educational stagnation' as far as Jamaica is concerned (4). If this statement is true of Jamaica it appears to be equally true of most of the remainder of the countries in the Caribbean and Guyana. It would be wrong to suggest, as some have done, that this stagnation was due entirely to the control which the churches have exerted over education; but it must be remembered that the West Indies are multiracial, and that a country such as Guyana, for example, is not even nominally Christian. R. T. Smith holds that

'The churches have played their part in the educational development of British Guiana just as they have in England but their day is done' (5).

There has always been a strong English orientation in the education of the British West Indies, and because of this the development of a really indigenous culture has been stultified. No one would deny the difficulties of achieving such a development in a country like Guyana; but, as R. T. Smith points out, so long as a state system of education is provided there is no reason why special schools for the learning of Hindu, Muslim or Christian scriptures should not be operated on the basis of small supplementary grants. The state schools would exist to provide as far as possible a common ground for integration or at least partial assimilation; the schools centred upon religious sects would be additional to the state schools, and their sole purpose would be the preservation of those elements of individual culture and belief peculiar to each religion.

But what has been said of Guyana applies in similar ways to other communities in the West Indian scene, such as Jamaica. Jamaica is nominally Christian, but it is nevertheless multi-racial and multi-cultural, and what R. T. Smith has said of Guyana applies equally to the rest of the Caribbean:

'When criticisms are levelled at the form and content of colonial education it is not so much the technical adequacy that is in question (though this has lagged a long way behind that of England during the twentieth century), but rather the psychologically damaging effect of teaching people to value what is alien to their own being' (6).

In the early days of the education of simple slaves and their descendants there was an argument for the development of some form of unity out of the heterogeneous population that existed. It seemed natural to establish such a unity through an English or British form of education; but once some form of unity had been established there was really little excuse for attempting to create another 'little England' wherever British colonizers were in operation.

C EDUCATION IN JAMAICA TODAY

The era of educational stagnation up to 1938 was followed by the war period during which there was very little opportunity for any radical change in educational provision or methods. It was not until after the Second World War that any real progress was made. In this section we shall concern ourselves with the developments made in Jamaican education during the past twenty-five years.

In order to improve learning and teaching situations it is obviously necessary to begin at the source, that is, it is essential to have better trained teachers, and facilities which permit of the exploration of new ideas and innovation generally. There are today some five teachers' training colleges in Jamaica in addition to the original Mico College established soon after emancipation. It is, of course, not sufficient just to have an increased number of colleges or amenities; the important thing is that they should provide and mediate the currently accepted methods of teaching and learning. Unfortunately, although founded and developed along the lines of English training colleges, those in Jamaica have always lagged behind in methodology. Katrin FitzHerbert quotes from a statement made by Elsa Walters, a former Deputy Director of the Institute of Education at the University of the West Indies, in which she says that in the schools a great deal of importance is attached to being able to give the right answer. She adds:

'There is little opportunity, and little encouragement, to think for oneself, or form one's own opinion. This is a handicap carried forward into secondary school, and even into training college and university, where hard work and diligent learning by heart appear, to the student, to be the only road to success' (7).

These things are, of course, a matter of degree. There is always a time-lag in educational development and in the mediation of change. And there is also a great need for consolidation and stability as well as for change and development. A prime function of education in such a country as Jamaica is not to establish a society which can compete on the same or equal terms with the rest of the world, but rather to elicit a social and cultural identity which will afford the people a sense of fulfilment as a group. Certainly the problem is not just one of method; it is also one of content. If, as Elsa Walters suggested, the teaching methods resemble those used in England a century ago, it is also true that the content of much Jamaican education is far removed from their own interests and needs.

Although fostered by the right sort of education, a sense of identity is something which grows through the application of critical analysis to what has happened in the social environment, and to what the society as a whole considers to be its social purpose. But it must be its *own* purpose. As Katrin Norris has rightly said, what the children require in order to fulfil their own potential educationally, as well as to develop a sense of identity and build a new society in Jamaican terms, is a teaching method and teaching material 'closely related to conditions of life which are familiar to them or understood by them'; moreover, they need to be given 'a critical understanding of their own country' (8).

Teacher-training remains very much a problem in Jamaica. And even though the question of supply may eventually be solved, the problems of methodology and the content of culture are ever-pressing ones. The question, 'What sort of society do we want?', is never an easy one to answer even for a society which is racially homogeneous, or relatively so. But for one which is heterogeneous or multi-racial, which has been largely a slave-labour and white-dominated society, and which is emerging into a colour-orientated one, the question is much more difficult to answer.

There are in Jamaica a number of teachers, referred to as 'probationers', whose sole qualification is that they have passed the Third Jamaica Local Examination, or the Jamaica Certificate of Education. These teachers, however, have not received any teacher-training, and they are really the equivalent in status of the five thousand or so 'unqualified teachers' in our own society (9). Some of these 'probationers' later go on to take a training. The training-college courses are, in the main, for three years, although two-year courses are also organized for students who are more mature, and who have had some practical teaching experience. There are also graduates who have taken the university diploma course in education. Three of the six training-colleges are co-educational, and the other three are at present for women only; one of these latter colleges is Roman Catholic and another Moravian.

The increasing importance of education in an island such as Jamaica becomes more obvious when one realizes that in 1943 Jamaica became the first black colony of Great Britain to receive universal suffrage. Since the masses are even now ill-informed and ill-educated, they are very susceptible to the blandishments and simple theories of the popular politicians. It is, of course, not *just* education that makes a people immune to political suggestion; it is the right sort of education through which individuals are encouraged to think independently, and to analyse critically what their purposes are.

The churches of all denominations still control the large number of primary schools in Jamaica, although they have never been able really to satisfy the needs or the demands of the Jamaicans. Gradually the Government has realized this need and has established a number of primary schools throughout the country. These primary schools are co-educational, and it must be appreciated that the word 'primary' here is not synonymous with the word 'primary' of the 1944 Education Act in this country.

Jamaican primary schools make provision for the education of children between the ages of six and fifteen years; that is, they are 'all-age schools'. In some areas children are admitted at the age of five.

Some of these all-age primary schools provide a type of education for senior children similar to that of the English secondary modern school. The curriculum, at first sight, appears broad enough, but an examination of the actual content reveals a paucity of depth and a somewhat slavish reproduction of the more conventional elements of English curricula. English language, including grammar, composition, spoken and written English, is a staple diet; this is supported by English literature, involving prose, poetry and drama. The difficulties of learning English, however, are revealed by Katrin Norris' statement that

'An indication of Jamaican children's handicaps was given in 1961 when 81 per cent of the candidates in the first public examination failed their English papers' (10).

The history taught is mainly that of England and the West Indies, and it is combined to some extent with a simple approach to civics. Mathematics is basically arithmetic, algebra and geometry; and the remainder of the curriculum includes religious knowledge, geography, health science, home economics, needlework, woodwork, art, theory of music and physical education. Some of the schools with senior sections also teach Spanish and Latin.

Naturally schools vary as much in Jamaica as anywhere else. There are primary schools in rural areas with about 450 or 500 children, in which classrooms are simply improvised divisions of a large hall or barn. These classrooms are tightly crammed with benches, and each room or 'division' may have to accommodate up to fifty or sixty children. When a teacher is absent through illness, two classrooms may have to be joined (simply by removing the blackboards) and another teacher will be landed with a class of about a hundred. It is perhaps fortunate that a large number of those children who are on the school register are not regular attenders. Many of the older children have to stay home in order to look after the younger ones; many are enforced truants because they have no clean clothes to wear; others are kept away in order that they may help with the household chores or assist in buying food from the markets.

Children in the primary schools suffer very much from the lack of properly trained teachers, from poor equipment and accommodation, and from textbooks which are redolent of a former age. The children's homes are equally impoverished so that as a result they are deprived both at school and at home where they have no toys or other play materials of any sort, no books or writing apparatus. At school really good visual aids are rare, and the chief method employed in learning is that of rote and choral repetition.

Writing in 1953 Henriques said that the 'elementary school population (children from seven to fourteen) for the whole of Jamaica is 234,519' (11). Out of this number he claimed that 80·6 per cent attended school, but he pointed out that this figure was misleading, and that attendance inevitably and progressively declined from Monday to Friday. This is still largely true, although the percentage of truants may be somewhat lower. Parents seem to have an ambivalent attitude towards the education available to their children. Whatever may happen in practice with regard to school attendance, in theory the view which parents consciously or unconsciously adopt towards education is that, ultimately, it is a means of elevating the individual in the social scale and of eliminating the stigma of manual labour.

Henriques holds that the Jamaican society is a *disnomic* one, as compared (say) with Britain which is *eunomic* (12). These terms were originally used by Professor A. R. Radcliffe Brown to delineate the degree of balance or integration which exists within any society. These are obviously relative terms only, since an absolutely disnomic society could not exist – there must be a minimum of integration for any society to survive. The disnomia in Jamaica is expressed by colour distinctions and the prejudices that attach to them and the resultant lack of total balance within the society. It is one of the purposes of education to help to restore this balance and to make society increasingly more eunomic. And it does this, eventually, by reducing the levels of poverty within the society.

In order to accomplish this aim it is obvious that all areas of education must be improved, including primary, secondary, and further or higher education, as well as the social values which education seeks to inculcate. Henriques, for example, complains that, whilst many teachers attempt to instil such virtues as gentleness, truthfulness and honour, it is in fact a losing battle. The home environment is too strong, and the child succumbs to his social *ambiance* with its meanness of accommodation as well as meanness of thought and attitude (13). What teacher has not complained of such depressing dichotomies between the standards and values of the school and those of the home? Part of the problem in Jamaica is the existence already of double standards in such questions as sex relations – there already exists the tacit prescription of 'Don't do as I do, but do as I tell you'. Children are no longer impressed with this principle, whether it be in Jamaica or England, or anywhere else. Although the problems of internationalization and socialization are universal, the acuteness of the problems in Jamaica derives largely from the attempt to introduce and impose standards and values of a society with a very different cultural history.

Although education is compulsory in the urban areas of Jamaica it is virtually impossible to enforce this. It is, however, the avowed aim of the Jamaican Government to work towards education for all from the ages of six to sixteen, with free secondary education from about eleven years of age. In 1957 a Common Entrance Examination was introduced to provide free places for children in secondary schools; and the Government esti- mates that during the ten years from 1957 to 1967 more than four thousand children were awarded secondary places annually as a result of their prowess at this examination. This compares very favourably with something like 150 per annum before the introduction of the Common Entrance Examina- tion.

The secondary schools owe their origin to the early establishment of secondary grammar schools and public schools for the children of planters during the days of slavery. They were naturally modelled upon English public schools, and they had a curriculum which was almost entirely classical. It is only within recent years that the curriculum has been extended to include modern languages and science. The children of planters were thus trained to play their part in government and in the higher levels of society generally. From his grammar or public school the student later went on to further education of one sort or another, and might then pass into commerce or the civil service.

As the examination system developed in England so it was passed on, practically without modification, to the grammar schools in Jamaica. At first the London Matriculation and the Cambridge Higher Schools Certificate were taken; since 1963, however, there has been a reorganiza- tion of the examination system, and pupils now sit for the Cambridge, or London examination boards' overseas General Certificate of Education. Those pupils who are incapable of reaching an 'O Level' standard may sit for the Jamaica School Certificate examination, which is roughly the equivalent of our Certificate of Secondary Education (C.S.E.).

Until 1955 the Senior Schools provided for those children whose parents were too poor to send them on to a secondary grammar school. At these schools, from about the age of twelve, children of average ability and intelligence have pursued a course of study leading to the First and Second Jamaica School Certificate Examination. The curriculum of the twelve Senior Schools develops the subjects taught in the primary schools, but in addition it provides some introduction to the technical skills, metalwork and technical drawing. These schools also make provision for additional courses for pupils of fifteen to seventeen years of age; such courses are of a pre-apprenticeship nature.

At present there are forty-two secondary schools in Jamaica, twenty of which are co-educational, nine for boys and thirteen for girls. In recent years there has been a tendency for the curriculum to lean increasingly towards mathematics, economics and the sciences, including physics, chemistry and biology. This developing interest in the sciences, and also in technology, is further demonstrated by the fact that until 1957 there was only one technical school in Jamaica; today there are six. The curriculum of these schools is similar in content to that pursued by the secondary technical schools in England; and the length of the course is at the moment a minimum of four years. A variety of examinations is offered including, on the technical side, stages one and two of the Royal Society of Arts, and on the academic side, the Jamaica School Certificate Examination and the G.C.E. 'O Level'. Three of the six technical schools provide day-release classes for apprentices working in industry.

In addition, there are two schools concerned with the theory and techniques of agriculture, a trade training centre, two technical institutes, and a vocational school. The agricultural schools afford training in the latest methods of agriculture, the rearing of poultry, general animal husbandry and breeding methods, soil and water conservation, and economics and accountancy. The trade training centre, vocational school, and the technical institutes provide training in crafts, the domestic arts, commerce and hairdressing for girls. Entry to these schools and centres usually occurs between the ages of twelve and fifteen years; and the courses themselves last for four or five years, and the examinations taken are the same as those offered in the technical schools.

One of the problems which many Jamaicans, and other West Indians, experience when they come to England is the disparity between their training or apprenticeship for skilled work and the skill levels of trained personnel within the English society. The Jamaican High Commission in London suggests that

'They came with great aspirations regarding apprenticeship here, often beyond what their capacities will permit, and sometimes both youngsters and parents cannot appreciate why such a lad cannot easily be apprenticed in the electrical trade for example' (14).

In the past 'apprenticeship' has been a very loose term in Jamaica for any sort of practical training undertaken by a young man in any craft or trade. No standards of attainment were laid down, nor was there any final inspection or certification; but after a certain period of apprenticeship the young apprentice would feel that he had become sufficiently proficient in his trade to regard himself as being 'skilled', and as a trained person ready to stand on his own feet or to join an established firm on equal terms with other trained employees.

In 1954 the Apprenticeship Law came into force in Jamaica. This was an initial attempt to establish some form of regularity in both the training of apprentices and in their final qualification and registration. Such an endeavour to regularize the situation was, of course, necessary within Jamaica itself; but it was doubly necessary for those apprentices who were emigrating to England, and who were seeking work on a basis of equality with English craftsmen and tradesmen. The system of apprenticeship is, broadly speaking, similar to that found in England (15), but obviously there has been some adaptation to the specific problems of Jamaica itself.

One of the areas in which education has considerably developed since 1955 is that of higher education. However belated this development may have been, it has been amazingly adventurous. The University of the West Indies is situated in a lovely plain at the foot of the hills near Kingston, at a place called Mona. It was founded in 1949 as a university college preparing its students for the degrees of London University; but in 1962 it was granted an independent Royal Charter by the British Government, which permitted it to award its own degrees. At the first the University faced the same problem as that of other developing countries seeking to improve or establish higher education, namely, that of lack of qualified staff. And so it depended heavily upon expatriates. As, however, West Indians themselves became qualified they were invited to become members of the staff, and there has emerged 'a steady policy of West-Indianization' (16).

The University of the West Indies serves Jamaica, Trinidad and the British Caribbean territories generally. In Jamaica it has faculties in arts, natural sciences, social sciences and medicine; there is a Department of Education and a Department of Extra-Mural Studies, an Institute of Trade Union Studies and an Institute of Social and Economic Research. This latter institute is doing some very intensive studies into the social problems of contemporary Jamaican society, as well as providing some valuable up-to-date statistics on such questions as religion, housing, population, emigration and employment. In 1960 the Department of Extra-Mural Studies produced a very important report on *The Ras Tafari Movement in Kingston, Jamaica* (17), which was notable for its expertise in its investigation of Rastafarianism and for its objective and balanced judgement.

In Trinidad the St Augustine campus of the University houses the faculties of engineering and agriculture, together with a College of Arts and Science; there is another such College at Cave Hill in Barbados. In 1965 there was an enrolment of 1,491 students at Mona, Kingston, 780 students in Trinidad and 185 in Barbados. Jamaicans, and the Caribbean people generally, are rightly proud of the expansion and achievements of the University, particularly in the fields of science and medicine. Henriques suggests that the 'theorizing' of those who work in the arts and social science faculties is not greatly appreciated, particularly by the non-academic; and he states that there is a feeling that the work of the social scientist has little practical application (18). There is a consciousness of a social gap between those – the academic élite – who live on the University campus, with a minimum of social contact with the rest of Kingston, and the mass of the Jamaican people.

A great variety of courses has been developed at the College of Arts, Science and Technology which provides some advanced instruction in such subjects as accountancy, company secretaryship, industrial management, and commercial enterprise and design on the arts side. On the science side there are courses in the physical sciences and their relation to industry, whilst the technology department is concerned mainly with training in industrial practice. Students eventually sit the examinations of the Royal Society of Arts, or the Ordinary and Higher National Certificates (O.N.C. and H.N.C.) of Great Britain.

The School of Arts and Crafts in Jamaica has developed specialist courses in all branches of art and craft, including painting, sculpture, ceramics, modelling and straw work. And in the nursing profession qualifications in general nursing may be obtained at the two nursing training hospitals situated in Kingston, namely the University Hospital and the Public Hospital. Midwives are trained at the Victoria Jubilee Hospital. General nurses who are also midwives may be trained as health visitors; and there are, in addition, courses in public health and public health inspection provided at the West Indies School of Public Health, situated in Kingston. These last-named courses are concerned with methods of sanitation, pest control, food handling, and the problems of communicable diseases.

D EDUCATION IN OTHER PARTS OF THE CARIBBEAN

It has been possible to give little more than the briefest outline of the educational background of children in Jamaica; but what has been said of that island applies to a large extent to other areas of the Caribbean. Although Jamaica has the largest population of the areas that we are concerned with here, its population density is not as great as that of Barbados or some of the Windward Islands. Both number and density of population create their own problems, but in general terms the same problems occur everywhere in this area: insufficient accommodation, a lack of qualified teachers, and a paucity of equipment, textbooks and general amenities.

In Trinidad and Tobago primary education is universal and compulsory; there are, in all, about 460 government and assisted primary schools, and in 1965 there were some 185,000 pupils attending them. Secondary education is provided at thirty-nine colleges and schools, and there are at present three government institutions at which vocational and technical training is given. In all these schools and institutions education is quite free, but there are also some institutions in which training is provided in industry. The extension of the University of the West Indies on the St Augustine campus in Trinidad has already been mentioned. Quite recently there has been established also a Liberal Arts College and an Institute of International Relations, the express purpose of the latter being to train specially selected West Indians for the diplomatic corps.

In his discussion of education in Guyana (then British Guiana), Professor R. T. Smith has claimed that, from the beginning of the nineteenth century,

'Schools and churches were held to be the best instruments for the transformation of a rebellious slave population into a peaceful and obedient working class' (19).

In spite of the contrary view expressed by the majority of the planters, there was a steadily developing belief that the best way to control slaves was by a canalization of their energies in activities which were useful and constructive. The Government and the colonial office considered education to be the very foundation of a civil society. But a 'civil society' in this context meant, in fact, one in which the language, culture and civilization of England were predominant. But English or British civilization was, and still largely is, the product of an alien culture – alien, that is, to their experiences, and alien to their inherited beliefs and ideas. Professor Smith emphasizes that, whilst the imposition of arbitrary English standards has in the past served the purpose of unifying a heterogeneous population, the time is long overdue when such standards should be revised.

Primary education has been legally compulsory in Guyana since 1876, but it is obvious that this compulsion has not been rigorously applied and is not being applied even now. There is a rapidly increasing school population, and there is a lack of accommodation to meet the educational demand since the school building and rebuilding programmes cannot keep pace with population changes. Coupled with the shortage of school places there is a shortage of adequately trained teachers. It is a somewhat familiar story, not merely in Guyana and the Caribbean but almost universally.

E LANGUAGE PROBLEMS

Not least fascinating of all the problems of the educational background of Caribbean immigrants is the linguistic one. The English language in our own society is a pretty heterogeneous affair, with Queen's English, 'Oxford' or public-school accent, Cockney, Brummagem, Geordie and many other accents. In considering the Caribbean dialects, however, we are not concerned with one island or one society; we are dealing with Guyana on the South American mainland, the islands of Trinidad and Tobago, Barbados, the Windward Islands, the Leeward Islands, the Virgin Islands, Jamaica and British Honduras – an arc of over a thousand miles involving peoples of many races and cultures. When one considers the geographical and historical facts, as well as the ethnological differences and the variety of political allegiances, perhaps the surprising thing is that

'there is so much of a common cultural heritage and so much linguistically in common between the different regions' (20).

One cannot speak of *the* native language of the West Indian child, in the sense that it will be common to all West Indian children. But certainly most immigrant West Indian children are likely to speak a Creole dialect of English; some may speak a Creole dialect of French; others may occasionally speak a form of Tamil or Hindi if they come from Guyana; or Amerindian, Carib or Spanish if they are from British Honduras.

The history and development of the various Creole dialects, and an analysis of their phonological, morphological and syntactic systems, as well as their semantic structure, would require a detailed study on their own. The interested reader is directed, in particular, to the writings of Professor R. B. Le Page, who is an authority on the Creole dialects of the Caribbean; to Beryl L. Bailey's *Jamaican Creole Syntax*; and to F. G. Cassidy's *Jamaica Talk*.

All the Caribbean Creole languages have developed from a pidgin used by people who spoke such West African languages as Ewe and Twi, and who in turn, through force of circumstances, acquired elements of a European language. Professor Le Page has pointed out that the degree to which the European language was actually learned depended very much upon 'the strength of one's motivation to learn the language in relation to other possibly conflicting motives' (21). West African traders were highly motivated by economics; slaves were motivated initially by the desire for survival. Later, in the medley of new and different languages in novel Caribbean surroundings, it was the children of the African slaves who were first forced, out of the sheer necessity of the situation, to develop a pidgin; and it was the children's children who grew up speaking a Creole language as their primary one. And today in Jamaica, for example, the children of the working classes will use Jamaican Creole almost exclusively in their daily commerce; Standard Jamaican English will be used only under duress in the classroom or in conversation with people of a higher social level. Immigrants to this country may, therefore, speak a Caribbean Creole which to untutored English ears might sound both foreign and unintelligible; others may speak an English not greatly different from our own.

REFERENCES

1 *Vide* Hoetink, H., *The Two Variants in Caribbean Race Relations* (O.U.P., 1967), Part One.
2 Ibid., p. 6.

3 *Vide* Tannenbaum, F., *Slave and Citizen* (Knopf, N.Y., 1947).
4 Jamaican High Commission, *Cultural and Educational Background of Jamaican Children* (H.C.O., London, Jan. 1967), p. 7.
5 Smith, R. T., *British Guiana* (O.U.P., 1962), p. 148.
6 Ibid., p. 147.
7 *Vide* FitzHerbert, Katrin, 'The West Indian Background' in Oakley, R. (ed.), *New Backgrounds* (O.U.P., 1968), p. 18.
8 Norris, Katrin (=FitzHerbert, Katrin), *Jamaica: The Search for an Identity* (O.U.P., 1962), p. 87.
9 *Vide* D. E. S., *Education and Science in 1969* (H.M.S.O., 1970), p. 32.
10 Norris, Katrin, op. cit., p. 87.
11 Henriques, F., *Family and Colour in Jamaica* (MacGibbon & Kee, 1953, 2nd edition 1968), p. 132.
12 Ibid., p. 161.
13 Ibid., p. 133.
14 Jamaican High Commission, op. cit., p. 15.
15 Ibid., p. 15.
16 Henriques, F., op. cit., p. 176.
17 Smith, M. G. *et al.*, *The Ras Tafari Movement in Kingston, Jamaica* (Department of Extra-Mural Studies, U.W.I., Jamaica, 1960).
18 Henriques, F., op. cit., pp. 176–7.
19 Smith, R. T., op. cit., p. 145.
20 Le Page, R. B., 'Incomprehensibility between West Indian English and other forms of English'; article in *Remedial Education*, Vol. 3, No. 3/4 (Pergamon Press, 1967), p. 130.
21 Ibid., p. 131.

BIBLIOGRAPHY

Bailey, B. L., *Jamaican Creole Syntax* (C.U.P., 1966).
British Honduras Government, *Seven Years Development Plan: 1964–70* (Belize City, Office of the Premier, 1965).
Cassidy, F. G., *Jamaica Talk* (Macmillan, 1961).
Cassidy, F. G. and Le Page, R. B., *Dictionary of Jamaican English* (C.U.P., 1967).
Evans, P. C. C. *et al.*, *The Education of West Indian Immigrant Children* (National Committee for Commonwealth Immigrants, London, 1967).
Henriques, F., *Family and Colour in Jamaica* (MacGibbon & Kee, 1968).
Jamaican High Commission, *Cultural and Educational Background of Jamaican Children* (H.C.O., London, Jan. 1967).
Le Page, R. B. (ed.), *Creole Language Studies, No. 1 – Jamaican Creole* (Macmillan, 1960).
Morgan, D. J., *Aid to the West Indies: A Survey of Attitudes and Needs* (Overseas Development Institute, 1964).
Oakley, R. (ed.), *New Backgrounds* (O.U.P., 1968), Chapter I by Katrin FitzHerbert, 'The West Indian Background'.
Smith, R. T., *British Guiana* (O.U.P., 1962).
Walters, E., *Learning to Read in Jamaica* (University of the West Indies, 1958).
Walters, E., *Language Teaching, Linguistics and the Teaching of English in a Multi-Racial Society* (U.W.I., 1965).

Chapter 5

Culture Contact
with the Host Society

In his *West Indian Migration to Britain*, Dr Ceri Peach argues that the number of arrivals here from the West Indies shows the same fall and rise as the employment index in this country (1), and he considers that on the whole conditions in Britain influence the proportion of returns to arrivals. He points out that, in the first year of the Commonwealth Immigrants Act of 1962, 26,040 West Indians arrived in this country whilst 19,176 left. This two-way migration occurred because, despite the economic conditions which favoured immigration, there were equally strong considerations which militated against it. It is not our purpose here to examine in any detail the statistical data which Dr Peach has thoroughly analysed in his 'social geography', but rather to look at some of the causal factors which he mentions as being, to some extent at least, responsible for the fluctuations in the migration figures. Such economic and social factors as the permanent shortage of houses and the chronically overloaded educational facilities were responsible for the decrease in the net immigration of West Indians after the Act of 1962. It is such factors as these that have never had the full consideration that they deserve – until it is too late.

In any discussion of the culture contact between the West Indians and the host society, one frequently reads of the 'disillusionment' of the immigrants, and their experience of lack of warmth, neighbourliness and hospitality. The Report on British Race Relations, published in 1969, claims that the disillusion and disenchantment were greater among the West Indians than among any other immigrant group because they expected so much (2). Whilst these things are in a very deep sense regrettable, they could not by any stretch of imagination have been unexpected. It is one of the tragedies of large-scale immigration to this country that it has just happened without the necessary education and informing of both the migrants and the host society in relation to what actually is occurring. Disillusionment can occur only where completely wrong impressions have been given in the first place; and a realistic appraisal of social, economic as well as psychological factors existing in the host society might at least have prepared the migrants more adequately for the different social ethos that they were about to experience.

But this argument is double-edged. It is equally true that the host society has been slow to educate itself with regard to the cultural and social back-ground of the immigrants. If we are to develop successfully a multi-cultural society we must have some sort of vision of the society we are building, and some idea of the way to build it. This is not the sort of thing that just happens; it requires planned and conscious effort; and it demands an educational programme which begins with informing teachers in training, who in their turn, in the schools, will make their pupils aware not merely of geographical distance but also of cultural and social distance, and of how the distance may be shortened.

There are some differences between the West Indian migrants and their hosts which are more obvious than others. They are coloured, even black. This fact immediately establishes a polarity, and it may arouse quite unsuspected prejudice on the part of white hosts. 'Colour shock' is not something confined to the uneducated, or to those with preconceived opinions about the 'blacks'; it is something we are all subject to, particularly in a society such as our own which has, until quite recent times, been almost exclusively a white society. Sheila Patterson has brought this fact vividly home in her study of West Indian communities in London. In her *Dark Strangers* she emphasizes the experience of 'colour shock' when she describes a preliminary reconnaissance which she made in the district of Brixton in May 1955, prior to making her detailed study. What struck her forcibly was the fact that almost everyone in sight had a coloured skin, and she experienced, she says, 'a profound reaction of something unexpected and alien'. She goes on:

'This first reaction of mine was, I think, similar to that of most people in the United Kingdom, following the recent large-scale immigration of West Indians and other coloured Commonwealth citizens into Britain. People in the United Kingdom knew that the majority of inhabitants of the Commonwealth have coloured skins; some had encountered them on their own ground; many were even used to the idea that there were old-estab-lished coloured communities tucked away in dock and port areas in Britain itself. But to be confronted with coloured people in highly visible groups in the centre of its large industrial cities – this was something that at first seemed strange and even out-of-place to most people here' (3).

This, of course, works equally in reverse. In the Census of 1946 there were in Jamaica, out of a total population of 1,237,063, only 13,809 people of white European stock, or just over one per cent. The rest were black or coloured. They too, on arrival here, must have felt something of this 'colour shock', and have sought refuge with people of their own kind and colour. It is a facile thing to say that it is simply a matter of time before we get used to colour; but one can survive the sort of 'colour shock' referred to by Sheila Patterson and yet have no general change of attitude towards those who are coloured. In fact, familiarity with what may already be regarded as contemptible may do little more than breed further contempt.

There are ingrained feelings and concepts about colour in our society that are not easily obliterated even by the closer presence of the coloured peoples or by the passage of time. 'Black' has always been associated with dirt, primitivity, and evil in the minds of white people; 'black' magic is bad, evil, sinister; 'white' magic is good and beneficent. Black is also unconsciously, or consciously, associated with more primitive levels of development, culture and thought. There is, for example, an initial and tacit assumption that the West Indian immigrant will be uneducated or ill-educated, and that he will introduce a hangover of African aboriginality which will represent a threat to our more developed, stable and sophisticated society. Dr P. C. C. Evans has emphasized the importance of seeking to eradicate 'racial stereotypes' (4), which have become ingrained in our thought and which are still the object of supercilious, or at least unthinking, derision. People who have grown up with phrases such as 'little nigger-boys', 'nigger in the woodpile', 'working like a nigger', and 'black as a nigger', do not find it easy to eradicate them from their vocabulary or their thinking.

Life in the West Indies is, for the most part, a life spent in the open air in a warm, sunny and friendly climate; and the warmth of the atmosphere is translated also in terms of human relationships. In the Caribbean people live together in crowded kin-group communities, and they share one another's hopes, fears, joys, sorrows, troubles and all family occasions. When they come here they find a climate which is cold, wet and highly unpredictable; they have to live most of their lives indoors, and there is no common 'yard' where all the street can congregate and engage in idle chatter. They begin to experience a pace of life which is greatly removed from the *dolce far niente* of the tropical Caribbean; its speed and unchanging, incessant routine are at first strange, and to some quite terrifying. If *we* suffer from 'colour shock', *they* suffer from climate and culture shock.

One of the most important factors for any migrant group is the ability to communicate with the host society. But the West Indians find, in addition to the other problems that they face, that their tacit expectation of at least a barrier-free system of linguistic communication is to a large extent unfounded. There is 'English' and 'English'; and the variety of Creole dialects are certainly not understood by many in our society any more than Neo-Melanesian pidgin English would be. Even Standard Jamaican English may remain unintelligible to the untutored ear.

Thus the West Indian finds himself in a new world of different sounds, in which he must acclimatize his hearing, his understanding and his expression to different accents as well as to a variety of social levels. These psycholinguistic problems can make him feel a total stranger, insecure, inferior and unadjusted. He may even find that the 'English' English accent, that he was at such pains to learn in his homeland, no longer carries with it in our society the sort of premium that he has been led to expect. Everything else that is attached to the concept of 'West Indian' or 'Caribbean' will outweigh every advance towards 'Englishness' that the individual has ever attained.

Verbal communication is, of course, very important; but there are deeper levels of communication where one might perhaps expect some sense of equality and identity. At the religious level, as we have already seen, there is at least the tradition of some form of Christianity. But here again a great deal of disappointment and disillusionment have been both experienced and expressed. The West Indians have found us cold, unemotional, unresponsive and unfriendly; and in consequence they have increasingly segregated themselves at the religious level from the host society. The picture which C. S. Hill provides in his *West Indian Migrants and the London Churches* is certainly a very pessimistic one; and he describes the frustration and bafflement experienced by the migrants. He claims that

'it is a measure of the church's failure that she is unable to make effective use of the number of contacts she has with the immigrant community' (5).

One of the interesting features of migration from the West Indies and Guyana to this country has been the way in which the immigrants have maintained the distance of their home societies. There are some areas such as Brixton, as Sheila Patterson has shown, where the settlements are composed predominantly of Jamaicans, with a few people from Guyana and Barbados (6). It is only gradually that other West Indian migrants have begun to mingle with Jamaicans even in a foreign land.

Large numbers of West Indian migrants begin their lives in this country in crowded slum dwellings, many of which have been purchased by other West Indians who are seeking quick returns by charging exorbitant rents. By the end of 1958 there were several hundred 'coloured-owned houses' in Brixton alone, and the number has certainly increased during the past decade (7). Many of these houses are overcrowded; and there are 'Box and Cox' arrangements whereby rooms and even beds are used by different people in rotation according to whether they are on day or night shift. Because there is a great demand for room in which to live, the rents and prices of houses inevitably soar, and this factor encourages even more sharing and cramming together. In fact, some houses are little more than dormitories.

'The worst-kept rooms are usually those in which live single men, or men with transient white girls. In such houses the individual rooms tend to be almost as dirty and untended as the shared parts, and tenants add little of their own, whether linoleum, wallpaper, pictures, or radiograms' (8).

In 1961 R. B. Davison reported that 83 per cent of West Indian migrants from outside Jamaica were living in three rooms or less. On an average almost 70 per cent of the population of coloured immigrants were in this type of accommodation, compared with 40 per cent of the English group. But at the end of the next five years these levels were reduced to 56 per cent for coloured immigrants and 22 per cent for the English group (9). Much is said about the undesirable development of ghettos in our society, and the term is invariably used in a pejorative sense. It is, perhaps, too late to redeem a term which, in its original Italian sense, meant 'a little borough' (*borghetto*), and was used in particular of the Jewish quarter in any city. A ghetto is, in fact, a minority group settlement, and the term itself does not describe the *quality* of the living conditions or of the life lived.

But, of course, since initially by the very nature of things immigrants are driven into the poorer areas of our cities there is always a tendency for a ghetto to perpetuate conditions of poverty as well as of racial distinction. A ghetto of white immigrants will tend to merge into the remainder of the society; but a coloured ghetto remains distinguishable, and because of that potentially dangerous. It is natural that an incoming people should seek identity and security in the company of others of a similar culture, colour and background. To Ceri Peach the ghetto represents 'the geographical expression of complete social rejection' (10); at the same time it may be of some considerable help in the immediate process of adjustment and accommodation to the strangeness of the new culture and society. Its greatest danger lies in its possibility of making a solid contribution to the 'hardening of the lines of racial division' (11).

There is, however, a fatal tendency for the ghetto to become poorer rather than to become enriched either through a deeper experience of the host society or by increased wealth. There are those who intend to return home anyway, and as soon as they have amassed the money they require they will leave. Others, who see clearly that the only way in which to improve their social position is to move out from the ghetto, also leave and make room for others entering at the lower levels of the social scale.

Another danger of the ghetto is the perpetuation of Caribbean familial concepts and values in the new society. Our discussion of the Jamaican family system has already demonstrated an entirely different attitude from that of the host society towards Christian marriage and illegitimacy. The isolation of immigrants in certain areas of our large cities will tend to encourage the retention of their own social systems rather than accom-modation to those of their hosts. Since they do not tend to join our social clubs or churches, nor to participate in our political activities, their social life tends to centre upon their own groups in their own homes, upon private parties and dances. As a society we may not accept that segregation is a sound policy, but voluntary segregation, or segregation which is forced upon immigrants through economic circumstances, is not something that can easily be prevented. According to Dr Peach the West Indians here experience 'both positive and negative impulses towards concentration' (12), and at the present time the positive reasons for seeking to cluster in particular areas, or ghettos, are dominant, and the negative impulses are latent.

One of the gravest features of West Indian immigration is the backwash which is felt in the West Indies themselves. Many of the men who migrate to this country are already involved in some form of non-Christian mar-riage, such as the faithful concubinage or keeper marriage type. They have children back home whom they would certainly have supported if they had been physically there. But distance inevitably removes something of the sense of obligation, particularly when the migrant finds a female friend in this country and begins another family here. There is nothing to prevent his marrying the girl here legally if he wishes, but whether he does or not he inevitably finds that he can no longer support the dependants he left behind. The latter, in their turn, have been left virtually penniless in order that their breadwinner might seek his fortune abroad. C. S. Hill has emphasized some of these social effects in the Jamaican society, and he quotes a senior Jamaican welfare worker as suggesting that migration to Britain was 'the greatest tragedy Jamaica has ever suffered', and was in fact responsible for the 'final break-up of Jamaican family life' (13). In the terms of Dr Henriques this means that the Jamaican society is becoming increasingly 'disnomic'; and that even what was formerly regarded as a tacit marriage contract, although no binding legal ceremony was involved, is no longer regarded as in any sense obligatory.

In Dr Peach's opinion the migration of West Indians to this country was the result of a demand for labour at the lowest end of the occupational ladder. And so long as they fill jobs at the lowest end they will also tend to cluster in dwellings which are the poorest in our society. The simple fact at the moment is that 86 per cent of West Indian immigrant heads of households are engaged in manual work, and another 3 per cent are shop assistants (14). Although there are other demographic factors to be taken into consideration in any detailed analysis and comparison of the economic circumstances of various groups of immigrants, it still remains a fact that the West Indian immigrants are heavily concentrated in the manual category, and at least 10 per cent more than Indian heads of households.

By and large, West Indian men will not do agricultural work and women will not engage in private domestic work. These jobs have a low status in their own country and so they reject them here. It is interesting to note that 60 per cent of the West Indian women here are economically active, compared with 48 per cent of the Indian women, 53 per cent of the Irish women, and 39 per cent of the English-born women. The women are engaged mainly in textiles, clothing, light engineering and nursing.

It is to be hoped that improved education, and general adaptation to English educational methods, will eventually assist the West Indians to develop a greater mobility in the occupational scale. It is in the school that West Indian children must ultimately find the means of equality. In this respect it becomes more clear every year that if these children really are to meet white children on equal terms, to learn to accept English values, and to acquire the requisite qualifications and skills to compete in the job market (15), there must be a clearly conceived educational policy, beginning with the training of teachers, the organization of schools in relation to immigrants and the methods to be employed in attempting to integrate them. The 1969 Report on Race Relations holds that

'Children of West Indian parents, the largest of all the immigrant groups, have been a source of bafflement, embarrassment, and despair in the education system. They have complicated the attempts to define the terms "immigrant pupil" and to assess the linguistic needs of immigrant pupils; in class, they have often presented problems which the average teacher is not equipped to understand, let alone overcome' (16).

The methods of teaching in the large majority of our schools are today quite alien to those used in West Indian schools, where crowded classrooms prevent mobility on the part of the children and the practice of those heuristic methods which have become almost second nature in our schools. The West Indian child is used to being told what to learn and how to learn it – mostly by simple repetition, and in chorus with other children. He is not expected to have a naturally inquiring mind, perpetually demanding to know the answers to his searching questions. On the contrary, he is expected to respond to a heavy discipline with the threat of a flogging if he doesn't do as he is told or learn what he should.

The West Indian child finds himself a coloured individual in a predominantly white society. He is faced with values and concepts which have originated in a *milieu* with an entirely different cultural history and background. He does not belong to the main stream of that culture or history; he is, in fact, that element in our colonial history which provokes in us a sense of shame, regret and guilt – an element which we might well prefer to forget. He finds himself in a society that, by and large, is still not yet fully acclimatized to colour, and that has not yet adjusted even to the concept or possibility of a multi-cultural or multi-racial society. Our teachers are still thinking in terms of assimilation: the assimilating of the immigrant child to white norms and white patterns of behaviour. The child discovers that his own values and cultural concepts are being rejected virtually without reference. Moreover, his own thought-forms are not easily communicable in the sort of English that he speaks and in which he thinks. He is caught up in culture tests and selection procedures that inevitably leave him at a disadvantage compared with white children of his own age, and even ability.

Most thinkers would perhaps agree that the concept of *negritude*, which involves 'the awareness, defence, and development of African cultural values' (17), is a misguided one if applied to West Indian immigrants in our society. There is no common West Indian culture to which West Indian children in this country may turn; leaders such as Neville Maxwell, a former Chairman of the West Indian Standing Conference, have, it is true, referred to 'our original African culture' and its suppression by the acquisitive whites, but this is more in the nature of an emotional appeal than an anthropological statement. There are, and have been, African 'cultures', many of them; but no single, or original, African culture. Nor is the West Indian immigrant child likely to discover one, unless some new Ras Tafari movement should develop in our midst and create a pseudo-African culture.

If, however, the recreation of a pseudo-African subculture is not a particularly viable proposition, nor is the 'flattening process of assimilation' a desirable one (18). Every racial group that enters our country has something to contribute to the enrichment of our society and its culture. To seek to assimilate every child, every immigrant adult, to our social norms would be to impoverish our society as well as our immigrants. The process of integration seeks to provide an equal opportunity for the immigrants without destroying their diversity of culture. The Report on British Race Relations refers to this type of integration as 'pluralism', and sees it as a process which may take one or more generations (19).

REFERENCES

1 *Vide* Peach, C., *West Indian Migration to Britain* (O.U.P., 1968), Chapter 4.
2 Rose, E. J. B., *et al.*, *Colour and Citizenship: A Report On British Race Relations* (O.U.P., 1969), p. 434.
3 Patterson, Sheila, *Dark Strangers* (Penguin, 1965), pp. 1–2.
4 Evans, P. C. C. *et al.*, *The Education of West Indian Immigrant Children* (National Committee for Commonwealth Immigrants, 1957), p. 22.

5 Hill, C. S., *West Indian Migrants and the London Churches* (O.U.P., 1963), p. 23.
6 Patterson, Sheila, op. cit., pp. 56–7.
7 Ibid., p. 164.
8 Ibid., p. 166.
9 Rose, E. J. B., *et al.*, op. cit., p. 140.
10 Peach, C., op. cit., p. xvi.
11 Hill, C. S., op. cit., p. 78.
12 Peach, C., op. cit., p. 84.
13 *Vide* Hill, C. S., op. cit., pp. 39–41.
14 *Vide* Rose, E. J. B., *et al.*, op. cit., p. 183, Table 14.1.
15 *Vide* FitzHerbert, Katrin, 'The West Indian Background' in Oakley, R. (ed.), *New Backgrounds* (O.U.P., 1968), p. 7.
16 Rose, E. J. B., *et al.*, op. cit., p. 281.
17 Ibid., p. 439.
18 Ibid., p. 25.
19 Ibid., pp. 25 and 439.

BIBLIOGRAPHY

Banton, M., *The Coloured Quarter* (Cape, 1955).
Banton, M., *White and Coloured* (Cape, 1959).
Borrie, W. D., *The Cultural Integration of Immigrants* (Paris, UNESCO, 1959).
Calley, M. J. C., *God's People: West Indian Pentecostalists in England* (O.U.P., 1965).
Carey, A. T., *Colonial Students* (Secker & Warburg, 1956).
Collins, S., *Coloured Minorities in Britain* (Lutterworth Press, 1957).
Collins, W., *Jamaican Migrant* (Routledge, 1965).
Davison, R. B., *West Indian Migrants* (O.U.P., 1962).
Davison, R. B., *Commonwealth Immigrants* (O.U.P., 1964).
Davison, R. B., *Black British: Immigrants to England* (O.U.P., 1966).
Eddington, Joyce, *They Seek a Living* (Hutchinson, 1957).
Eisenstadt, S. N., *The Absorption of Immigrants* (Routledge, 1954).
Evans, P. C. C. and Le Page, R. B., *The Education of West Indian Immigrant Children* (National Committee for Commonwealth Immigrants, 1967).
FitzHerbert, K., *West Indian Children in London* (Bell, 1967).
Glass, R. and Pollins, H., *Newcomers: The West Indians in London* (Allen & Unwin, 1960).
Griffith, J. A. G. *et al.*, *Coloured Immigrants in Britain* (O.U.P., 1960).
Hawkes, N., *Immigrant Children in British Schools* (Pall Mall Press, 1966).
Hill, C. S., *West Indian Migrants and the London Churches* (O.U.P., 1963).
Hooper, R. (ed.), *Colour in Britain* (B.B.C., 1965).
Institute of Race Relations, *Coloured Immigrants in Britain* (O.U.P., 1960).
Little, K. L., *Negroes in Britain* (Routledge, 1948).
MacInnes, C., *City of Spades* (MacGibbon & Kee, 1957).
Patterson, Sheila, *Dark Strangers* (Penguin, 1965).
Patterson, Sheila, *Immigration and Race Relations in Britain: 1960–1967* (O.U.P., 1969).
Peach, C., *West Indian Migration to Britain* (O.U.P., 1968).
Richmond, A. H., *Colour Prejudice in Britain: A Study of West Indian Workers in Liverpool, 1941–1951* (Routledge, 1954).
Richmond, A. H., *The Colour Problem* (Penguin, revised edition 1961).

Rose, E. J. B. *et al.*, *Colour and Citizenship: A Report on British Race Relations* (O.U.P., 1969).

Ruck, S. K. (ed.), *The West Indian Comes to England* (Routledge, 1960).

Tajfel, H. and Dawson, J. L. (ed.), *Disappointed Guests* (O.U.P., 1965).

Watson, A. R., *West Indian Workers in Britain* (Hodder & Stoughton, 1942).

Wickenden, J., *Colour in Britain* (O.U.P., 1958).

Wright, P. L., *The Coloured Worker in British Industry* (O.U.P., 1968).

Part Two
The Indians

Chapter 6

General Background
of India

A THE LAND AND ITS PRODUCTS

India, with a land area of some 3,268,090 square kilometres, is the seventh largest country in the world, and her estimated population in May 1969 was 524 millions (1). Thus, with only 2·4 per cent of the world's land area, India is attempting to support about 14 per cent of the world's population. That this is a frustrating and stultifying task is well illustrated by the Government's advertisement on Family Planning. It opens with the story of the boatman who rowed all night on the River Padma, but found next morning that he was still at his starting point. The advertisement goes on to state that, after twenty years of hard and earnest efforts to improve the people's standard of living, they had not in fact gone far from where they had started. During the fourteen years from 1951 to 1965 food production had gone up 17 million tons, but the actual amount of food available for each person had 'decreased by 0·4 oz.' (2). With a birth rate of 40 per thousand, and a death rate of 17 per thousand, this means that there is a natural increase in population of 23 per thousand per year, or about 12 million people.

India lies entirely in the northern hemisphere, between 37°6′ N. and 8°4′ N. (3). In the north she is flanked by the Himalayas and is adjoined to China and Nepal; she is bounded in the east by East Pakistan, and in the north-west by West Pakistan and the border of Afghanistan. India derives her name from 'Sindhu', the Sanskrit name for the River Indus; and from Sindhu are derived the word 'Ind' and 'Hind', signifying the land beyond the Indus, and later referred to as India or Hindustan, the land of the Hindus.

Physically India is divided into three major regions: the mountain zone of the Himalayas, the almost level Indo-Gangetic plain, and the southern Deccan peninsular plateau. The Himalayan mountain wall possesses some of the highest peaks in the world, including Mt Everest which is 29,141 feet. The Indo-Gangetic plain has hardly any variation in relief and is one of the world's largest stretches of alluvial soil; it is also one of the most densely populated areas on our planet. The southern peninsula juts into the Indian Ocean, with the Arabian Sea on the west and the Bay of Bengal on the east.

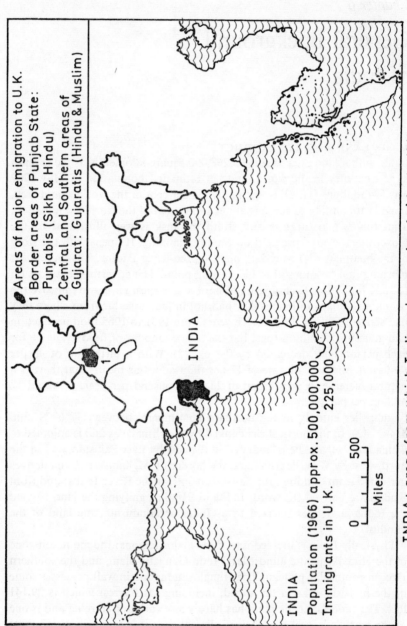

INDIA

Population (1966) approx. 500,000,000
Immigrants in U.K. 225,000

Areas of major emigration to U.K.
1 Border areas of Punjab State:
Punjabis (Sikh & Hindu)
2 Central and Southern areas of
Gujarat: Gujaratis (Hindu & Muslim)

INDIA

INDIA: areas from which Indians have emigrated to the U.K.

The river system of India includes some of the largest rivers in Asia. The Himalayan rivers are snow-fed, flow continuously throughout the year, and flood during the monsoon season; the Deccan rivers are rain-fed and fluctuate in volume; the coastal rivers are short in length and supply limited catchment areas; and, finally, there are the rivers of the inland drainage basin, which drain towards individual basins or salt lakes, or are lost in the sands, having no outlet to the sea. In West Rajasthan, in the north-west of India, the rivers are few and ephemeral in nature.

The largest river basin in India is that of the Ganga (or Ganges), which receives water from an area comprising 25 per cent of the total area of India. The second largest is that of the River Godavari, and it comprises 10 per cent of India's land area. The basins of the Brahmaputra in the east and of the Indus in the west are of about the same size, whilst the Kistna (or Krishna) basin is the second largest in Peninsular India. The bed of the Kistna is some half or three-quarters of a mile across, but during the month of March it may contain no more than a mere trickle of water.

The climate of India is divided into four seasons. The cold weather season is from January to February, and is fairly mild in most parts of the country except in the north where it can be very severe indeed. The hot weather season is from March to May, and during this period the temperatures rise rapidly and pressures decrease. In March the mean maximum temperature in the Deccan peninsula has already risen to over 100° F.; and by May, which is the hottest month in most areas, the temperature has risen to over 105° F. In the Punjab temperatures reach over 110° F.

The monsoon, or rainy period, extends from June to September. The word 'monsoon' is Dutch in origin and probably derives from the Arabic *mausim*, which means literally 'season'. It is now used in popular language to refer to the rainy season, although in nautical terms it specifically implies the great N.E. and S.W. air-currents. The monsoon rains are highly predictable, particularly their onset in the coastal areas where strong and violent winds are experienced from the sea, with torrential rainfall and a quite dramatic fall in the temperature. The precision of their arrival is expressed by Professor Spate in the following terms:

'The S.W. monsoon breaks on the Bombay coast about June 5th, in Bengal about June 15th, and by July has spread over nearly all India, advancing on a broad turbulent front aptly likened by Eliot to an estuarine bore' (4).

The period from October to December is the season of the retreating S.W. monsoon. The change does not occur with the abruptness of the onset of the rainy season, but towards the end of September drier conditions become increasingly prevalent, particularly in northern India. During the month of October temperatures are reasonably uniform throughout India, rising slightly after the rains to between 77°F. and 81°F. It is a humid, hot, uncomfortable season.

India is rich in mineral and power resources, and she has begun to exploit those resources both in terms of her internal expansion and industrialization and in terms of international trade. It is impossible here to consider those resources in any detail, but her power resources include coal, lignite, oil and water-power. India has a large number of hydro-electric and power generation projects under way, and some of these involve the areas (Punjab and Gujarat) from which most of our immigrants come. India has also the largest iron deposits (including hematite, magnetite and spathic ore) in the world. In fact, her iron ore reserves are assessed as representing a quarter of the world's total deposits; whilst her manganese deposits are the third largest in the world.

Other mineral resources include widespread deposits of bauxite, three main mica belts, two copper belts, chromite, gold, ilmenite, gypsum and such refractories as magnesite and kyanite. There are also huge reserves of thorium, and there is a great variety of other minerals of less importance. India has long been aware of the abundance of her natural resources: what she has lacked has been the capital, the expertise and the united energy to initiate the plans of industrialization required to maximize those resources. A measure of her increasing awareness is the fact that in 1967 the total value of mineral production in the country, excluding petroleum, atomic and minor minerals, was more than three times the total value in 1951.

India now has twelve councils whose sole concern it is to promote and regulate certain industries. These industries are as follows: paper and pulp; drugs and pharmaceuticals; inorganic chemicals; sugar, automobiles, tractors and transport vehicles; heavy electrical equipment; leather and leather goods; textile machinery; man-made textiles; non-ferrous metals and alloys; food processing; and oil, detergents and paints. During the fifteen years between 1951 and 1966 factory production went up by 160 per cent.

Tea, coffee and rubber plantations today provide employment for over 1,200,000 persons: and together the plantations cover about 0·4 per cent of the cropped area, being concentrated mainly in the north-east and along the south-west coast. Agriculture accounts for over half of the total national income, and at least 70 per cent of the people are still dependent on the land for their living. Of the cereals which are grown rice is the most important, and it is the staple food of southern and eastern India. Wheat, which is the staple diet of northern India, is the next in importance, whilst other crops include barley, maize, millets and legumes. India leads the world in the production of peanuts and tea, and in 1967 the production of the latter was the highest ever recorded. She is, in addition, the second largest producer of jute, raw sugar and rice, and the third largest grower in the world of tobacco.

Bearing in mind the extent of village life, the Indian Government has done its utmost to encourage the development of small-scale and cottage industries (5). This means, in practical terms, that the government has developed a programme of technical assistance to these minor industries, and has provided training facilities and technical advice to small units. Village industries include coir spinning and weaving, sericulture, handicrafts, homespun cloth (*khaddar*), handmade paper and soap.

India realizes that no economy today is self-sufficient and her export trade figures over the last decade indicate a steady expansion and diversification of exports. In order to promote this trade India has established nineteen export promotion councils, each council being responsible for the developmental activities of those concerned with a particular commodity or group of commodities, such as tobacco, sports goods or silk and rayon textiles.

B THE PEOPLE AND THEIR HISTORY

Perhaps one of the most amazing things about the Indian society is that, despite its considerable diversity of peoples, there is a basic cultural unit within the Indian Union of States. This cultural unity may be summed up in the word 'Hinduism', which represents not merely a religion but also the basis, in real terms, for a social structure and a pattern of life. We shall consider the details of the religion of Hinduism in Chapter 7; we are here concerned with the way in which a great variety of races and ethnic stocks have somehow become welded into a major society which recognizes differences and yet has integrated those differences into a common society.

In describing any group of people and its origins it is difficult to find a set of categories which are valid and acceptable to all scholars. In his *The Human Species*, Anthony Barnett has an interesting chapter on 'Human Types' in which he divides the human species into four main groups, namely Negriforms, Mongoliforms, Australiforms and Europiforms; the latter group he subdivides into Mediterranean, Alpine and Nordic types (6). Barnett defines a race as

'a group which shares in common a certain set of genes, and which became distinct from other groups as a result of geographical isolation' (7).

Professor Morris Ginsberg lists such hereditary traits and characteristics as:

1 *Hair form*: smooth, wavy, curly, woolly.
2 *Pigmentation*: colour of hair, eyes, skin.

3 *Head formation*: ratio of breadth of skull to length.
4 *Stature and bodily proportions.*
5 *Facial traits*: nasal form, lip form, eyelids (8).

It has been suggested that other, and perhaps more sophisticated elements enter into 'race' classifications, such as similarities in blood grouping, or the ability to taste phenyl-thio-urea (which appears to be absent in American Indians and possibly in Mongolians). T. Dobzhansky has dealt with the 'blood' theory of heredity in an interesting chapter in *Evolutionary Thought in America* (9), whilst experimentation with regard to taste seems to have been limited.

The aboriginal inhabitants of India appear to have been negroid types of small stature, usually referred to as 'Negritos'. These elements are still to be found on the mainland of India in the Rajmahal Hills of Bihar, as well as in the East Indian islands of the Andaman group. The Negritos were followed by the Australoid peoples, who are to be found among the tribal populations of central and southern India, among the lower or 'exterior' castes generally, and among the Veddas of Ceylon. The next to arrive were the Mongoloids. Many of the tribal peoples of the north are Mongoloids, and they inhabit a broad expanse of Himalayan country from Kashmir in the north-west to Bhutan in the east.

The hills on each side of the Assam valley are the habitat of a dolichocephalic, or long-headed, Mongoloid type; whilst a brachycephalic, or broad-headed type of Mongoloid is dominant in Burma. In the Assam valley itself there is a mixture of Mongoloids and the Mediterranean sub-group of the Caucasoids. Of the first three main ethnic stocks so far mentioned Professor Spate makes the comment that

'The populations which show the most marked evidences of these three major stocks (Negroid, Australoid and Mongoloid) are mainly tribal, though of course these elements are not confined to the tribes, nor are they represented in all tribes. The "higher" populations are more complex still' (10).

The Caucasoids followed the Mongoloids and were of the Mediterranean sub-type, dark in complexion, of slight build, moderate in stature and dolichocephalic. This type is dominant in northern India and among the upper classes generally. Finally, about 1500 BC an Aryan group of pastoralists entered northern India; they were tall, fair Caucasoids referred to as Proto-Nordics, and they are now found mainly between the Indus and the area in the north of Madhya Pradesh known as Bundelkhand.

When the Proto-Nordics entered India, the ancient Indus civilization, which centred upon the cities of Mohenjo-Daro (the 'Mound of the Dead')

and Harappa, had already decayed and disintegrated. The Harappa culture was essentially an urban one, with something like forty sites scattered over the Indus plains; and Spate's estimates of the general impression of 'a utilitarian business culture', and the high standard of drainage as being one of its most striking features (11), seem to be the sort of judgements accepted by other scholars. Professor E. O. James, for example, suggests that although the cities were well planned, the bare red-bricked, two-roomed cottages were 'devoid of any semblance of ornament', and bore every indication of a 'utility' motive (12); whilst Professor Stuart Piggott compares them to 'contemporary coolie-lines' (13).

It would certainly be mistaken to suggest, as some have done in the past, that the invading Indo-Aryans, or Proto-Nordics, destroyed a superior civilization. The 'bourgeois mediocrity' of Harappa, to use Piggott's phrase, was over; the light-skinned, cattle-breeding *aryas* began to settle in small forest clearings where they established villages and gradually developed agriculture. They were essentially a simple society based upon a family unit, and wherever they went they developed the village type of life.

It is obviously not possible here to detail the remainder of the history of India down to modern times, which is not, in any case, the purpose of this section. The rise and fall of kingdoms and empires centred upon India make a fascinating story, and the reader is referred to the works of Romila Thapar and Percival Spear who have, between them, brought the story down to modern times (14).

There are, however, some important facts in that history worth noting here. It is believed that the Aryans invented the decimal system of notation as well as 'Arabic' numerals, the Arabic name for which is 'Hindsa', meaning 'from India'. India has been the home of a great variety of cults and religions which have originated or found some sort of refuge there, including Hinduism, Buddhism, Jainism and Sikhism. Zoroastrianism, which today is represented by some 110,000 Parsees (or 'Persians') who worship the Creator God and Lord of Light called Ahura Mazda, originally developed in Persia. In the early eighth century the Parsees fled from Persia and made their way by sea and by the coastal route to western India, in order to escape from the Arab and Islamic rule to which they had been subjected.

Islam initially came to India in the seventh century through Arab traders; and after the Arabs there came the Afghans and the Mogul (or Mughal) conquerors. One of the most enlightened of these was the Emperor Akbar, who ruled from 1556 to 1605, and who was responsible for the growing synthesis of the best in Hindu and Muslim religion, philosophy and art. Today there are more than 50 million Muslims in India.

Christianity originally came to India during the first century AD but its full impact was not really felt until the seventeenth century when a direct sea-route from Europe was established. During the ensuing years there was considerable rivalry among the Portuguese, Dutch, French and British for markets in India, as well as for commercial, economic and political control. Eventually the British emerged dominant over the whole of India, and the reign of the East India Company lasted from about 1753 until 1813, when its absolute monopoly of Indian trade was abolished. In 1833 its powers were limited to administration, and after the Indian Mutiny in 1857–9 the East India Company was liquidated and the Crown took over complete responsibility for India. The British Raj reigned supreme until India's struggle for freedom eventually culminated in partition and independence on August 15, 1947. On January 26, 1950, India adopted a new Constitution and was declared a sovereign democratic Republic.

C THE NEW INDIA

The head of the State under India's new Constitution is the President, who is elected by an electoral college composed of the members of the two Houses of Parliament (the *Rajya Sabha* or Council of States, and the *Lok Sabha* or House of the People) and of the Legislative Assemblies of the States. The President must not be less than thirty-five years of age, he must be a citizen of India and eligible for election as a member of the House of the People. He holds the office for a term of five years and is eligible for re-election; but he does not normally exercise any constitutional powers on his own initiative. The Vice-President is similarly elected. The Prime Minister is, in theory, appointed by the President, who is also responsible for appointing the other ministers on the advice of the Prime Minister. In fact the Prime Minister is chosen by the members of Parliament, and then he or she will form the Cabinet. All these appointments must, however, be ratified by the President.

The aim of the Constitution, in general terms, is to secure for all citizens of India political, social and economic *justice*; *liberty* of belief, faith, worship, thought and expression; *equality* of status and opportunity; and *fraternity* which will assure the dignity of the individual and the unity of the nation. Entitlement to citizenship of the Union of India may be acquired through birth within the territory of the Union, or descent from Indian parents, or residence for a period of at least five years within India at the commencement of the Constitution. Individuals of Indian origin residing abroad could become citizens by registering themselves as such with Indian diplomatic or consular representatives in countries of their residence. By Article 6 of the Constitution, displaced Pakistanis were permitted to become citizens. Article 326 of the Constitution enfranchised all persons of twenty-one years and over who were not otherwise disqualified through non-residence, criminality, corruption or unsoundness of mind (15).

The Constitution seeks to guarantee seven broad categories of fundamental citizen rights which are justiciable:

1 The right to equality before the law; to the prohibition of discrimination on the grounds of religion, colour, caste, race or birth; and to equality of opportunity in the matter of employment.
2 The right to freedom of speech and expression; of assembly, association or union; of movement, residence, and acquisition or disposal of property; and the right to practise any profession or occupation subject to the security of the State, friendly relations with foreign countries, public order, decency and morality.
3 The right against exploitation, prohibiting all forms of forced labour, child labour and traffic in human beings.
4 The right to freedom of conscience and free profession, practice and propagation of religion.
5 The right of minorities to conserve their culture, language, and script, and to receive education and to establish and administer educational institutions of their choice.
6 The right to property, subject to the right of the State to compulsory acquisition for public purposes after due payment of compensation.
7 The right to constitutional remedies for the enforcement of fundamental rights (16).

Local government is organized through local self-governing institutions which are broadly of two categories – urban and rural. The large cities are administered by corporations, and the smaller cities and towns by boards or municipal committees. The rural areas are governed by what is termed *panchayati raj*. Whilst India is becoming increasingly industrialized by her succession of Five-Year Plans, she is still essentially an agricultural country with something like 560,000 villages. These villages are suffering, generally, from a weak local economy with low incomes, poor productivity and a lack of continuous employment. The aim of the *panchayati raj*, which is a form of self-government by means of a council, or *panchayat*, composed of village elders, is to effect a more productive and efficient economy with a greater range of both agricultural and domestic or village occupations. The basic village institutions are the *panchayat*, the co-operative and the school.

The *panchayat* is ultimately responsible for local agricultural production, rural industries, medical relief, child and maternity welfare, the management of common grazing grounds, the maintenance of village roads, streets, tanks and wells, and the provision of drainage and sanitation. Naturally much of the organization and administration is handed on to the co-operative, which functions in the economic sphere, and to associate bodies such as women's and youth organizations, artisans' associations, farmers' unions and so forth. The *panchayat* may also be responsible for primary education, the maintenance of village records, the collection of land revenues, and even the levying of taxes on lands and houses. At the end of 1968 it was estimated that over 210,000 village *panchayats* were already functioning in India (17).

REFERENCES

1 Ministry of Information and Broadcasting, *India Today: Basic Facts* (Ministry of Information, New Delhi, May 1969), p. 2.
2 Research and Reference Division, Ministry of Information, *India – A Reference Annual, 1968* (Publications Division, Ministry of Information and Broadcasting, Government of India, 1968), Advertisement 1, p. 629.
3 I am indebted throughout this chapter to Spate, O. H. K., *India and Pakistan* (Methuen, 2nd edition 1957), to which the reader should refer for a more detailed account of the geography and ethnology of this region.
4 Spate, O. H. K., *India and Pakistan: A General and Regional Geography* (Methuen, 2nd edition 1957), pp. 43–4.
5 See *India – A Reference Annual, 1968*, pp. 334–6.
6 *Vide* Barnett, A., *The Human Species* (Penguin, revised edition 1961), Chapter 7, pp. 133–51.
7 Ibid., p. 151.
8 Ginsberg, M., *Sociology* (Home Univ. Lib., O.U.P., 1934), Chapter III.
9 *Vide* Dobzhansky, T., 'The Genetic Nature of Differences Among Men' in Persons, S. (ed.), *Evolutionary Thought in America* (Yale Univ. Press, 1950), Chapter III, pp. 86–155.
10 Spate, O. H. K., op. cit., pp. 123–4.
11 Ibid., p. 145.
12 James, E. O., *The Ancient Gods* (Weidenfeld & Nicolson, 1960), p. 26.
13 Piggott, S., *Prehistoric India* (Penguin, 1950), p. 169.
14 *Vide* Thapar, Romila, *A History of India*, Vol. I (Penguin, 1966), and Spear, P., *A History of India*, Vol. II (Penguin, 1965).
15 See *India – A Reference Annual, 1968*, pp. 22–4.
16 Ibid., pp. 22–3.
17 Ibid., p. 50.

BIBLIOGRAPHY

Agarwala, S. N., *Some Problems of India's Population* (Vora & Co., Bombay, 1966).
Aurora, G. S., *The New Frontiersmen* (Popular Prakashan, Bombay, 1967).
Basham, A. L., *The Wonder That Was India* (Sidgwick & Jackson, 1954).
Bauer, P. T., *Indian Economic Policy and Development* (Allen & Unwin, 1961).
Campbell, A., *The Heart of India* (Constable, 1958).
Chaudhuri, N. C., *The Continent of Circe: Being an Essay on the Peoples of India* (Chatto & Windus, 1965).
Dubey, R. N., *Economic Geography of India* (Kitab Mahal, Allahabad, 1964).
Edwardes, M., *A History of India: From Earliest Times to the Present Day* (Thames & Hudson, 1961).

Griffiths, P., *Modern India* (Benn, 4th edition 1965).

Hanson, A. H., *The Process of Planning: A Study of India's Five-Year Plans 1950–1964* (O.U.P., 1966).

Lamb, B. P., *India: A World in Transition* (Pall Mall Press, 1963).

Lewis, O., *Village Life in N. India: Studies in a Delhi Village* (Random House, N.Y., 1965).

Majumdar, D. N., *Races and Cultures of India* (Asia Publishing House, 4th edition 1961).

Majumdar, R. C. *et al.*, *An Advanced History of India* (Macmillan, 2nd edition 1961).

Mamoria, C. B., *India's Population Problem* (Kitab Mahal, Allahabad, 1961).

Mehrotra, S. R., *India and the Commonwealth 1885–1929* (Allen & Unwin, 1965).

Morris-Jones, W. H., *The Government and Politics of India* (Hutchinson, 1964).

Nanda, B. R., *Mahatma Gandhi: A Biography* (Allen & Unwin, 1959).

Neale, W. C., *India: The Search for Unity, Democracy and Progress* (Van Nostrand, 1965).

Panikkar, K. M., *Survey of Indian History* (Allen & Unwin, 1960).

Panikkar, K. M., *Commonsense About India* (Victor Gollancz, 1960).

Piggott, S., *Prehistoric India* (Penguin, 1950).

Rawlinson, H. G., *A Concise History of the Indian People* (O.U.P., 2nd edition 1950).

Registrar General of India, *Census of India, 1961* (Manager of Publications, Registrar General, Delhi, 1962).

Schmid, P., *India: Mirage and Reality* (Harrap, 1961).

Segal, R., *The Crisis of India* (Penguin, 1965).

Sharma, B. M., *The Republic of India, Constitution and Government* (Asia Publishing House, 1966).

Spate, O. H. K., *India and Pakistan: A General and Regional Geography* (Methuen, 2nd edition 1957).

Spear, P., *A History of India*, Vol. II (Penguin, 1965).

Srinivas, M. N. (ed.), *India's Villages* (Asia Publishing House, 2nd edition 1960).

Srinivas, M. N., *Social Change in Modern India* (Univ. of California Press, Berkeley, 1966).

Stamp, L. Dudley, *India, Pakistan, Ceylon and Burma* (Methuen, 1957).

Thapar, Romila, *A History of India*, Vol. I (Penguin, 1966).

Varma, B. N. (ed.), *Contemporary India* (Asia Publishing House, 1964).

Williams, L. F. R. (ed.), *Murray's Handbook for Travellers in India and Pakistan, Burma and Ceylon* (Murray, 20th edition 1965).

Wolpert, S., *India* (Prentice-Hall, 1965).

Zinkin, M. and T., *Britain and India: Requiem for Empire* (Chatto & Windus, 1964).

Zinkin, T., *India* (Thames & Hudson, 1965).

Chapter 7

Some Indian
Religions

A HINDUISM

> Lead me from the unreal to the real.
> Lead me from darkness to light.
> Lead me from death to immortality.

(From the Upanishads)

1 *Caste*

It is not easy to get inside the thoughts and beliefs of other races; moreover, there is always a tendency to misrepresent what we do not or cannot understand. When we have done our best, and unfortunately sometimes our worst, we present those elements of another religion which are clearly strange, intriguing, different and perhaps sufficiently 'inferior' as to give us more confidence in our own belief. If we were going to introduce Christianity to a non-Christian society (or even our own) we certainly would not begin with the Spanish Inquisition or with some of the more sordid aspects of the Crusades. Similarly, in introducing Hinduism we shall avoid emphasizing some of those elements which tend to alienate the reader because of their apparent or overt grossness. To understand the rituals and forms of worship of any faith one needs to know a great deal of the myths, patterns and symbols of comparative religion, and we cannot attempt to do this in the space at our disposal. But one must recognize that many of the encapsulated oddments purporting to provide the 'essence' of Hinduism, or any other religion, more often than not offer a completely superficial, if not perverted, view of what that religion provides.

Excavations in the 1920s revealed a pre-Aryan civilization in the Indus Valley at Harappa and Mohenjo-Daro, in the north-west of India. This culture dates from about 3000 BC and it continued to flourish until about 2000 BC, when it began to wane. By 1500 BC, according to the archaeological evidence, the Harappa culture had virtually disappeared. About this time the Nordics, variously called Aryans and Indo-Aryans, left the northern plateau of Iran where they had settled and wandered into northern India. The Aryans were a light-skinned race who were proud of their origins, their purity and their nobility – *aryas* means 'the noble ones'. Most of the indigenous people whom they gradually conquered, subdued and colonized were darker in colour; and the Aryans eventually made them their workers and slaves. The term which was used to describe them was *dasas* – a word of contempt, later signifying slaves.

The story of the gradual development of the caste system during something like a millennium cannot be told in a few words. There were obviously struggles for power, particularly between the two castes of *brahmins* (or *brahmans*) and *kshatriyas*, and there were long periods when first one, and then the other, appears to have been in the ascendancy. The Aryans themselves were already, according to Romila Thapar (1), divided into three social classes when they first arrived in India. These social classes comprised the aristocracy, who were the warriors, the priests, and the commoners; and this division of the Aryan society was largely an economic one. In general terms, however, the great division was not within the Aryan society itself, but rather between the Aryans and the non-Aryans. Gradually the Aryans assumed the status of the three upper castes and the indigenous non-Aryans became the fourth caste.

It has frequently been pointed out that the Sanskrit word for caste is *varna*, which means colour. And there can be little doubt that the original caste system was a form of colour discrimination that was reinforced by the fact of conquest. Taya Zinkin, in an attempt to delineate the position of caste today, has said that

'A Brahmin is no less a Brahmin if he is born jet-black; an Untouchable is no whit less untouchable if she happens to be fair' (2).

She rightly points out that white men are, after all, Untouchables. But if caste is not colour today it certainly was in origin, if only by reason of the fact that the conquerors were, fortuitously, lighter-skinned. The three upper castes, formed from the Aryans, were known as 'twice-born' for they had gone through the process of physical birth and also of initiation. They were the *brahmins*, or priestly caste, the *kshatriyas* or warriors, and the *vaishyas* or agriculturalists. The conquered *dasas* formed the lowest caste who were the labourers, the herdsmen, the serfs and slaves, and were called the *shudras*.

These four broad divisions, however, do not by any means constitute the total complexity of the caste system. Zinkin states that there are over two thousand *jatis* or sub-castes among the *brahmins* alone, so that altogether there are literally thousands of sub-castes and kin-groups. The ramifications of caste structure are so many and complicated that the most that can be done here is to make one or two generalizations about it. According to orthodox Hinduism inter-caste marriage was not permitted; in fact, a caste has been defined as

'a group of families whose members can marry with each other and can eat in each other's company without believing themselves polluted' (3).

But, despite this, one form of inter-caste marriage seems to have been permitted, namely that termed *anuloma* marriage, in which the bridegroom was of a higher caste than that of the bride. Children born of such a marriage generally belonged to their father's caste. It would be true to say today, however, that marriage customs vary with caste and sub-caste, and that the orthodox ideals of non-intermixture of caste are obsolescent. One group, nevertheless, remains outside the caste system and is referred to as 'outcastes'; they number at least fifty million, that is, about 10 per cent of the population.

Formerly known as untouchables, or pariahs, these people were not only without caste, but were also social outcasts without opportunities of labour or contact with members of the caste system. Their chief occupation was that of begging and making sure that they did not pollute their benefactors by personal contact. K. M. Sen maintains that there is no certainty about when the idea of untouchability originated; and although the scriptural support for it is indeed slender it does not seem to be of recent origin. Sen states that

'Quite conceivably, some form of untouchability might have existed in pre-Aryan India. It is perhaps of some significance to note that untouchability is strongest in south India and that it applies not merely to low castes *vis-à-vis* higher ones, but sometimes even between different low castes' (4).

So that almost every group, caste or *jati* appears to be in a state of 'untouchability' to another group, caste or *jati*. These ideas of untouchability when first encountered, seem alien and odd to us when we freely mix with others in markets, shops, places of entertainment, homes and on public transport. But Taya Zinkin has argued that caste and untouchability are not exclusively Indian or Hindu. Indeed, in most societies there appear to be first- and second-class citizens, according to birth, or colour, or capital, or earning capacity, even though there may not be a political or social policy of apartheid. Zinkin further suggests that this segregation has occurred even within Christian churches in parts of India; she maintains that

'Some South Indian churches have always made their ex-Untouchables sit apart from their ex-Brahmins' (5).

Mahatma Gandhi worked very hard on behalf of the untouchables during his lifetime, and he refused to accept that any sort of contact with them incurred pollution. Indeed, we are told that his wife had considerable problems with drinking vessels and toilet facilities in her *ménage* because her Gandhiji would invite into his home, and at the same time, people who in normal Hindu society would have avoided one another because of the danger of pollution; and these would include not merely untouchables but also members of different sub-castes of the same main grouping who had certain avoidance laws or dietary tabus. Outcastes were first referred to as *harijans* by Gandhi – the 'children of God' – and this name has remained with them. Today there exist laws against the deliberate practice of untouchability; but one cannot, by legislation, change overnight the habits and customs of three or more millennia. Discrimination against members of lower castes when being interviewed for a job is also illegal; but, as some high-caste Hindus have not hesitated to point out, this sort of legislation tends to act in reverse and can very quickly lead to discrimination against the so-called privileged members of the *brahmin* and *kshatriya* castes.

There is, of course, a strong link between the social fact of the caste system and the religious beliefs of the Hindus. Myth and reality are inevitably mingled in religious faith and dogma, and this is clearly so in respect of caste. A hymn in the *Rig-Veda* suggests that

When the gods made a sacrifice with the Man as their victim . . .
When they divided the Man, into how many parts did they divide him?
What was his mouth, what were his arms, what were his thighs and his
   feet called?
The brahmin was his mouth, of his arms were made the warrior.
His thighs became the vaishya, of his feet the shudra was born (6).

This hymn, dating back to at least 1000 BC, provides a presumption concerning the position and office of each of the castes. The *brahmins* were intended to be the priests or the mouthpieces of the gods; the *kshatriyas* were to become the warriors, using their arms to promote the will of their gods and to increase their territory; the *vaishyas* would bear the weight and burden of the work to provide the gods and their highest servants with sustenance; and the *shudras* would perform the laborious work of fetching and carrying under the control and direction of the *vaishyas*.

This mythical view, however, has never remained unchallenged even within Hindu religious literature. Thus, for example, one of the *Puranas* argues that

'Since members of all the four castes are children of God, they all belong to the same caste. All human beings have the same Father, and children of the same Father cannot have different castes' (7).

Such an argument is difficult to combat even for a Hindu; but the fact is that he is faced with a *fait accompli* in the established and formalized caste system itself. It is a system which has operated socially as well as religiously;

and a myth which provides a rationalization of what actually exists is likely to be preferred to a philosophy of what might, or ought to be. It is true, as Zinkin suggests (8), that the average Hindu really believes that his religion demands the observance of caste, and that many of the evils of his world have arisen from the pollution of caste intermixture. Even in the *Bhagavad-Gita* there is an explicit acceptance of caste and all that caste implies, when Arjuna says to Krishna:

> We know what fate falls
> On families broken:
> The rites are forgotten,
> Vice rots the remnant
> Defiling the women,
> And from their corruption
> Comes mixing of castes:
> The curse of confusion
> Degrades the victims
> And damns the destroyers (9).

But implicitly there is also an acceptance throughout, in the words of Krishna, that caste like war is really incidental to life in the body; the only true reality is the indwelling Godhead, the *atman*, which is ultimately the same for all men. In other words, caste itself is unimportant in absolute terms, *sub specie aeternitatis*, provided one understands the nature of It, the *atman*, in all its wonder.

2 *Reincarnation*

Thus, caste may be accepted at different levels and for different reasons, by different Hindus. But the end-result is the same: a resignation to what is god-ordained, socially acceptable and sanctioned, or even just adventitious. Resignation to it results from an inner realization that this present life is but a brief incident and time-span within eternity. The fact that one is born into a particular caste, and that there is no possibility of advance up the caste scale in this life, pales into insignificance when one realizes that there is a certain inevitability about return after death. Such return and its nature are contingent upon the sort of life one has lived here and now: this is the important thing in the philosophy of caste – not the fact that I am born a humble *shudra*, but the fact that if I want to return next time in a more favourable position in a higher caste, as a *vaishya* for example, I must live as near a perfect life as possible in my present condition.

The philosophy of *samsara*, or reincarnation, is far-reaching and capable of an ever developing sophistication. It is not to be confounded by mathematical arguments about increasing or decreasing population, or by the discovery of other planets and their possible habitation. The Hindu, the thinking Hindu, regards his present span of life as merely an episode in a long succession of lives, some already lived, some yet to come; some human and some possibly animal; some here on earth, some elsewhere on other planets or in other dimensions. The universe is his oyster. But he is also part and parcel of its physical and moral causation – he cannot escape his total participation in all that happens throughout the universe.

The concept of *karma* involves complete personal responsibility for what the individual does; every embodied being, in close connection with its environment, is the product of its own past. None can avoid *karma*: it is the debt we have to pay, the work and the deeds we have to do in order to work out our own personal salvation. Just as we have complete responsibility for our actions, so also we have freedom of will, for our present joy or sorrow is contingent upon our free activity in the past – back to the first choice we ever made for good or ill. Nor is 'we reap what we sow' a doctrine peculiar to Hinduism. The prophet Jeremiah, in the sixth century before Christ, stated that 'each shall die for his own sin, and he who eats the sour grapes, his own teeth shall be set on edge' (10). And Ezekiel, who also flourished in the sixth century BC and supported the doctrine of individual retribution in a similar passage, maintained that the evil man was as responsible for his own death and dying as the good man for his own life and living: 'The soul that sins, that soul shall die' (11). Nor did the Christian philosophy change anything in this respect for St Paul when he wrote to the Galatians:

'Make no mistake – God is not mocked – a man will reap just what he sows; he who sows for his flesh will reap destruction from the flesh, and he who sows for the spirit will reap life eternal from the spirit' (12).

The burden of Emerson's essay on *Compensation* (13) is that you cannot do wrong without suffering wrong; that every point of pride a man has is injurious to him, that the exclusionist in religion shuts the door of heaven on himself and not upon others, and that we live in a universe in which the tear of a child cannot possibly occur in isolation, for it will have some effect upon a star. For Hinduism, as apparently for some Old Testament prophets and for Emerson, the universe is a continuum in space and time in which there is an inextricable confluence of all our individual thought and activity, and in which we are all responsibly involved in the pain, disappointment and sorrow of others as well as in their joy, success and happiness.

Ultimately, the individual will be released from the apparently ceaseless round of *samsara*, or rebirth, only when his karmic debt is fully paid, and his personal purification leads to an acceptance of the *dharma*, or universal law of goodness, truth and righteousness. The final goal is one of 'no return'; the chains of desire and of the illusion (*maya*) of life are broken, and *moksha*, or salvation, is attained.

3 *The Nature of Brahman or God*

The Creed of Saint Athanasius (the 'Quicunque Vult') was appointed to be read or sung upon thirteen occasions during the religious year of the Church of England, and one phrase in the Creed refers to

'The Father incomprehensible, the Son incomprehensible; and the Holy Ghost incomprehensible' (14).

This humble attitude towards God's incomprehensibility is intrinsic also to the Hindu belief. Ultimately Brahman, the Absolute and Supreme Reality, can be expressed only by the sort of negation implicit in the word 'incomprehensible'. Brahman cannot be defined: It can be described only negatively – *neti, neti*; It is 'not this, not that'. One can exhaust the universe itself in seeking this identification of Brahman; and everywhere one goes one has to admit that Brahman is not this, Brahman is not that. But, like Saint Athanasius and those who still claim some allegiance to his creed – however tenuous that allegiance may be – the Hindu realizes that man cannot live for long in the realm of abstractions. Saint Athanasius went on to define the indefinable in some desperate attempt to comprehend the incomprehensible: one must worship one God in Trinity, Unity in Trinity and Trinity in Unity – until gradually the hardened dogmas begin to emerge and end with 'life everlasting' or 'everlasting fire'.

Hinduism, too, has its unity and diversity, the One and the Many. The reader will find Hinduism placed into every conceivable category of religious belief: it is pantheism or monism (15); it is monotheistic (16); it has a kathenotheistic tendency at the Vedic stage (17); it is a dualism and polytheism (18); it is, in fact, none of these but rather panontism (19) or panentheism. One cannot, without going into all the nuances and niceties of distinction between these terms, assign Hinduism here to any particular philosophical-cum-theological position. Nor is it very important. Like almost every other great world religion, Hinduism has passed through every stage of development in its evolution: and each stage lingers on with some worshipper or group of worshippers. Hinduism does not pretend to be any more homogeneous than Christianity; there is room in it for almost every shade of belief. Its own 'honest to God' reformation led to an intellectualization of Brahman, the Impersonal, the Transcendent, the Infinite and the Absolute. At the warmer, personal though still transcendent, level it produced Ishwara, an object of worship and love.

Brahman is 'not this' and 'not that' because Brahman is *advitiyam,*

5. *Top:* Delhi State Assembly candidate setting out on an election campaign,
(bottom) Electioneering procession in New Delhi during the fourth General Election,
1967.

6. Loading and unloading at Cochin Port, Kerala, India

'without a second'; Brahman is the sum-total of all that exists; Brahman is all-Being (hence panontism). Yet all things consist in Brahman (hence panentheism), and are permeated by It.

> With bliss ineffable
> I felt the sentiment of Being spread
> O'er all that moves and all that seemeth still.

This sentiment that Wordsworth experienced was the awareness of the Hindu's all-pervasive Brahman; it was the same consciousness of 'the All', the totality of Being, that moved the author of the third-century Gnostic *Gospel of Thomas*, which was discovered at Nag Hammadi in 1945, to exclaim:

> I am the All;
> (from me) the All has gone forth,
> and to me the All has returned.
> Split wood: I am there.
> Lift the stone, and you will find me there (20).

Hinduism has, apparently, some interesting psychological as well as spiritual insights. According to C. G. Jung, the concept of the trinity, or triunity or triad, is an archetype existing preconsciously and forming a structural dominant of the psyche in general; and he traces the existence of triads of gods at very primitive levels and in the religions of Babylonia, Egypt and Greece (21). Ishwara, the personal God, became a triad of gods or trimurti, each being a representation of a particular function of the supreme God. The three-faced God incorporated Brahma the Creator, Vishnu the Preserver, and Shiva the Destroyer. Brahma was originally Prajapati, or God in creativity, who was responsible for the projection of the universe as an extension of himself. Vishnu's function was to preserve the world from evil and destruction, and to make personal intervention in the cosmic process. Shiva's function was closely associated with the essential destruction of evil in order that the natural cycle of creation, preservation and re-creation might be maintained. There is no precise equation between the Christian concept of the Trinity and the Hindu concept of the trimurti; but there is an obvious similarity in the context of role or function. Brahma is God the Father bodying forth creation; his popularity has declined over the years and very few temples were built to celebrate his worship. Vishnu is God the Son and man's perpetual saviour; his worship is performed in temples dedicated to him by his followers, the *vaishnavas*. Shiva is God the Dissolver, that is, the spiritual element in the trimurti which discerns good and evil and divides them asunder in order to destroy the evil; and his worship is supported by the *shaivas*. But this is a similarity of function which must not be pressed too far in theological terms, even though it may provide some preliminary 'common ground' for discussion.

Professor R. L. Slater further maintains that

'this reference to a Hindu trinity may again be misleading because there is nothing in Hindu thought which corresponds to the central conception of a Christian Trinity' (22).

There might be some room for argument as to what exactly 'the central conception of a Christian Trinity' is, but this is not the place for theological discussion. The correspondence is mainly at the archetypal and psychological levels; and if we are prepared to accept that theological dogmas are largely the excrescences of age – inessential to fundamental belief, and often simply morbid outgrowths of ossified ideas – we may find an even greater identity between the Hindu and Christian concepts.

But the Hindu, like the Christian, is not content to leave his God either at the impersonal, absolute level, or at the personal, transcendent level, or at the level of a mystical triunity. God must still, for him, find expression in human form, in incarnation. The *avataras* are regarded as mediators between man and God: saviours who reject the ultimate joy of union with Brahman in order to assist mankind to find that union for themselves. The *Bhagavad-Gita*, which was written somewhere between the fifth and second centuries BC, has as one of its speakers the Lord (or Sri) Krishna. Krishna was an *avatara*, the great divine incarnation of Indian history, who was also called Govinda, or the 'Giver of Enlightenment'. In conversation with Arjuna, the Lord Krishna says:

> When goodness grows weak,
> When evil increases,
> I make myself a body.
>
> In every age I come back
> to deliver the holy,
> to destroy the sin of the sinner,
> to establish righteousness (23).

Krishna was a non-Vedic and non-Aryan deity, and K. M. Sen is of the opinion that it is at least not improbable that the *avatara* concept was present in non-Aryan Indian thought for a long time. Whether that is so or not, it is a concept that has continued down to modern times. Most recently Mahatma Gandhi has been accorded the reverence due to an *avatara*, whilst earlier *avataras* have included Rama, and Gautama the Buddha.

God, Brahman, is the Absolute and the undifferentiated; but within every man is the *atman*, the soul or inner self. The *atman* is God immanent in each and everyone, and this is expressed in the *Chandogya Upanishad* in the statement *tat tvam asi*, 'Thou art That'. The Brahman and the Atman are one and the same, and this doctrine provides for a non-duality in the concept of God: man does not stand over against Him, for when Brahman projected out of Himself the universe He entered into every being, and 'All that is has its self in Him alone'. The *Chandogya* goes on with the identification of Brahman with everything that exists – with earth, food, fire and sun. Indeed, just as formerly it was said that Brahman was not this, not that (*neti, neti*), now it is said that Brahman is this, He is that (*iti, iti*).

'He who glows in the depths of your eyes – that is Brahman: that is the Self of yourself. He is the Beautiful One, he is the Luminous One. In all the worlds, forever and ever, he shines' (24).

Only when the individual has a realization of this ultimate inner identity between himself and God does he obtain release from the illusion (*maya*) of life; then he reaches the state of *moksha* or liberation; this is the passionless peace, the emancipation of Nirvana. Nirvana is not a place but a different dimension or state of consciousness, and an awareness of union with God, who is finally seen as the only Reality. Brahman is *Sacchidananda*, that is, He is Infinite Being (*sat*), Infinite Consciousness (*chit*) and Infinite Bliss (*ananda*). To enter into His Being is not to be snuffed out like a candle, as many Western writers have suggested; it is to cease to operate as a small, partial being and to extend one's consciousness and beingness to the infinite dimensions of Brahman.

For the Hindu, Truth is at the mountain top. We all begin at different points at the foot of the mountain, and there are many ways up the mountainside. But there is only one crest where ultimate Truth abides. The Hindu believes that as long as a man persistently climbs his own particular path, and refrains from merely running around the mountainside, he must in the end find what all men find who climb – Brahman, the Ultimate Truth.

4 *Yoga*

How can man reach this mountain top? How can he attain to the ineffable goal of union with God? There are techniques which may be developed to reach this union, or *samadhi*, which means 'together with the Lord'. The West knows Yoga mainly through popular advertisements showing devotees in strange and awkward positions, or *asanas*. But this is only one form of Yoga. The word 'Yoga' has the same origin as the English word 'yoke' and the Latin 'iugum'; it means a discipline, a way, a union. The man who pursues the way is a yogi. When Jesus said to his disciples, 'Take my yoke upon you and learn from me,' he implied that knowledge of God demanded a certain discipline. In Hinduism the *guru*, or teacher, yokes himself, metaphorically speaking, to the *chela*, or disciple. The discipline and the goal are one.

In the relics of the Harappa civilization, archaeologists found sculptured figures in a variety of the yogic *asanas*; and there is certainly a presumption among many writers on India and Hinduism that at least the physical practice of yoga (that is, hatha yoga) is of greater antiquity than the Aryan invasion. Although there are seven distinct schools of yoga, with differing practices and techniques, the aim of yoga is one – to find union with Brahman. E. W. F. Tomlin states that:

'When, sometime between 300 and 150 BC, the sage Patanjali composed the *Yoga Sutras*, he was probably engaged in the codification of many ancient traditions. Men who devote a lifetime to the practice of ascetic meditation must evolve a great variety of techniques; but the comparative simplicity of Patanjali's rules must not blind us to the elaborate metaphysics upon which they are based. The practice, however scrupulous, of such rules of posture, breathing, etc., by the enthusiastic Westerner can scarcely do harm; but abstract gymnastics are no substitute for the arduous consecration of a lifetime to reflection, *askesis*, and worship' (25).

And this admirably sums up the whole business and difficulty of yoga: it is a way of life, it is the totality of living, it is the perpetual practice of the presence of Brahman. As, in the Chinese religion Taoism, the Tao is the way, the goal and the way-goer, so in Hinduism yoga is the discipline, the end and the practice; and the yogi is not an exhibitionist displaying to the world his conquest of space, time and consciousness, but one whose sole, all-consuming aim is to reach the state of *samadhi*, or union with Brahman. If this intensification of consciousness should result in what we are pleased to term 'supernormal' experience, or psi-phenomena, he certainly will not reject them; nor will he seek to exploit them. Such phenomena are, again, but extensions and diversifications of Brahman within his creation and, in particular, within the *atman*. Patanjali held that

'The student whose mind is steadied by meditation obtains mastery which extends from the atomic to the infinite' (26).

The *Bhagavad-Gita* provides a synthesis of at least three forms of yoga: the path of knowledge, or *jnana*; the path of work, or *karma*; and the path of devotion, or *bhakti*. The way of the yogi is the way of knowledge, the knowledge of the Absolute Ground, of the Truth, of the Reality, of the self. Knowledge of the self or *atman* is also knowledge of God or Brahman, and such knowledge is increased and developed by being yoked to a great Master – for Arjuna, the hero of the story, the Master is Krishna. Self-knowledge is also assisted by meditation. Patanjali once described the mind as being akin to an inebriated monkey, suffering from St Vitus' dance, and stung into uncontrollable fury by a wasp. Patiently and gradually the individual must free himself from all mental distractions and fix his mind upon the *atman*; always, however much his thoughts may wander, he must bring them back to this focal point (27).

Such a practice of meditation, however, does not imply inaction, but only non-attachment to the results of action, or *karma*. The yogi must be involved in life and its problems, since freedom from activity is never achieved by abstention from action. Actions, however, must be disinterested and must be performed sacramentally (28). This view is summed up in the statement of Krishna:

> Brahman is the ritual,
> Brahman is the offering,
> Brahman is he who offers
> To the fire that is Brahman.
> If a man sees Brahman
> In every action,
> He will find Brahman (29).

Such a union with God is both the end and the means: to reach Brahman one must be absorbed into Brahman; and this absorption is achieved by devotion (*bhakti*) to God, or to Krishna his *avatara*. The *Bhagavad-Gita* emphasizes, in all this, the importance of human relationships: one must be friendly and compassionate to all, and one should not hate any living creature. One should no longer think in terms of 'I' and 'mine', for these are delusions; there is only Brahman. Pleasure and pain must be accepted with equal equanimity – they cannot change or affect the essential and eternal self. Only if the devotee sets his heart upon his Lord in this way, and takes him for his ideal above all others, will he come into the Being of God.

B JAINISM

1 *Mahavira* (*fl.* 500 BC)

What is the point of including an account of Jainism in a book on the background of immigrants and immigrant pupils, when it is more than likely that there are no Jains amongst those immigrants? The answer is a simple one – the background of immigrants includes the totality of their cultural history and experience. It is clearly not possible in a book of this length to consider in detail their whole history, culture and socio-economic background, and so we must be selective. Jainism, like Sikhism and

Buddhism, has arisen within the religion of Hinduism itself in the form of a reaction to certain of its beliefs and tenets – just as within Christianity sects and schisms have developed during the last nineteen-hundred years. These sects – both within the history of Hinduism and Christianity – have had their effect upon the main streams of religion and upon society as a whole. Hinduism and India are different today because of the Jains, the Sikhs and the Buddhists, however small their present number of followers might be. Jainism entered the very soul of Hinduism at its best and highest level.

The founder of the Jains, Vardhamana, was born during the sixth century before Christ, probably about 540 BC, near Vaishali in Bihar. His father was a very wealthy *kshatriya* chief, who, with his wife, practised extreme forms of fasting in the hope that eventually rebirth might be averted through starvation and suicide. In fact both his father and mother eventually succeeded in their efforts and left their son to his own devices at the age of thirty-two. Mahavira became depressed about the whole business of life and death, and began a serious, intellectual search for truth, knowledge and understanding. He renounced the wealth and social position which he inherited from his father and began to withdraw from all the splendour of the rich *kshatriya* life to which he himself had been accustomed, despite his parents' nihilistic views.

Tradition claims that for twelve or thirteen years Vardhamana wandered around the country of Western Bengal, during which time he practised extreme forms of asceticism and rejected every sort of property, including personal clothing. Perpetually seeking liberation (*moksha*) from the illusions of life, Vardhamana eventually sat under a tree by the side of a river where he meditated and, eventually, attained the liberation he sought; from now on he was known as Mahavira, the great man or hero.

Mahavira held that eternal truths were revealed to him during this critical period of meditation. These truths were revealed in this way only to the *jinas*, the conquerors or saviours of the world who appeared from age to age, and he was, therefore, one of these *jinas*. The function of a *jina* was to reform the older, orthodox teaching and to highlight its essence. Mahavira began to preach and draw around him followers who accepted his call to asceticism, and discipleship brooked no barriers of caste or sex. His disciples were, and still are, known as Jains, that is, those who conquer and are victorious over the evils and distractions of life. The Sanskrit root *ji* means 'to conquer', and there is in this religion a consciousness of the conquest of karmic matter. The body was, for the Jain, no longer in command. As E. O. James has indicated,

'for Mahavira the fundamental ill was the association of the soul with the body' (30).

The body was the product of *karma*; the elimination of *karma* would result in liberation from the prison of the body.

After Mahavira attained to his perfect spiritual knowledge, or *kevala*, he continued his wanderings for thirty years during which the religion, or sect, of Jainism became established.

2 *The Essence of Jainism*

The Jain took five vows based upon the three 'jewels' of right faith, right knowledge and right action. These three jewels were essential possessions if the devotee were to reach the everlasting peace and inaction of *moksha* or *nirvana*. For the Jain the latter state meant a complete dissociation from *karma* and all that it implied. The first vow was concerned with the preservation of all forms of life, since killing, or *himsa*, was the worst possible action, whether the object of the action were a human being or an insect. The concept of non-killing, or *ahimsa*, however, went further than the mere action of killing; it involved thought, word, and all deeds including eating and drinking which resulted in the deprivation of life. This principle of *ahimsa* excluded the Jain from any form of industry that involved the destruction of any sort of life; thus he could not, and still cannot, engage in agriculture, hunting or fishing. For this reason a strict Jain will avoid disturbing the earth in any way; he will sweep in front of him wherever he walks in order not to tread upon an insect; and he will strain his drinks and wear a cloth over his mouth for the same reason.

The second vow was concerned with the jewel of right knowledge and truth: there was to be no uttering of a lie. Actually, once more, the vow concerns more than the mere telling of a lie – there is to be no lie in the soul, no deceit, no rejection of what is intuitively known to be the truth. The third vow was concerned with property: no Jain could take that which belonged to another unless it were clearly a gift. According to his fourth vow the Jain must not indulge in any sensual pleasures, particularly sexual intercourse. Clearly, however, if all Jains made and kept this vow the whole sect would die out; and so, as in other religions, there are two levels of discipleship: those who are completely involved in the asceticism of the religion and all its rigours; and those who in any case are unable to go to such extremes but who, nevertheless, are responsible for the continuance of the sect physically speaking. His fifth vow involved the renunciation of all interests in worldly affairs: he must have no personal attachments in this life.

The Jains developed, during the first century AD, two schisms – the *svetambaras*, or white-robed ones; and the *digambaras*, or sky-clad ones. Whilst the former wore a simple white robe, the latter insisted upon the rejection of all forms of ownership and went about naked. Both groups, however, practised much the same sort of austerities, involving intense meditation, and physical and emotional control. The concept of God, however, is completely denied in their scheme of things, and the Hindu's search for Brahman is useless. This does not mean that Jainism is purely materialistic: the very concept of the *jiva*, or soul, which is the equivalent of the Hindu *atman*, is opposed to this. Moreover, any belief in reincarnation, or the transmigration of souls, implies a spiritual dimension within the universe. When, however, the soul is finally liberated from material obstacles, the *jiva* reaches a state of omniscience, or perfect knowledge (*kevala-jnana*). The liberated *jiva* is referred to as the *jivanmukta*, and rising it reaches the top of the universe (*lokakasa*) where it remains eternally. There are some individuals referred to as *arahats* because, although they have reached a stage of enlightenment and sainthood, they have not yet reached liberation (*moksha* or *mukti*) although they live without amassing any further *karma*.

The whole philosophy of the Jains is summed up in their *Akaranga Sutra*:

'He who knows wrath, knows pride. He who knows pride, knows deceit. He who knows deceit, knows greed. He who knows greed, knows love. He who knows love, knows conception. He who knows conception, knows birth. He who knows birth, knows death. He who knows death, knows hell. He who knows hell, knows animal existence. He who knows animal existence, knows pain. Therefore, a wise man should avoid wrath, pride, deceit, love, hate, delusion, conception, birth, hell, animal existence and pain' (31).

True knowledge will so inform a man that henceforth he will avoid all those things which result in *karma*, and consequently the continuance of rebirth or *samsara*. Only when nothing is deliberately desired or sought after will the individual disciple reach the state of 'beyond good and evil', in which the *jiva* remains unmoved, unaffected and eternally unchanged.

The Jains, because of their peculiar position in relation to the sanctity and inviolability of all life, are naturally vegetarians and pacifists. But, in addition, because they cannot hunt, fish or participate in agriculture, they have become a race of bankers, lawyers, merchants and landowners – a prosperous community representing probably less than one-third per cent of the Indian population. Their contribution to Indian culture, through their brilliantly carved and decorated temples, their fine white marble images which represent the *jinas*, and their whole ethos of *ahimsa*, cannot be overestimated. It is clear that Mahatma Gandhi was considerably influenced by their thought and action – or, perhaps more accurately, their inaction or passivity in the face of violence. Moreover, much of the reform spirit of Jainism in regard to such practices as vegetarianism affected a large body of Hinduism.

C BUDDHISM

1 *Gautama* (563–483 BC)

Doubt has always been cast upon the very existence of the great religious leaders of the world, such as Mahavira, the Buddha, Zoroaster, and the Christ. And the dates provided by the scholars for the period of their earthly existence have been so widely variable that detailed scholarship and research often seem to lend weight to certain mythological views about these leaders, avatars and saviours. The Southern Buddhists date Gautama between 624 and 544 BC, whilst other scholars would place him as late as the fourth century before Christ.

Gautama Siddhartha Shakyamuni was born in north-east India, in the foothills of the Himalayas at a place called Kapilavastu. One cannot ignore the various accounts of his miraculous birth, the consequence of some sort of 'immaculate conception'; they reflect that wisdom which so many religions have in retrospect, feeling as they do that such incredible leadership and insight must result from supernatural powers. His mother, Maya Devi, was the wife of an exceedingly wealthy *kshatriya*, possibly a prince or king. The legend has it that she had a dream of a white elephant which entered her womb, and Gautama was conceived. There were many supernatural manifestations at the birth of Gautama, comparable with those at the birth of Jesus. The *Jatakas*, or Birth Stories, are a collection of legends, or myths, which reveal the sense of awe and wonder which for ever accompanied the life of Gautama. They speak of the way in which the world was flooded with light at his birth; how the blind received their sight in order to have the vision of his glory, and the deaf and dumb freely conversed in the ecstasy of expectation. Even the fires of hell were quenched and the crimes of beasts were hushed as the peace of Brahman encircled the earth. Mara, the Evil One, alone refused to rejoice.

Tradition holds that Gautama had a very luxurious life in his father's palace, and that at the age of sixteen years he married a princess called Yasodhara. The latter bore him a son, Rahula. Gautama was perpetually protected from the evil, dirt and ugliness of life: he was not permitted to have any contact with sickness, old age or death, and always, when he went out walking or riding, he was shielded by a court entourage provided by his father. But Gautama was discontented with the life he was living, despite the exaggerated traditions of three palaces and forty thousand dancing girls which his father thoughtfully provided for him.

It was contact with the realities of life which first made Gautama aware of his utter ignorance of the deeper, spiritual levels of being. Somehow one day he escaped his ever protective entourage and he experienced the 'Four

Passing Sights' of old age, disease, death and withdrawal from life. He saw an old man, broken and bent, leaning upon his stick, ugly, decrepit and in despair. Then he saw what has always been a common sight in India – a disease-ridden body lying by the roadside, and near it a corpse, rotting in the heat and the sun, and overrun with insect life. Finally, he saw a monk with his head shaven, wearing a single threadbare robe and carrying a begging-bowl. Here was a man who had withdrawn from life with all its personal problems and involvements. Gautama began to reflect upon this new vision of the world as a place where life was tortured and subject to death; and so he asked the question, 'Since life is subject to old age and death, where is that realm of living where neither age nor death have any dominion?'

Therefore, at the age of twenty-nine years, Gautama left his wife, his son, his palaces and his possibilities of pleasure, and become a mendicant, meditating, fasting and practising yoga. One day, after considerable wandering and agonizing Gautama eventually rested under a bo-tree, or fig-tree, at a place now called Bodh Gaya in Bihar. As he meditated beneath this tree he was presented with three temptations by Mara. The first temptation was at the level of desire, and here Mara seems to have been somewhat unperceptive – a man who had not been imprisoned by a delightful wife and forty thousand dancing girls was not likely to succumb to the three voluptuous goddesses whom Mara presented to him. The second temptation was to destroy himself. During a period of torment in which he experienced hurricanes, rain and darkness, Gautama saw the whole of human misery presented before him. The temptation here was to invite, or accept, death in order to escape from the whole catena of life's sorrows. But Gautama did not succumb and it was, apparently, at the end of this temptation that he reached enlightenment (*bodhi*), and became the 'enlightened one' or the Buddha.

But it is one thing to know the truths and realities of life, to become 'enlightened', it is quite another to mediate the truth one knows to others, and this was perhaps for Gautama the greatest temptation of all – to accept one's enlightenment and keep it to oneself because of an awful sense of the impossibility of transmitting to others such ineffable knowledge. Gautama the Buddha, however, whilst aware of all the problems that would face him, accepted that there would always be some, perhaps the few, who would understand what he was trying to say. For the remaining fifty years of his life the Buddha wandered around India teaching what he felt had been vouchsafed to him through his own personal enlightenment.

The Buddha taught of sufferings and the end of suffering; he attacked the caste system and the conventional rites, celebrations and prayers of the Hindu religion and of the Brahmanistic system. He saw a people who, desperately needing spiritual release, were chained by the oppressive and obscurantist teachings of traditionalists. To these people he said, 'Be ye lamps unto yourselves.' They were not to accept what they heard by report or received through tradition or scripture; not even what their teacher taught them; they were to search within themselves, for enlightenment came from within. They had to work out their own salvation with considerable concentration and diligence. Just as Jeremiah appealed to the individual, so also did the Buddha.

2 *The Four Noble Truths*

The Buddha taught the Four Noble Truths, the Middle Way and the Noble Eightfold Path, and his starting point was suffering, that fact in life which had shaken his youthful innocence and joy. All life is suffering, or *dukkha*; it is out of joint or off-centre, just like a wheel that has slipped off its pivot. This is the first noble truth. The stress, strain, pain, misery, sorrow and unhappiness of life were all an expression of this friction caused by dislocation. Healing could occur only when the cause of this dislocation had been discovered.

The second noble truth is the recognition that desire, or *tanha*, is the cause of all suffering. *Tanha* is a selfish or blind craving or demandingness; it is the desire to find fulfilment in the fleeting pleasures as they arise, in a part of the self. The fact of *tanha* is best illustrated by a circle. Perfect integration of the personality occurs when life operates from the centre; there is no friction, no suffering. When, however, life operates from off-centre, a partial self is set up. It is this new, partial self that is being fulfilled; but the mere fact that only part of the self is being satisfied causes suffering, disappointment, frustration and pain.

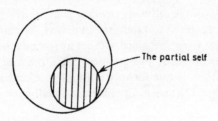

The partial self

This partial fulfilment leads to self-centredness, and in the extreme pathological state this can mean, as with some psychotic patients, a complete solipsist existence in which no communication may be made with another person for many years. As Anthony Storr remarks:

'And so we have the paradox that man is at his most individual when most in contact with his fellows, and is least of all a separate individual when detached from them' (32).

To get back 'on-centre' implies an extension of the self; it implies a recognition that we are members one of another, and that all others are extensions of ourselves.

Thus we come to the third noble truth which is simply and explicitly stated in the sentence 'We must overcome desire'. We can become free from suffering and torment only if and when we become released from the narrowness of our self-interest and extend our interest to all mankind. This is man's search for his original wholeness; it represents his recognition that only as he gets back 'on-centre' can he really *be* himself. The fourth noble truth is the actual overcoming of desire and the techniques involved in doing so. What the Buddha proposes is certainly not 'instant salvation'; anyone who looks for an easy or immediate conversion would assuredly have to look elsewhere. To become integrated or 'total' one must practise integration; and this involves the Eightfold Path. But before one can even begin upon this path one has to create a right association, that is, the right *guru-chela* relationship.

3 *The Eightfold Path*

The way, the truth and the life were, for the Buddha, one and the same; they are called the *dharma* (or *dhamma*). This *dharma* was expressed in the Middle Way of the Eightfold Path – a middle path between the extremes of complete self-mortification and the quest of emancipation through knowledge and works. The Path begins with *right knowledge*: one must understand what one is about and have a correct view of things. We must, in fact, know ourselves in order to rule ourselves, and our self-knowledge must be based on a complete acceptance of the four noble truths already discussed.

Right knowledge of the self will provide a plan for living, an understanding of what is yet required to attain to wholeness. We must then consider what we really want from life, since without a *right aim*, hope or aspiration we shall make no progress. For progress there must be consistency – a consistent acceptance of our identity with all mankind and our involvement in the welfare of all; we must reject continually our separateness, our discreteness.

In this progression towards the goal of integration our speech and speech patterns are vitally important. What we say is some indication of what we think and what we are; it is an index of our being and character, and there should clearly be some correspondence between what we think and say and do. If we deviate from the truth we should understand what element in the self is seeking private satisfaction and bring it under control. Our efforts to deceive others harm not only them but also ourselves – they reduce our very being. Plato once remarked that the mask an actor wore was apt to become his face; our behaviour-patterns eventually become our selves, for we are judged by them and our whole activity is predicted by them. This is the path of *right speech*, and it is one in which slander, gossip and lack of charity are alien to the whole concept of union with others. We cannot have identity with others if we are forever driving a wedge between ourselves and them; the principle of *noli me tangere*, whether practised by forms of isolation or by forms of verbal attack, is self-destructive.

Right behaviour can be achieved only by self-examination, by a careful reflection upon our daily activity, and a very close look at our motives in whatever we do. But, in more general terms, there are some things that no one on the path can find it within himself to do. He cannot kill, for all life is sacred. He cannot steal, for such activity reflects the very covetousness of the soul and the deprivation which we seek to bring upon others. He cannot lie, for lying presupposes a lack of integration within the self, a hiatus between thought and word, and between word and action. It is not simply that others may be deceived by such activity; in Platonic terms, the 'lie in the soul' is destructive of the individual self. He cannot be unchaste, for this involves the rejection of the total self in favour of a partial self. And, finally, he cannot drink intoxicants or take drugs, for these lead to a lack of control by the central consciousness of the self and, once more, a partial element of the self takes over. A man who travels on the path must, at all times, be fully aware of who is travelling and also of the nature of the journey.

It is, moreover, important that the traveller should have the *right livelihood*, the right occupation, in life. There are some things which the way-goer cannot honestly and sincerely engage in, for if his work pulls in a direction opposed to spiritual progress then that work is deleterious. Life in all its fullness must be promoted by whatever labour one is involved in, for labour is but the means to the ultimate goal of the spirit in Nirvana. Nirvana is the state of supreme enlightenment beyond the conception of mind and thought; it is the annihilation of the personal or separate self.

Once the right occupation has been chosen the individual must perpetually engage in making the *right effort*. This is not a question of wishful thinking, it is a matter of enormous personal effort which each one on the road must exert steadily and daily without intermission. Life is a serious business; it demands the fullest possible identification with the end in view and an unrelenting participation in the effort of will required to reach the goal.

Man *is* essentially what he thinks, and his thoughts go out to others and affect them for good or ill. We must be concerned to fill our world with loving and sympathetic thoughts so that we may participate positively in the lives of others. *Right mindfulness* demands that we should closely examine ourselves, our minds, our thinking and our personal relationships. This self-analysis is not a selfish or unhealthy introspection, but a purposeful consideration of one's thoughts in relation to others and an acceptance that, with Tennyson's Ulysses, 'I am a part of all that I have met'. Our lives, which are essentially our thoughts, go out towards and into others.

If the disciple follows the path with complete determination and *right absorption*, he cannot fail to reach the end, for the end and the way are one. The techniques of raja yoga, the royal yoga, will lead ultimately to the realization of the fact that Being itself is infinite, eternal, cosmic, and within ourselves. It is beyond description and beyond analysis, for all words are limiting, even those that seek to express the endless infinitude of cosmic consciousness. It is in a state of absolute contemplation and right absorption that one can say:

'Now I realize that the present moment contains all time and within it is all that can be hoped for, done and realized.

Now I realize that wherever I am contains all places; and the distance that I walk embraces all distances' (33).

4 *The Subsequent History of Buddhism*

In 270 BC Ashoka Maurya became king and, like his father, he continued to campaign in order to extend his empire. Ten years after his ascension to the throne he became master of virtually all India, having completely routed his remaining enemies, the Kalingans. The destruction was terrible, involving hundreds of thousands of Indians; and Ashoka, eventually revolted by the horrors of the wars and battles in which he had participated, was filled with remorse and sought consolation in Buddhism and its doctrine of *ahimsa* or non-violence. Christmas Humphreys (34) states that Ashoka united his people in the *dharma*, and that Buddhism became the established religion of India. Romila Thapar, however, emphasizes that the Buddhism which he inculcated and developed was not simply a religious belief, but 'a social and intellectual movement at many levels', which in consequence had an influence upon all the ramifications of society (35). Ashoka was, in a very real sense, a humanist desiring that his people should be non-violent and should uphold the dignity of man. He signed his edicts 'Piyadassi' meaning 'The Humane One'.

Soon after Ashoka died in 232 BC the empire began to break up. The fundamental loyalty to the person of the King had so far held it together; but after his death brahmanic teachings gradually returned within the national religion, and Buddhism itself became fragmented. By the end of the seventh century AD it was a dying religion. Geoffrey Parrinder remarks that Buddhism 'remained a cultural force till the twelfth century AD, and so had almost as long an influence on Indian culture as Christianity has had on Europe to date' (36).

By the time the invading Muslims entered India with the message of Islam, Hinduism had already absorbed, in principle at least, some of the finer elements of Buddhism; whilst what little remained of Buddhism had become infected by some of the baser Hindu practices. Indeed, by about the eleventh century AD Buddhism, as a separate religion, was virtually non-existent in India. But its spirit still remains even in modern times, for the Maha Bodhi Society, which Anagarika Dharmapala of Ceylon founded in 1891, is very active throughout the whole of India, whilst Gautama the Buddha remains for the Hindu the great 'Enlightened One' who enlightened, and continues to enlighten, others. He also remains for his followers the supremely 'Compassionate One', filled with compassion (*karuna*) for all suffering humanity.

D SIKHISM

Today there are about six million Sikhs, most of whom live in the Punjab. When India was partitioned in 1947 the Sikhs combined in an attempt to gain complete independence for themselves and a state of their own. There resulted a bloody struggle in which Hindus, Muslims and Sikhs were all involved, and eventually the Sikhs were driven from the Pakistan area of the Punjab.

During the fifteenth century AD there were several reform movements both within Islam and Hinduism. Kabir (1440–1518), a Muslim weaver who lived in Benares, became a disciple of the Hindu teacher Ramananda, and composed hymns, songs and poems. When he was eventually expelled from Benares he began to wander around the country with a number of disciples, seeking to convert others to a more tolerant and universal belief in God.

Nanak (1469–1538) was clearly influenced by the broad approach of Kabir's teaching and its acceptance of all men of good will. Nanak was born in a rural environment near Lahore in the Punjab; his parents were Hindus, and he himself married and became the father of two children. One day, like the Buddha many hundreds of years before him, he decided to leave his family in search of the truth, and he became an ascetic, joining the Sufis who were a mystical sect of the Muslims. He experienced and seemed to understand the deep conflict between Hinduism and Islam; and whilst touring the sub-continent of India he attacked the priesthood for their ostentation and encouragement of idolatry, and also the caste system which was responsible for so much division in his society. At the age of thirty, he resolved the dilemma of sectarianism by the dictum, 'There is no

Hindu, there is no Muslim, but only one human being; he is the Sikh'. The 'Sikh' is simply 'a disciple' of God.

Nanak believed in the fundamental, innate goodness of man: if only he were set free from the domination of conventional and sectarian beliefs he would find God everywhere and in every man. He believed that rituals came between God and man, not as a mediation of God's grace, but as an unwarranted intrusion and obstacle between man and his ultimate realization. And so Nanak did not hesitate to ridicule brahmanic rituals; but equally he flouted the religious customs of Islam and other religions. It is said that on one occasion Nanak was reproached for sleeping with his feet towards Mecca: this was to him one of the puerilities of pettifogging religious convention, and he replied in kind: 'All right, put my feet in a place where God is not.'

In Nanak's view there was no real divorce between man and God, and there should be no separation between man and man either. Caste was criminal to Nanak simply because it erected social, personal and religious barriers between God's children. All men were equal in God's sight; there were no kings or *kshatriyas*, no serfs or *shudras*, only people. In his simple uncomplicated way Nanak saw society as possessing the possibilities of the sort of primitive socialism reflected in the life of the early Christian Church – all wealth was to be divided evenly among all people according to their basic needs.

Not surprisingly the Sikhs became the object of some persecution. Nanak, however, was determined that the reforms he had begun should continue, and so he nominated his successor who was referred to as a *guru* or teacher. There followed a line of *gurus* who were peaceful men refusing to participate in any form of violence or warfare. All was well until one *guru* was put to death by an invading Mogul emperor, after which the Sikhs developed a strong sense of self-preservation. The tenth and last *guru*, Govind Rai, organized the sect of the Sikhs into a strong, militant group who were able, should the occasion arise, to defend themselves and to destroy the aggressor.

Guru Govind decided before he died that the reign of the *gurus* was over; in future the essence of Sikhism should be the holy book of the Sikhs, the *Adi Granth* or the 'Original Book', written in Punjabi. This book is somewhat like the Christian Bible, namely, an anthology of compositions by a variety of authors, including poems by Ramananda, Kabir and the Muslim Sheik Farid. The poems and hymns composed by the *gurus* are set to classical Indian music and sung somewhat like plain-song.

Govind regarded his disciples as the elect or pure ones, the *Khalsa*, who should model their lives upon the ten *gurus* who had been their leaders. His male disciples were lions in the battle for truth and right, and henceforth they were to be called 'Singh' or 'lion'; female disciples were to

7. The Engineering College at Chandigarh in Punjab, India.

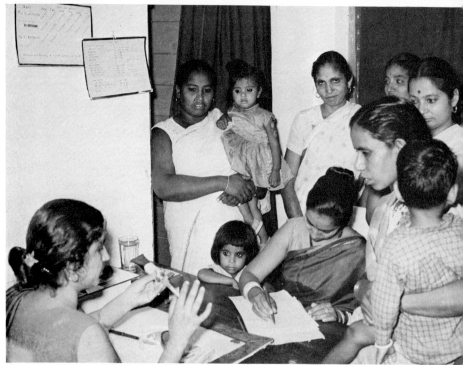

8. *Top:* A scene from the ancient Indian folk art of Uakshagana, (*bottom*) An Indian family-planning centre.

receive the appellation 'Kaur', meaning 'princess'. These names were to be added at a baptismal rite called *pahul*, normally performed by several devout Sikh laymen some few years after the birth of a child; the ritual involved the sprinkling of the latter's eyes and hair with *amrita*, a concoction of sugar and 'holy' water.

The Sikhs, the *Khalsa*, were committed to a way of life which would ensure their spiritual purity. They were permitted by Govind to eat meat, except beef, provided the animals were killed at one stroke. Whilst they were permitted alcohol, they were strictly forbidden to smoke tobacco. There were five visible signs of membership of the *Khalsa*, known as the Five K's: *kesh*, or beard and uncut hair covered by a turban; *kangha*, or comb to keep the hair clean; *kirpan*, or short sword to be used if necessary in self-defence; *kara*, or steel bangle representing the law of God to which the wearer is bound; and *kachha*, or short pants worn beneath the trousers. All these elements are symbolic in much the same way as crosses, crucifixes and clerical collars.

Sikhism is a syncretic religion, seeking to bring together the best in Hinduism, Islam and Buddhism with their various sectarian groups. It is monotheistic in essence: there is one God called the Name (*Nam*), who is creator, eternal, omnipresent, absolute and formless. But although God is absolute he is also personal; although transcendent he is also immanent in man, and he reveals his presence and his will through the *gurus* and the *Adi Granth*. This ubiquity of God in Sikhism is similar to that already noted in *The Secret Sayings of Jesus* (37), for the *guru* says:

Why dost thou go to the forest in search of God? He lives in all, yet is ever distinct; he lives in thee too.

As in Hinduism there may be the use of words or sounds for God other than *Nam*, but God is One, and there is no second. There is also a firm belief in reincarnation, obviously derived from Hindu philosophy.

The sacred city of Sikhism is Amritsar where there exists the small but impressive Golden Temple. But for Sikhism worship in a 'temple' is not essential for communion with God: since God is everywhere, worship can occur wherever man seeks that presence. There is, however, a meeting-place where communal religious observances may take place, and where members are taught the elements of their faith. This is the *gurdwara*, or the place of the *guru*, which is a simple, bare hall without chairs or stools, but with a simple platform and lectern to support the *Adi Granth*. The congregation, who are all equal before God, sit or squat on the floor. Most *gurdwaras* are open for short services every day and for longer services once a week; but they are also social and community centres where Sikhs meet to discuss their problems, share experiences, learn more of their faith, and even share meals.

Sikhism is a religion which believes that as far as possible the course of nature should not be disturbed. The *kesh* or uncut hair, for example, is a symbolic expression of the continuity of nature, which must not be opposed in its prolific development except for the sake of human survival. The Sikh is opposed to all forms of selfishness, immorality, cruelty, greed or excess; and in this respect he obviously has a great deal of common ground with both Judaism and Christianity. Indeed, despite the fact that, at first sight, Sikhism appears to be a minor syncretic sect, it offers in fact a major contribution to unity in religious philosophy and thought, and it possesses something of that 'perennial philosophy' which has always attracted some of the world's greatest minds.

REFERENCES

1 Thapar, Romila, *A History of India:* Vol. I (Penguin, 1966), pp. 38–9.
2 Zinkin, Taya, *Caste Today* (O.U.P., 1962), p. 1.
3 Wint, G., *The British in India* (Faber, 1947), p. 41.
4 Sen, K. M., *Hinduism* (Penguin, 1961), p. 28, n. 1.
5 Zinkin, Taya, op. cit., p. 2.
6 Basham, A. L., *The Wonder That Was India* (Sidgwick & Jackson, 1954), pp. 240–1. This particular passage is a translation of the *Rig-Veda,* x, 90.
7 *Bhavishya Purana, Brahma Parva,* 41, 45.
8 Zinkin, Taya, op. cit., p. 2.
9 Prabhavananda, Swami and Isherwood, C. (tr.), *Bhagavad-Gita* (Phœnix House Ltd, 1947, 5th impression 1956), p. 36.
10 Jeremiah 31, v. 29 (Moffatt's translation).
11 Ezekiel 18, vv. 1–20 (Moffatt's translation).
12 Galatians 6, v. 8 (Moffatt's translation).
13 See *The Works of Ralph Waldo Emerson* (George Routledge & Sons Ltd, 1900), pp. 21–9.
14 See *The Book of Common Prayer* ('At Morning Prayer – Quicunque Vult').
15 *Vide* Parrinder, G., *The World's Living Religions* (Pan Books Ltd, 1964), p. 42.
16 *Vide* Oakley, R. (ed.), *New Backgrounds* (O.U.P., 1968); Chapter III, 'The Indian Background' by Roger T. Bell, p. 55.
17 James, E. O., *Comparative Religion* (Methuen, University Paperbacks, 1961), p. 151.
18 Sen, K. M., *Hinduism* (Penguin, 1961), p. 37.
19 Eliade, Mircea, *Patterns in Comparative Religion* (Sheed & Ward, 1958), pp. 459–60.
20 Grant, R. M. and Freedman, D. N., *The Secret Sayings of Jesus* (Collins, Fontana Books, 1960), p. 167.
21 *Vide* Jung, C. G., *Psychology and Religion: West and East* (Routledge, 1958), pp. 107–200.
22 Lewis, H. D. and Slater, R. L., *The Study of Religions* (Penguin, 1969), pp. 33–4.

23 Op. cit., p. 60.
24 Prabhavananda, Swami and Manchester, F. (tr.), *The Upanishads* (The New American Library, 1957). This and previous quotations are from pp. 64–78 of the *Chandogya Upanishad*.
25 Tomlin, E. W. F., *The Eastern Philosophers: an Introduction* (Hutchinson, 1968), p. 232.
26 Coster, G., *Yoga and Western Psychology* (O.U.P., 1934), p. 107 (Sutra 40).
27 Op. cit., p. 83.
28 Ibid., p. 52.
29 Ibid., p. 64.
30 James, E. O., *Comparative Religion*, p. 167.
31 *Akaranga Sutra*, Book VI, quoted in E. W. F. Tomlin, op. cit., p. 189.
32 Storr, A., *The Integrity of the Personality* (Penguin, 1963), p. 36.
33 Gibran, Kahlil, *Thoughts and Meditations* (Heinemann, 1969), p. 20.
34 Humphreys, C., *Buddhism* (Penguin, revised edition 1955), p. 46.
35 Thapar, Romila, op. cit., p. 85.
36 Parrinder, G., *The World's Living Religions*, p. 86.
37 See reference 20 above.

BIBLIOGRAPHY

A GENERAL
Bouquet, A. C., *Comparative Religion* (Penguin, 1946).
Eliade, M., *Patterns in Comparative Religion* (Sheed & Ward, 1958).
James, E. O., *Comparative Religion* (Methuen, 1961).
Jurji, E. J., *The Great Religions of the Modern World* (Princeton Univ. Press, 1946).
Kellet, E. E., *A Short History of Religions* (Penguin, 1962).
Parrinder, G., *Comparative Religion* (Allen & Unwin, 1962).
Parrinder, G., *What World Religions Teach* (Harrap, 1963).
Spiegelberg, F., *Living Religions of the World* (Thames & Hudson, 1957).

B HINDUISM
Bouquet, A. C., *Hinduism* (Hutchinson's Univ. Lib., 1948).
Daniélou, A., *Hindu Polytheism* (Routledge, 1964).
Hiriyanna, M., *The Essentials of Indian Philosophy* (Allen & Unwin, 1949).
Panikkar, R., *The Unknown Christ of Hinduism* (Darton, Longman & Todd, 1964).
Parrinder, G., *Upanishads, Gita and Bible* (Faber, 1962).
Prabhavananda, Swami and Isherwood, C. (tr.), *Bhagavad-Gita* (Phœnix House Ltd, 1956).
Prabhavananda, Swami and Manchester, F. (tr.), *The Upanishads* (The New American Library, 1957).
Radhakrishnan, S., *The Hindu View of Life* (Allen & Unwin, 1927).
Radhakrishnan, S. (tr.), *The Bhagavadgita* (Allen & Unwin, 5th edition 1956).
Renou, L., *Hinduism* (Prentice-Hall, 1961).
Sen, K. M., *Hinduism* (Penguin, 1961).
Srinivas, M. N., *Caste in Modern India* (Asia Publishing House, 1962).
Zaehner, R. C., *Hinduism* (O.U.P., 1962).
Zinkin, T., *Caste Today* (O.U.P., 1962).

C YOGA

Coster, G., *Yoga and Western Psychology* (O.U.P., 1934).
Déchanet, Dom J-M., *Christian Yoga* (Burns & Oates, 1960).
Eliade, M., *Yoga, Immortality and Freedom* (Routledge, 1958).
Evans-Wentz, W. Y., *Tibetan Yoga and Secret Doctrines* (O.U.P., 1935).
Prabhavananda, Swami and Isherwood, C. (tr.), *How to know God: The Yoga Aphorisms of Patanjali* (Allen & Unwin, 1953).
Wood, E., *Yoga* (Penguin, 1959).
Wood, E., *Practical Yoga* (Rider, 1940).

D JAINISM

Jaini, J., *Outlines of Jainism* (C.U.P., 1940).
Schubring, W., *The Doctrines of the Jainas* (Delhi).
Stevenson, S., *Notes on Modern Jainism* (Blackwell, 1915).
Stevenson, S., *The Heart of Jainism* (Oxford, 1915).

E BUDDHISM

Burtt, E. A., *The Teachings of the Compassionate Buddha* (New American Library, 1955).
Conze, E. (ed.), *Buddhist Texts Through the Ages* (Cassirer, 1954).
Conze, E., *Buddhism, Its Essence and Development* (Cassirer, 1953).
Hamilton, C. H., *Buddhism: A Religion of Infinite Compassion* (Liberal Arts Press, N.Y., 1952).
Humphreys, C., *Buddhism* (Penguin, 1955).
Lévy, P., *Buddhism: A 'Mystery Religion'?* (University of London Press, 1957).
Morgan, K. W. (ed.), *The Path of the Buddha* (Ronald Press, 1956).
Pe Maung Tin, *Buddhist Devotion and Meditation* (S.P.C.K., 1964).
Percheron, M., *Buddha and Buddhism* (Longmans, 1957).
Pratt, J. B., *The Pilgrimage of Buddhism* (Macmillan, 1928).
Smith, F. H., *The Buddhist Way of Life* (Hutchinson's Univ. Lib., 1951).
Suzuki, D. T., *The Essence of Buddhism* (Buddhist Society, 1957).
Thomas, E. J., *The History of Buddhist Thought* (Routledge, 1951).
Wilhelm, R., *The Secret of the Golden Flower* (Routledge, 1931).
Zürcher, F., *Buddhism* (Routledge, 1962).

F SIKHISM

Archer, J. C., *The Sikhs* (Princeton Univ. Press, 1946).
Field, D., *The Religion of the Sikhs* (Murray, 1914).
Keay, F. E., *Kabir and His Followers* (O.U.P., 1931).
Singh, K., *A History of the Sikhs* (O.U.P., 1963).
Singh, K. (ed.), *Selections from the Sacred Writings of the Sikhs* (Allen & Unwin, 1960).
Singh, T., *Sikhism* (Longmans, 1938).
Tagore, R., *Kabir's Poems* (Macmillan, 1915).

Chapter 8

Social Background
of the Indians

A SOCIAL STRUCTURE

In our discussion of Hindu religion it was inevitable that we should consider something of the origin and religious significance of caste. In the present chapter we are concerned not so much with its origin as with its structure, functions and sanctions. Caste permeates the whole of Hindu life, and although Taya Zinkin has maintained that caste is not class, not colour, not occupation, and not exclusively Hindu or Indian (1), there is a sense in which caste is involved in class, colour (or *varna*) and occupation; and although there are undoubtedly institutions analogous to caste elsewhere, the Indian system is unique. The latter theme is expanded fully in Hutton's *Caste in India* (2).

The caste system has repeatedly come in for attack both from egalitarians outside India as well as from reformers within. At the same time others have seen some of the dangers of the iconoclastic attempts to destroy caste, and they have sought to rationalize the system in terms which could only be acceptable to one who is already in a high caste. Just as in England the common people were eventually no longer convinced that their 'station' in life was God-ordained and that they must therefore make the most of it, so there are those in India at the present time who are questioning the whole business of caste – even the superstition reiterated by J. H. Hutton that caste appears to be of some definite help to the Hindu 'in his superlative anxiety for male offspring' (3).

At the same time, however objectionable caste may appear to be, it is possible to oppose it on the wrong grounds. Professor O. H. K. Spate's statement about the theory of caste, for example, would seem to go too far and to ignore some of the unifying functions of caste in a plural society. Spate argues that

'the theory of caste, like all *Herrenvolk* theory, whether in Nazi Germany or contemporary S. Africa, rests finally on the assumption that all of one group are superior in things of the mind and spirit to all of another. Quite apart from ethics, this is simply contrary to human experience' (4).

This is, however, too much of an over-simplification. There are some 3,000 castes at least in India, and a large number of sub-castes; and it would be impossible to put them in the sort of rank-order that Spate's statement seems to suggest. There is a complexity and elaboration about the Hindu caste system that defies any easy generalization or simplification. Whilst it is, of course, true that the prestige of the *brahmin* has been the basis of the hierarchical system, apart from the four main castes, the *brahmins*, the *kshatriyas*, the *vaishyas* and the *shudras*, castes and sub-castes may be 'superior' in occupation and yet be 'inferior' in a more ritualistic context. To explore fully the cross-cultural relations of one caste with another would require an encyclopaedia; and certainly at the end of it the whole business would not be capable of analysis in terms of *Herrenvolk* theory.

It is also true that a man's caste is virtually determined for the whole of his life from birth, although he may be expelled for some violation of its tabus and strictures. J. H. Hutton, however, states that there is the possibility of the transition from one caste to another in places on the fringes of northern India where in the course of several generations the offspring of a low-caste mother and high-caste father may be accepted as belonging to the higher caste. That caste is often linked closely with occupation is indicated by the fact that certain castes, such as 'cattle-keeping castes', have combined to form a new caste; and other castes, such as the Khatiks, a caste of butchers, develop sub-castes (for example, the Bekenwalas or pork butchers). There is thus both a conjunctive and a fissiparous nature about caste; the former in order to concentrate social and political power and influence, the latter to extend the division of labour and area of economic influence (5).

Thus, whilst there is a certain rigidity about the caste system it would be wrong to suggest that there is no mobility whatsoever. It is argued that caste has in the past provided social stability, even if the lower castes have seen their role as one of privileged servitude. But again, it would be wrong to over-emphasize the servitude, however privileged, of the lower castes only. This is merely to look at caste structure without viewing more closely its functions and sanctions. The strictures *within* an endogamous caste are as great as any tabus which exist between the castes. J. H. Hutton has suggested that the tabu on marriage, or caste endogamy, is 'the necessary and inevitable outcome of the tabus on drink and food rather than the cause of it' (6).

Without attempting to detail all the tabus and the rituals involved in the full observance of caste, it is sufficient to mention here that ceremonial purity has been, and for most remains, of paramount importance. Restrictions apply not merely to food but also to eating and drinking vessels and cooking utensils. Earthenware vessels, for example, are tabu to all the higher castes; whilst untouchables, such as the Chamar who are leather-workers, are the only people who will eat beef. Some castes are completely vegetarian, whilst those who are meat-eaters may restrict their diet to goat meat or mutton. Pollution, whether through eating the wrong foods or through making bodily contact with the wrong people, can be eradicated only by ceremonial purification.

Whilst much of this sort of purification has been modified in recent years, largely as a result of increasing mobility and contact generally through travel, in the past the cult of ceremonial purity has been

'carried to pathological lengths – in Kerala, Nayadis (quasi-aboriginals) could not approach within 72 feet of a Brahmin without occasioning defilement, and as late as 1932 the existence in the same region of an "unseeable" group, emerging only at night, was reported: these unfortunates washed the clothes of untouchables' (7).

The Ernadans, a small jungle tribe of Malabar, could not come within 400 yards of a village, or within 100 yards of a man of high caste; and if any man were polluted by a member of such tribes he was obliged to bathe in seven streams and to let blood from his little finger. Hutton's book is replete with the most bizarre examples of both contamination and purification; what is important, however, is the general principle that the strictures of caste provide *in toto* a way of life, a life-style, directions for living, or a code of behaviour. Some of the exhortations and prohibitions may appear risible to the western mind; they may seem stupid, repressive and unfair; but, together, the tabus of the caste system deal with every aspect of life from birth to burial or burning, from the commission of sin to its dispensation, from pre-existence to the period of *kamaloka*, the twilight of the waste land between death and reincarnation.

Such a complete guide to spiritual, physical and social living is not easily given up whatever the value-judgements of other societies may be, and however strong the impact of culture contact. Something that has worked, however badly, for two or three millennia, is not easily swept aside even by the advancing forces of technological society. Whilst the caste system is not well adapted to accept change and development, it is fitted to pass on and maintain culture patterns and social structures. On the other hand, the caste can, if feeling is sufficiently strong, modify in any way its social and ethical standards as well as its religious observances. And, as Hutton indicates, there is

'no reason why caste should not be activated in the opposite direction to liberalize the Hindu tradition, but in point of fact it generally seems to have functioned hitherto in the direction of increasing restraint, and, in view of the element of tabu in its origin, this is perhaps only what could be expected' (8).

When W. H. Gilbert wrote his study of the *Peoples of India* during the Second World War he argued that the system of castes, which as a scheme of social adjustment had developed in India, compared quite favourably with the European system of warring nations (9). India, with its vast catena of tribes and groups, its varying colours and races, its differing religions and cultures, has nevertheless been integrated into one society and one community. This is more than Europe has ever accomplished. J. H. Hutton has developed this theme and claims that India has effectively dealt with the sort of problems that the United States, South Africa and other societies have failed to solve; and that caste, moreover, has been an 'integrator of peoples' (10). This is not intended in the present context as a defence of caste in a modern world; it is simply a statement of what has happened in the past. Nor is it an attempt at the sort of rationalization or apologia which Professor Spate so rightly criticizes as amounting to a disputation on the 'precedence between a louse and a flea' (11).

It is not suggested here that the *pariahs*, the untouchables, the *harijans* – whatever one cares to call them – are in any way honoured by being able to serve in such a lowly station. Nothing in life ultimately justifies the degrading subordination or subjugation of one group of people by another, or the treatment of any human beings as if they belonged to some lower order. But a 'civilization', which can destroy cities with atom bombs, which can use flame-throwers to shrivel men into a macabre charade of blackened bones, which can kill babes as a petulant reprisal for bombing raids, and can infect civilians with bacteria, has little right to moralize about 'emergent' nations and the solution of their internal problems.

Caste may certainly have served a unifying purpose in the past, but it has come to the parting of the ways in a rapidly expanding society, which is becoming increasingly mobile, industrialized and technological. Professor Spate is clearly right in his analysis of the crisis which caste faces at the present time. The increasing urbanization of India makes the avoidance of daily, if not hourly, contamination something quite impossible. Nor is it any longer reasonable to expect those who have suffered pollution on public transport, or in public places, to undergo perpetually the purificatory rites which caste strictures have always demanded. Moreover, the new complexity of modern living, with its unfriendly and escapist anonymity, makes it impossible for the individual to pursue the older caste complex at the same time. Indeed, it is a relief for many to evade the suffocating sanctions of the village caste and tribal groups, and to flee to the virtually unrestricted freedom of town and city life.

All this must inevitably have its dangers; all people seek an identity of some sort with one group or another. The loss of one form of identity can leave a void which must be filled; and it must be filled by a new identity. The worst features of caste at the level of untouchability are gradually being eradicated: it was Gandhi who sought to give dignity to all human life, and who made a determined attempt to reform social attitudes towards the untouchables. But caste cannot be eradicated overnight: its disappearance would require not only a social revolution but also a religious reformation.

There is, in fact, nothing theologically inevitable about caste; what *is* inevitable in the Hindu scheme of things is that, because of man's karmic debt which he must irrevocably pay, men will be born into a situation of inequality at least in terms of genetic endowment if not also in terms of environment. We may do our utmost to provide equality of opportunity as regards those elements under our control, but we cannot *make* people equal. Hinduism, at least, accepts this: caste has simply been the social medium for the expression of man's inequality; the latter could just as easily be expressed through one of the western forms of democracy – or even through communism. A theological dogma, once established and crystallized, is not easily disturbed by social change or evolution; *karma* can certainly survive the disappearance of caste, since it is no more than the philosophical expression of the practical experience of the principle that 'whatsoever a man soweth that shall he also reap'.

The untouchables are now officially referred to as Scheduled Castes and Scheduled Tribes. The Constitution explicitly prescribes protection and a variety of safeguards for these castes and tribes, and 'other backward classes', in order to promote both their educational and their economic interests (12). Article 17 establishes the abolition of untouchability and the forbidding of its practice in any shape or form; Article 46 demands that the former untouchables should be protected from all expressions of social injustice and every form of exploitation. Hindu religious institutions of a public character had always been closed to untouchables, but Article 25 of the Constitution insists upon the opening up of all such public institutions to all the Scheduled Castes. Similarly, Article 15 seeks to remove all disabilities, liabilities, restrictions or conditions with regard to access to shops, restaurants, hotels and places of public entertainment, the use of wells, tanks, bathing pools, roads and places of public resort maintained wholly or partly out of state funds or dedicated to the use of the general public.

Further Articles are concerned to end the curtailment of the general rights of citizens of any caste, colour or creed to move freely, to settle in any area of their choice within the Union, to acquire land or property, or to practise any business or trade. There is an obligation now upon the state to consider the claims of any members of depressed groups in the making of any appointments to public service, and, moreover, to ensure that they are adequately represented. The Constitution further prescribes special representation for Scheduled Castes in Parliament and the State

Legislatures, and provides for the establishment of advisory councils and departments in the states for the promotion of their welfare and the protection of their interests.

According to the Census of 1961, there were 64,500,000 members of the Scheduled Castes and 30,200,000 members of the Scheduled Tribes; which means that out of a population of some 439 million at that time about 21·5 per cent belonged to the deprived and underprivileged groups. In Uttar Pradesh alone there were over 15 million members of Scheduled Castes. On June 1, 1955, the Untouchability (Offences) Act came into force, whereby penalties were provided for anyone who prevented another person, on the ground of untouchability, from entering any place of worship, offering prayers in any holy area, or taking water from a sacred well, spring or tank. Sanctions were also established against the enforcing of such social disabilities as denying access to any sort of public place or institution. The Act is very specific, detailed and comprehensive and seems to have taken into account every conceivable possibility of the practice of untouchability.

'The Act similarly lays down penalties for refusing to sell goods or render services to a *harijan* because he is a *harijan*; for molesting, injuring or annoying a person or organizing a boycott of, or taking any part in the excommunication of a person who has exercised the rights accruing to him as a result of the abolition of untouchability' (13).

One of the interesting features about the enforcement of the provisions of this Act is the fact that the onus of proving innocence has been placed upon the accused. At first sight this principle appears to be in opposition to the sort of democracy that the Act claims that it is seeking to achieve. The reform, however, is in itself so drastic that none but the most stringent measures could ever hope to effect a change. On the other hand, it would be tragic for Indian social development if this principle were to create a precedent for all legal procedure.

The absolute eradication of untouchability, both in theory and practice, is viewed by the Government of India as of paramount importance, and since 1954 she has consistently provided financial support to this end. District Officers and other officials have allocated 'Harijan Days' and 'Harijan Weeks' during which public attention has been deliberately focused upon the whole problem. Pamphlets, books, handbills and audio-visual aids have all been published and prominently displayed as effective media for awakening the public conscience and creating new attitudes to a problem which has always existed in India.

There is, therefore, no lack of goodwill on the part of the Government, and there exists an obvious determination to tackle the worst features and effects of caste before approaching the more fundamental and radical questions of social hierarchy and structure. And there is a sense in which this is a much more realistic approach than any general philosophical or theological moralizing, however sincere and humane. The erosion of caste, through accepted and acceptable public and individual action, will achieve – without disruptive and even bloody revolution – a far more permanent social change. Whilst it is certainly no longer true, as C. Bouglé wrote in 1908, that 'L'Inde ne veut pas connaître la figure du "parvenu"' (14), the contentions of Professor F. C. Bartlett in his Huxley Memorial Lecture of 1943 are still sound. There are certain 'hard points' in social cultures and structures that must be clearly and rationally as well as sympathetically understood, if one is to help to modify the stratification of any particular society (15). J. H. Hutton argues that caste is one of the 'hard points' of Hindu culture, and that any *direct* attack upon it could do little more than provoke a heavy resistance to it and a resultant social discord (16). Evolution, though apparently slow – perhaps more slow to those outside its operation than to those within – is safer and more generally acceptable than sudden revolution.

B THE FAMILY

Despite the size of India, both geographically and in population, there is an amazing social and cultural unity which will permit of a certain amount of generalization on a subject which is, nevertheless, one about which many volumes have been written. In our own society the family is usually referred to as a 'nuclear' unit consisting of the father, the mother and the children. It is a nuclear unit which has become steadily smaller since the Victorian era and since the introduction of family planning and a large variety of contraceptive devices. Thus today it makes an even greater contrast with the Indian familial concept.

The Indian family is generally referred to as 'joint' or 'extended', and such families are invariably male dominated, the eldest living male taking charge of the whole household or group of houses, and making any vital decisions concernings its members. Thus in the extended family there will be included the grandfather and grandmother, their married sons and their families, and their unmarried sons and daughters. Obviously the actual composition of such extended families will vary considerably, but the underlying principles of that composition will be the same. There is a communal attitude towards property which is shared, and if the house is large enough the joint family will live together; if it is not they will live close together in the same village or town.

Such a concept makes for strong blood-ties which are extended ulti-mately to the whole kin-group. This will include a variety of people in the village related through endogamous rules of marriage, and closely linked by linguistic and cultural ties. In a society with such a variety of languages, and of local dialects, the spoken word may well be one of the external symbols of kin-group or sub-caste identity. It is hardly surprising that in such a vast society of over 500 million there will often be greater identification with a local group or village than with Mother India.

Within the home of the joint family everything is 'arranged', and the futures of some children are virtually preordained in such a way that they have never had, and in certain instances never will have, any control over their own lives. This means that there can be very little training in actual decision-making for the younger members if the head of the household lives to a ripe old age. In this respect it is perhaps worth noting that, although the expectation of life at birth has made great strides during the present century, and particularly during the past four decades, it is still within the region of some forty years or so. The family head may arrange marriages, control the family finance, and consult the horoscopes, oracles and astrologers to decide the future of his kin, even when he is economically dependent upon his children and perhaps his grandchildren. The aged within the joint family are the responsibility of the remainder of the group, and so under this system there is – or more accurately was – little problem of the lonely and neglected parent or spinster aunt. The traditional Indian family is, in fact, a welfare society within itself, looking after its own sick, injured, weak, aged and unemployed.

Because of the inherited social system a girl has always been regarded as a liability within the family since she has no economic value. Not only is she in the position of being unable to earn money, she must also be hedged about in order that she may still be a virgin when she is ready for marriage. And whilst her marriage is in one sense an occasion for rejoicing in that the liability has at least been handed over to another joint family, it is also an occasion of loss in that an agreed dowry must be provided to go with her. Not only does a father lose a daughter, he may also lose a number of valuable cows as well.

Times change, however. The sense of kin hospitality still exists, but the view that a woman should be trained simply to be her husband's submissive servant is undergoing some revision. There are a variety of reasons for this, some of which we shall consider presently when we discuss India's family-planning programme. India needs not merely a literate society but also an educated one; she needs in addition a labour pool which will include women as well as men for the expanding variety of occupations in industry, commerce and light engineering. The more Indian women become educated the less likely they are to wish to remain simply decorative housewives, or even members of a limited number of professions such as nursing or medicine.

The rapidly increasing urbanization and urbanism in India has meant that the extended family has already begun to become smaller, and many of the traditional kinship groups are breaking up. As Roger Bell remarks,

'The joint family . . . is under pressure to change even in India, since it has within itself certain centrifugal forces which if controlled tend to its destruction' (17).

This statement epitomizes the problem. It is not so much the clash of cultures which will eventually lead to the breakdown of the joint family system and its replacement by the nuclear family. It is the increasing industrialization of the Indian society and the introduction of money values in areas where they have hardly existed before. Sharing earth products and scarce property is one thing; sharing individually earned money is quite another. Indeed, the mere measurement of labour in monetary terms must inevitably lead to comparisons of worth, in terms of market value, within the home. And even kinship affinities are unlikely eventually to survive the all too human proneness to compare one's own abilities and rewards with another's.

It may take time, but the gradual development of the western concept of the nuclear family must lead also to the abandonment of the arranged marriage and its antiquated dowry attachment. This, indeed, may be accelerated by increasing culture contacts through emigration and travel generally. And whilst it must be understood that arranged and early adolescent marriages are still in vogue, they may not last very much longer.

C THE FAMILY-PLANNING PROGRAMME
Another development which will tend to decrease both the size and importance of the joint family is the vast birth-control programme which India has developed, quite suddenly and explosively, since 1952. In its formulation of the Third Five-Year Plan (1961–6), the Government stated that

'the objective of stabilizing the growth of population over a reasonable period must be at the very centre of planned development' (18).

In consequence India launched the largest family-planning programme in the world. In 1967 Dr S. Chandrasekhar, then Minister of State for Health, Family Planning and Urban Development, saw the programme as one calculated to ensure the emancipation of the women of India, and the adoption of a small family as the norm of Indian society (19).

There can be little doubt about the thoroughness of the programme envisaged. By mid September 1967 the estimated population of the Indian Union was in the region of 511 millions, and the annual growth rate was put at 13 millions or 2·5 per cent, which would indicate a population of some

1,000 millions in less than thirty years. Dr Chandrasekhar was nothing if not frank in his report. India has certainly made great strides in the cumulative rate of growth of her economy from less than 1 per cent per year before Independence to 3·8 per cent per year at the present time. Educational facilities had trebled by 1967; and the major communicable diseases had been brought under control largely through the establishment of twice as many dispensaries and hospitals, three times the number of hospital beds, twice the number of doctors and six times the number of nurses as compared with 1947. But all these gains – and they were no mean achievement by any standards – had 'been liquidated by the population growth' (20); 63 million children were still unable to get places in schools, 10 million youths were unemployed, and there were 74·1 million houses short in urban and rural areas.

The objective of the family planning was to reduce the birth rate and stabilize it at a level considered to be consistent with the requirements of the national economy. This would mean a reduction from the existing 41 per thousand to 25 per thousand in the shortest possible time – say, by 1976 – and it was hoped that this could be done by the participation in the programme of some 90 million couples. It has been thoroughly understood from its inception that this programme deals with a very difficult and sensitive problem, and that if tackled in the wrong way it could easily antagonize a people with religious and moral scruples and tabus.

The emphasis of the programme has been upon a mass education and motivation of the people towards a limitation of the size of their families. This, in turn means a determined effort to overcome the limitations imposed by illiteracy, prejudice, resistance to change, and the diversity of customs and languages, to say nothing of the vastness of the territory to be covered. In order to cope with the problems, personnel at all levels – educational, medical, technical, ancillary – have to be trained.

At the beginning of 1967 there were 14,148 centres, of which 12,665 were in rural areas, providing family-planning advice and contraceptives free. A year later, in 1968, this number had increased to nearly 24,000 centres working on a regular, full-time basis. After extensive experiment and trial the intra-uterine contraceptive device (I.U.C.D.), or 'loop', was found to be a very suitable method and was introduced in July 1965; but other forms of contraceptive, such as condoms, diaphragms and foam tablets have also become increasingly popular. In this programme there has been no attempt to compel any of the population to participate, although every conceivable means of propaganda and indoctrination have been employed in order to convince the masses. During the year 1967–8, however, just on 1·4 million sterilization operations were performed, making a total of nearly 3·8 millions since the beginning of the programme. The number of I.U.C.D. insertions up to January 1968 was 2·2 millions (21)

The Ministry of Health, Family Planning and Urban Development is clearly not satisfied with this progress, and it has launched research programmes in demography, communication action, reproductive biology and medicine. Studies in the biological and medical aspects of the whole problem of family planning are under way in a variety of institutions and universities under the auspices of the Indian Council of Medical Research; this research includes an attempt to find a safe and easy oral form of contraceptive.

Certainly the traditional extended family is under attack from the 'centrifugal forces' within itself, from the generally changing structure and nature of Indian society, and from the declared policy of the Indian Government. There must be some inevitable repercussions also, through increasing literacy and education, upon both the family and the system of caste. And immigrants of the future to this country may well be more adapted than their predecessors to the western nuclear family. Indian womanhood is beginning to become the controller of her own destiny and to find a new freedom and sense of identity; soon she will cease to be the submissive servant of her husband and become an equal partner in a new familial enterprise.

REFERENCES

1 Zinkin, Taya, *Caste Today* (O.U.P., 1962), pp. 1–2.
2 Hutton, J. H., *Caste in India* (O.U.P., 4th edition 1963), pp. 133–48.
3 Ibid., p. 132.
4 Spate, O. H. K., *India and Pakistan* (Methuen, 2nd edition 1957), p. 139.
5 Hutton, J. H., op. cit., pp. 49–51.
6 Ibid., p. 71.
7 Spate, O. H. K., op. cit., pp. 136–7.
8 Hutton, J. H., op. cit., p. 115.
9 Gilbert, W. H., *Peoples of India* (Smithsonian Institution War Background Studies, No. 18, Washington, 1944), p. 82.
10 Hutton, J. H., op. cit., p. 120.
11 Spate, O. H. K., op. cit., p. 139.
12 *Vide* Research and Reference Division, Ministry of Information, *India – A Reference Annual, 1968* (Publications Division, Ministry of Information and Broadcasting, Government of India, 1968), pp. 121–9.
13 Ibid., pp. 122–3.
14 Bouglé, C., *Essai sur le Régime des Castes* (Travaux de l'Année Sociologique, Paris, 1908), p. 212. Quoted in Hutton, J. H., op. cit., p. 122, note 20.
15 Bartlett, F. C., *Anthropology in Reconstruction* (Huxley Memorial Lecture, 1943), p. 5.
16 Hutton, J. H., op. cit., p. 130.
17 Bell, R., 'The Indian Background', in Oakley R. (ed.), *New Backgrounds* (O.U.P., 1968), p. 60.
18 Research and Reference Division, Ministry of Information, op. cit., p. 103.

19 Information Service of India, *India 1967 – Annual Review* (Information Service of India, London, 1967), p. 26.
20 Ibid., p. 22.
21 Research and Reference Division, Ministry of Information, op. cit., p. 104.

BIBLIOGRAPHY

Bailey, E. G., *Caste and the Economic Frontier* (Manchester Univ. Press, 1957).
Darling, M. L., *The Punjab Peasant in Prosperity and Debt* (O.U.P., 1925).
Desai, A. R., *Rural India in Transition* (Popular Book Depot, Bombay, 1961).
Dey, S. K., *Community Development* (Asia Publishing House, 1964).
Dube, S. C., *Indian Village* (Routledge, 1955).
Dube, S. C., *India's Changing Villages* (Routledge, 1958).
Gilbert, W. H., *Peoples of India* (Smithsonian Institution War Background Studies, No. 18, Washington, 1944).
Gore, M. S. (ed.), *Problems of Rural Change* (University of Delhi, 1963).
Hinnells, J. R., (ed.), *Comparative Religion in Education* (Oriel Press, 1970).
Hiro, D., *The Indian Family in Britain* (Community Relations Commission, 1969).
Hutton, J. H., *Caste in India* (O.U.P., 4th edition 1963).
Karve, I., *Kinship Organization in India* (Poona, 1953).
Karve, I., *Hindu Society, an Interpretation* (Poona, 1961).
Majumdar, D. N., *Caste and Communications in an Indian Village* (Asia Publishing House, 1958).
Mayer, A. C., *Caste and Kinship in Central India* (Routledge, 1960).
Mukherji, B., *Community Development in India* (Orient Longmans, Bombay, 1961).
Panikkar, K. M., *Commonsense about India* (Victor Gollancz, 1960).
Ross, A. D., *The Hindu Family in its Urban Setting* (Toronto, 1961).
Segal, R., *The Crisis of India* (Penguin, 1965).
Singh, K., *A History of the Sikhs* (O.U.P., 1963).
Srinivas, M. N., *Caste in Modern India* (Asia Publishing House, 1962).
Srinivas, M. N., *India's Villages* (Asia Publishing House, 1960).
Vaid, K. N., *State and Labour in India* (Asia Publishing House, 1965).
Williams, L. F. R. (ed.), *Murray's Handbook for Travellers in India and Pakistan, Burma and Ceylon* (Murray, 1965).
Zinkin, Taya, *Caste Today* (O.U.P., 1962).

Chapter 9

Education of
the Indians

A TRADITIONAL EDUCATION AND THE PROBLEM OF ILLITERACY
It has already been noted that Indian culture and civilization are very
ancient, extending in the past to the third millennium BC when the
Harappa culture of the Indus Valley was flourishing. A number of in-
scriptions on a variety of seals still remain to be deciphered, but they
clearly relate to some form of mercantile activity during this period.
By about 1500 BC this culture had gone into decline, and was finally
destroyed by the Indo-Aryans who were entering the north-west of India.
The earliest literary source of this period is the *Rig-Veda*, of which parts
were composed before 1000 BC; other literature, such as the *Ramayana*,
the *Brahmanas* and the *Upanishads*, was composed from about 800 BC
onwards.

There is, therefore, a tradition of creative literary culture as well as
utilitarian literary usage in India from earliest times; certainly the Harappan
people employed a script even though the Aryans may not have developed
one until 800 BC or later (1). The method of learning, from the earliest
times, was a systematic repetition of the lessons after the teacher, and
learning has remained very much the same ever since. Education as such
was the almost exclusive prerogative of the higher castes, and some of it –
the esoteric philosophy and theology of Hinduism – was the specific
province of the *brahmins* alone. This was so much so that

'Sanskrit soon became the language of the educated upper castes, amongst
whom it remained a unifying factor throughout the sub-continent for many
centuries. But as it tended to isolate these castes from other articulate and
significant sections of society who used other languages, it later became
obscured' (2).

Illiteracy, therefore, has over the years been produced and promoted by
the class distinctions of the caste system. Sanskrit became the language of
the learned *brahmins* and of any official proclamations; and a popular form
of it, namely Prakrit, took its place with a number of local variations in the
towns and the villages. Pali, another form, was also based upon and
derived from Sanskrit, and it was the language used in the canonical books

of Buddhists. During the lengthy period of conflict in the southern kingdoms, between about AD 500 and 900, entry into Hindu colleges (or *ghatikas*) was restricted to the top three castes of the caste system. Sanskrit was the language used in these colleges, it was the official court language, and it was adopted in literary circles.

The educational system has always been closely linked with the class structure. Brahmanical forms of education were becoming more and more theological in content as time went on, and their institutions were increasingly restricted to the use of the *brahmins*. During the period from AD 800–1200 the greater proportion of villages had schools which were attached to local temples. Romila Thapar points out that, with the perpetuation of the system of formal education, by means of statement and repetition or rote learning, there developed a growing contempt for technical knowledge, whilst education for castes below the *brahmins* took the form of professional training only (3). The medium of instruction remained Sanskrit which had now become, like Latin in this country in the Middle Ages, the language of the privileged.

The inevitable results of this brahmanical inbreeding were the isolation of its own cultural and educational development, and the emergence of a very large number of parochial and regional vernaculars which were to become, and to remain, the media for popular views and ideas. Indeed, the hieratic contempt for technical know-how did nothing but weaken formal as well as technical education.

During the period of strong culture contact between Hindus and Muslims, and the partial assimilation of the latter from about AD 1200 to 1500, the *ulema*, or Muslim theologians, refused all attempts at full integration. Education provided by the Muslim element was attached to their mosques in the form of *madrassahs*, or colleges, which were financed by the state and which provided a variety of theological training only. It has been estimated that during the fourteenth century there were approximately a thousand educational institutions in Delhi itself. Outside the theological backwaters there was some intellectual contact, in the areas of medicine in particular, but in general the intellectual exchange that occurred was 'confined to limited sections of society and did not influence the core of the educational tradition' (4).

The 'classical' tradition of education in India developed into a regularized system of teaching and learning by oral repetition and written reproduction. Since the sixteenth century the system has hardly changed, and the British imperial modification of it, in order to produce a certain type of English-speaking government civil servant, did very little to improve upon it. In fighting the present illiteracy situation India is faced with the problem of several hundred different languages and a multitude of dialects. Many of these languages and dialects are confined to a few hundred people belonging to single villages, whilst other languages may be spoken by a population of more than twenty-five millions.

Professor J. H. Hutton, first writing in 1946, claimed that there were some thirty different groups of languages spoken in India, and that each group consisted of from one to five or more different vernaculars. We shall not discuss his classification here since the typology he uses, such as Kolarian and Mon-Khmer, does not appear to be universally adopted (5). But his general statement of the number of languages and dialects indicates that there are something in the region of a hundred. The 1931 Census indicated 225 Indian and Burmese languages, of which 135 were Tibeto–Burman and confined in the main to Burma. Six languages accounted for the speech of 65 per cent of the 1931 population; although, according to Professor O. H. K. Spate, one language was quite solemnly recorded in the *Imperial Gazetteer* as spoken by one person – 'a lonely soul', he adds (6).

According to Spate there are only some twelve to fifteen really 'major languages', and some of these have a close kinship. The greatest distinction is, in fact, between the north and centre of India, where Indo–Aryan languages are spoken, and the south where the languages are mainly Dravidian. About three-quarters of the sub-continent speak Hindi and its variants, whilst the chief Dravidian languages of the south are Tamil and Telugu. As Spate indicates, bilingualism and even trilingualism are not uncommon, and a traveller who understood and could speak Hindustani (a patois of Hindi), English and Tamil would probably be comprehended in most market towns in India (7).

Much of the development and popularization of some of the more important languages of India occurred during the religious revivals of the late fifteenth and early sixteenth centuries. From about 1440 to 1533, during the period of the *bhakti* (devotion) saints, literary compositions including poems and hymns were created in the vernaculars of the people being taught and evangelized. Such saints as Kabir, Nanak, Shankaradeva and Chaitanya helped the common people to see their own languages as instruments of creativity; moreover, they also got to know a great deal of their Sanskrit heritage in translation, as well as commentaries on such sacred texts as the *Bhagavad-Gita* and the original works of their religious leaders. Romila Thapar emphasizes that

'Literature in the regional languages was strikingly different from Sanskrit literature in one main respect; it was as spontaneous and imbued with genuine sentiment as the latter had become artificial and forced. The themes of the new literature were often of common interest to more than one religion, and literary innovations travelled quickly and widely in northern India' (8).

Chaitanya (1485–1533) used the eastern language, Bengali; Shankaradeva made the use of Assamese popular in the Brahmaputra valley during the sixteenth century; and Gujarati was used by the Jaina teachers in western areas of India. Hindi had developed in the area around Delhi and was being used by the devotees of the *bhakti* movement; and, finally, Urdu developed as a 'camp-language', originally between Muslim conquerors and their subjects. Urdu steadily developed as a *lingua franca*, evolving as a combination of Hindi syntax and grammar and Persian–Arabic vocabulary. It will become the official language of West Pakistan by 1974.

Like Pakistan, India is anxious to minimize the problem of illiteracy before the end of the present century – if not by 1980. In a question of this sort it is virtually impossible to give precise figures, but it was estimated in 1950–51 that there was something like 83 per cent illiteracy. Ten years later, in 1960–61, this proportion had fallen to 76 per cent, whilst in 1966 it was reduced to 70 per cent (9). In actual figures this means that, out of an estimated population of 490 million Indians, 343 millions were illiterate. This has been an uphill fight, and at first sight might appear even depressing. Looked at in a more positive way, however, it is somewhat commendable that since Independence in 1947 the number of literates has nearly doubled. By the turn of the century India aims to reduce the proportion of illiterates to 40 per cent at the most.

India 1968 provides a summary of literacy figures based on the Census of 1961, and the following Table provides a selection of some of the highest and lowest literacy percentages in India, including some of the areas from which emigrants to this country come (10). A study of

TABLE OF LITERACY IN INDIA

| | Percentage of Literacy | | |
	Persons	*Males*	*Females*
INDIA	24·0	34·5	13·0
Delhi	52·7	60·8	42·5
Madras	31·4	44·5	18·2
Gujarat	30·5	41·4	19·1
Manipur	30·4	45·1	15·9
Assam	27·4	37·3	16·0
Punjab	24·2	33·0	14·1
Orissa	21·7	34·7	8·6
Uttar Pradesh	17·7	27·3	7·0
Himachal Pradesh	17·1	27·2	6·2
Jammu and Kashmir	11·0	17·0	4·3
Dada and Nagar Haveli	9·5	14·7	4·1

the total figures provided reveals, not surprisingly, two things in particular: illiteracy is much higher among women than men, and it is greater in the rural than in the urban areas. It is, of course, also true that illiteracy is heaviest amongst the older members of the population. These facts underline something of the traditional development of the educational system in India, and also the innate social and religious prejudices of the Indian society. Women have never, until recent times, been regarded as the intellectual equals of men nor as members of society requiring any form of socialization other than their necessary subservience to man as wife, helper and worker. Knowledge was essentially the commerce of men.

It is important to note that the immigrants in our country, who come from Gujarat and the Punjab, are from states whose literacy rate is higher in the case of the Gujaratis and about the same in the case of the Punjabis as the average for all India. Rashmi Desai points out that almost all male Gujarati immigrants are literate, and many of them have been to a college or a university; and that whilst almost all Gujarati immigrant women are literate, very few of them have been to a university. The degree of education and literacy among the Indian Punjabis is lower than that of the Gujaratis, and fewer of their women are literate. Desai further emphasizes the fact that education in India, and in particular university education, is synonymous with some knowledge of English. All Indians who have received a university education have had the experience of reading and writing English, but perhaps little experience of speaking it.

'Hence almost all immigrants need a severe adjustment in their knowledge of English before they are able to communicate with the English. Those who are not well educated have a meagre vocabulary, few phrases, little grammar and a sing-song accent. At best they achieve bare mutual intelligibility in everyday situations' (11).

India is still faced with the problem not merely of illiteracy but also the lack of a common language. According to Article 343 of the Indian Constitution, Hindi became the official language of the Union with effect from January 26, 1965. The Official Languages (Amendment) Act of 1967 provided that English would be used for purposes of communication between the Union and a state which had not adopted Hindi as its official language. In addition, where Hindi was used for purposes of communication between one state and another which had not adopted Hindi as its official language, any communication in Hindi had to be accompanied by an English translation.

The Government has proposed a number of schemes for the propagation and development of Hindi as the official language of the Union. The schemes suggested very clearly present a major task for scholars, teachers and administrators, for the official publication of the Ministry of Information lists twenty-two elements in the programme (12). It is the object of the programme to review, co-ordinate and finalize Hindi terminology; to standardize a keyboard for Hindi typewriters and teleprinters; to evolve a standard system of Hindi shorthand; to organize Hindi teachers' training-colleges on a zonal basis in the areas in which Hindi is not spoken; to compile encyclopaedias and standard manuals in Hindi; to prepare indices of selected Hindi poets and novelists and to publish omnibus volumes of the works of eminent writers; to prepare multilingual and bilingual dictionaries; to prepare bilingual alphabet charts in Hindi and in other regional languages; to translate standard works in foreign languages into Hindi; to finalize the form of Devanagari script; to translate and publish standard works on scientific and technical subjects; and to establish the Central Hindi Directorate and its regional offices for the propagation and development of Hindi.

All this, and indeed more, represents a formidable task of permeating a whole society with a language and a culture in that language. It is true, as Professor Spate suggests, that the many languages of India are very interesting to philologists, but not 'insuperable obstacles' to the unity of the Indian people (13). But it will all require a determined and unified effort if this tremendous goal is to be achieved. Local dialects and vernaculars, however divisive, are treasured and sacrosanct. Prejudice against what is different and novel is not easily overcome, and more will undoubtedly be done with the education of the young than with the conversion of the old.

B DEVELOPMENT OF PRIMARY AND SECONDARY EDUCATION

The combating of illiteracy has necessarily been a slow process, but as we have seen there are signs of increasing success. One of the more perceptive comments on the process has been made by Professor Spate when he suggests that, whilst 'widespread analphabetism' has its dangers, the danger of low standards might be even worse. He goes on to say that

'Education, however, remains badly balanced: the imposing concrete buildings of the universities rest on the timber and brick of the Government High Schools, they in turn on the mud or thatch hut of the primaries' (14).

As with Pakistan, the educational system has been geared in the past to produce a vast corps of clerks and professional people whom the social machine has never had a hope of completely absorbing. It has frequently been said in our own society that more attention should be paid to the primary schools which are, after all, the foundation of the whole educational structure. How much more true is this of India where what is immediately required is the extension of initial literacy to the exploding population of an estimated 511 millions in 1967 (15), rather than a vast expansion of higher education. At the upper end the most urgent need is a reallocation of students to science, technology and commerce, and away from the arts and legal subjects which have overloaded the labour market with a superfluity of litigiousness-prone *babus*.

Considerable progress has been made in at least a minimum provision of elementary or primary education for all children. By the end of 1961 primary education had, at least in theory, become compulsory and free for all children between the ages of six and eleven. In fact, in 1967 eight out of ten children in that age-group attended school regularly, as against four out of ten in 1952. Under a Directive Principle of the Constitution, free and compulsory elementary education must be provided for all children up to the age of fourteen. The terms 'primary' and 'elementary' appear from official documents to be used interchangeably (16). In addition to legislation for compulsory primary education, schemes have been drawn up for intensive enrolment in schools and for the training of teachers. During the years from 1950 to 1965 the number of primary schools increased from 209,671 to 385,250; the number of pupils on rolls went up from 18,293,967 to 33,578,000; and the number of teachers from 537,918 to 906,900 (17). This means that the quantitative progress in all these areas had practically doubled in fifteen years; whilst expenditure in cash terms had in fact trebled.

In 1952 the Secondary Education Committee was appointed by the Government, and as a result of the recommendations it made, and of the suggestions put forward by the Central Advisory Board of Education, the following pattern of education was decided upon:

(a) Eight years of elementary, or basic, education (6 to 14 years).
(b) Three or four years of secondary education with diversified courses (14 to 17/18 years).
(c) Three years of university education after the higher secondary school, leading to the first degree.

The Annual Review, *India 1967*, stated that in that year primary education was free throughout the country up to the fourth standard, whilst it was free in all union territories and in nine states up to the eighth standard. It added that

'The total number of schools is a little over 500,000 with nearly 2·1 million teachers, including about half a million women teachers' (18).

In fact, all state governments with the exception of those of Uttar Pradesh, Kerala, Madras, Gujarat and Nagaland have taken the necessary steps to reorganize their secondary education along the lines suggested by the Secondary Education Commission. Lack of trained teachers, problems of administration and paucity of finances have all contributed to the slow pace of reorganization. It is perhaps not very helpful to quote the breakdown statistics since, in the words of Professor Spate, the figures of the sub-continent are very subject to 'the malign influence of the three Bad Fairies, Not Available, Not Comparable, Not Reliable' (19). For example, the figures for secondary education between the years 1950 and 1965 appear to refer to both the secondary type of education which existed before the development of the integrated elementary education (that is, between the ages of 11 and 14 years), and that which has existed since (that is, between the ages of 14 and 17/18 years). It is this type of confusion which makes Indian statistics difficult to analyse (20).

The Education Commission has been seeking a more systematic and uniform pattern of education throughout the country, and it has suggested a duration of fifteen years leading to a first degree: that is, ten years of 'high school' education, two years of 'higher secondary' education, and three years for the first degree course. This suggestion is still 'under consideration', although apart from the actual terminology used it does not seem to differ fundamentally from the recommendations of the Secondary Education Committee and the Central Advisory Board of Education in 1952. The term 'high school' here seems to include education from the age of six to sixteen years, in much the same way as the term is used in our own country to cover the primary or preparatory department (junior high school), and the secondary department (secondary high school, or just high school) of certain voluntary and/or independent schools.

In 1956 the National Institute of Basic Education was set up, and it later became a constituent unit of the National Council of Educational Research and Training (N.C.E.R.T.). Its purpose is to engage in research and provide training and guidance to teachers and administrators of basic education; in addition, it seeks to provide suitable material and literature to both teachers and pupils. The Education Commission has stated that the essential principles of 'basic education' should shape and guide the educational system at all levels; and therefore 'no one stage of education may be designated as basic education' (21).

C OTHER FORMS AND STAGES OF EDUCATION

Vocational and technical school education includes a variety of institutions such as those involved in the teaching of agriculture, forestry, commerce, industry, arts and crafts, engineering, medicine, veterinary science and physical education. There are also polytechnics concerned with a variety of subjects and forms of training. All these institutions have increased in number from 2,339 in 1950 to 4,137 in 1964. Statistics after that date are somewhat unreliable, but the great increase in the interest expressed in technical and vocational education, both on the part of the Government and of the people, is clear from the fact that in 1964–5 there were seven times as many teachers involved in this type of education as there were in 1950–51, and about fourteen times as many students on the rolls.

The development of higher education has been quite spectacular during the past two decades. In 1950 the number of universities was 27, in 1967 there were 70; the number of colleges, both general and professional, was 798 in 1950 and by 1967 had risen to 3,976. The University Grants Commission (U.G.C.) was constituted in 1953 as a result of the recommendation of the University Education Commission, set up in 1948 to investigate the possibilities and methods of university expansion. In 1956 the U.G.C. was granted an autonomous statutory status by Act of Parliament, and it was required by the same Act to take the steps it considered necessary to promote and co-ordinate university education, and to maintain the standards of teaching, examination and research. The composition of the Commission includes a chairman, a secretary, and eight other members and it has the power to make grants to various universities, and to implement schemes for development and augmentation. Since its inception the Commission has helped the universities and their constituent colleges to improve their laboratory and library facilities. In addition, it has assisted in improving the pay-scales of lecturers and teachers in order to attract young and brilliant people to the profession.

As school education has rapidly expanded so there has been the need for an increasing number of teachers. The number, in fact, increased from 750,000 in 1950–51 to close on two million in 1965–6; whilst the number of *trained* teachers during this period increased from 430,000 to 1·4 million, which means that the percentage of trained teachers rose from 57 to 70. In order to meet the increasing demand for trained teachers there has been an expansion of teacher training institutions. Such institutions for elementary teachers have increased from 649 in 1946–7 to about 1,350 in 1965, with an annual intake capacity of about 103,890. The number of training-colleges at the secondary stage has, during the same period, risen from 41 to more than 268, with an annual intake capacity of about 26,000.

It is clear that India is making considerable progress in teacher training, but whilst her annual intake capacity is higher than it has ever been and is steadily increasing, in terms of a society whose population has increased from 439 millions in 1961 to 511 millions in 1967, or 72 millions in six years, this is still not enough. India has, nevertheless, indicated her ability to develop in the field of education once freed from outside restrictive influences. In addition to initial training, twenty-five training-colleges have facilities for courses and research leading to the post-graduate degrees of M.Ed. and Ph.D. (22).

In-service training courses are being organized by Extension Services Departments in about a hundred secondary teachers' training-colleges. Several state governments have set up institutes in order to provide training in the teaching of English and to prepare textbooks and a variety of teaching aids. The U.G.C. and the N.C.E.R.T. have also initiated a programme of Summer Schools for school teachers and college lecturers. These Summer Schools are particularly concerned to mediate new knowledge and modern methods in science and mathematics.

Between the years 1950 and 1966 there was a considerable expansion in facilities for higher technical and technological education. In 1950–51 there were 142 institutions providing degrees and diplomas in engineering and technology; by 1966 the number had reached 407 (23). The increase in admission capacity and in success rate has been sevenfold. The Government has accepted that the expansion of her economy and her future affluence depend very much upon the organization of technical education. Thus, fresh facilities have been provided for industrial engineering, printing technology, aeronautical engineering, mining, petroleum technology and architecture. The Third Five-Year Plan (1961–6) aimed at the establishment of 23 engineering colleges, 8 regional colleges and 94 polytechnics; and whilst this programme had not been completed by July 1968 the Government could claim that 21 colleges and 77 polytechnics were already functioning. A college of architecture had been established at Chandigarh, and 18 out of 24 polytechnics planned for women under the state programme were then operating. There were also 19 centres set up to provide part-time and sandwich diploma courses in engineering for persons working in industry.

All forms of research are promoted by the N.C.E.R.T. whose function it is to undertake and assist research in every branch of education. The Council is also concerned to organize pre-service and in-service training, and one of its important functions is the dissemination of improved techniques and methodology, and a scrutiny and analysis of the examination systems in order to ensure both a more liberal form of education and a more objective method of assessment.

In addition to all the foregoing efforts made by the Indian Government to raise the general level of education throughout the country, the authorities are deeply concerned with what they are pleased to call 'social education' (24). The purpose of social education is to provide education to the adult population for the enrichment of their lives, and in order to motivate them to help in the change from a 'traditional' to a 'progressive' society. The state governments and the union territory administrations have taken on the responsibility for the field programme of social education, with adult literacy as its central concern. It is the role of the Ministry of Education to co-ordinate programmes and to provide supporting services and pilot projects for the social education of the whole of Indian society. There are a number of schemes concerned with the welfare of youth and the promotion of social service, physical education, community living and training in civil defence.

It is very difficult to appreciate the sort of expenditure which the Indian Government is prepared to make upon the whole educational programme. The actual amounts in hard cash have certainly increased over the years; but crores of rupees in themselves have very little significance for the British mind, even when crores are translated in terms of tens of millions and rupees in terms of pounds. The only really useful indication of expenditure in this context is in terms of a proportion or percentage of the gross national product. In 1960–61 the expenditure on education represented about 2·3 per cent of the gross national product; in 1961–2 it rose to 2·4 per cent, and in 1962–3 to 2·5 per cent. This proportion, however, was a peak in education expenditure, for 1963–4 saw a fall to 2·4 per cent; and in 1964–5 the proportion was even lower, namely 2·2 per cent (25). One thing must be clear, and that is that the percentage of expenditure on education should be increasing, and not decreasing; and that it should be approaching a figure between 3 and 4 per cent if education is to keep pace with the expanding economy and the explosion of population.

REFERENCES

1 Thapar, Romila, *A History of India*, Vol. I (Penguin, 1966), p. 42.
2 Ibid., p. 48.
3 Ibid., pp. 241–65.
4 Ibid., p. 303.
5 Hutton, J. H., *Caste in India* (O.U.P., 4th edition 1963), pp. 4–5. The first edition of this book was published by the C.U.P. in 1946.
6 Spate, O. H. K., *India and Pakistan: A General and Regional Geography* (Methuen, 2nd edition 1957), p. 125. Professor Spate adds an interesting footnote in which he quotes the remark by R. Palme Dutt in *India Today* (1940) to the effect that 'the philosophical conception of language as a means of communication between human beings will have to be revised in the light of Andro; Nora, with a grand total of two speakers, just scrapes through'.
7 *Vide* ibid., pp. 124–8, for an excellent and authoritative summary of the 'Language and Literacy' situation.
8 Thapar, Romila, op. cit., p. 312.
9 Information Service of India, *India 1967 – Annual Review* (Information Service of India, London, 1967), p. 59.
10 Research and Reference Division, Ministry of Information, *India – A Reference Annual, 1968* (Publications Division, Ministry of Information

and Broadcasting, Government of India, 1968), p. 64, Table 28, 'Literacy in India'.
11 Desai, Rashmi, *Indian Immigrants in Britain* (O.U.P., 1963), pp. 8–9.
12 Research and Reference Division, Ministry of Information, op. cit., pp. 73–4.
13 Spate, O. H. K., op. cit., p. 125.
14 Ibid., pp. 127–8.
15 Research and Reference Division, Ministry of Information, op. cit., p. 8.
16 *Vide* ibid., pp. 63–5.
17 Ibid., p. 65, Table 29, 'Primary Education'.
18 Information Service of India, op. cit., p. 117.
19 Spate, O. H. K., op. cit., p. ix.
20 *Vide* Research and Reference Division, Ministry of Information, op. cit., p. 65.
21 Ibid., p. 66.
22 Information Service of India, op. cit., p. 62.
23 *Vide* Research and Reference Division, Ministry of Information, op. cit., p. 69, Table 36, 'Higher Technical Education'.
24 Ibid., pp. 72–3.
25 Ibid., pp. 61 and 156. Table 23 gives the 'Progress of Expenditure' on Education; Table 56 provides the 'National Product and Some Other Related Aggregates'. The percentages are derived from the expenditure on education expressed as a fraction of the gross national product at market prices.

BIBLIOGRAPHY

Aiyar, C. P. R., *Indian Universities: Retrospects and Prospects* (Annamalai University, Madras, 1964).
Chaube, S. P., *A Survey of Educational Problems and Experiments in India* (Kitab Mahal, Allahabad, 1965).
Dayal, B., *The Development of Modern Indian Education* (Orient Longmans, Bombay, 1953).
Dongerkery, S. R., *University Education in India* (Manaktalas, Bombay, 1967).
Gokak, V. K., *English in India: Its Present and Future* (Asia Publishing House, 1964).
Information Service of India, *India 1967 – Annual Review* (Information Service of India, London, 1967).
Kabir, H., *Education in New India* (Allen & Unwin, 1956).
Mani, R. S., *Educational Ideas and Ideals of Eminent Indians* (New Book Society of India, New Delhi, 1965).
Misra, A., *Educational Finance in India* (Asia Publishing House, 1962).
Mudaliar, A. L., *Education in India* (Asia Publishing House, 1960).
Mukherjee, D. P., *Modern Indian Culture* (Hind Kitabs Ltd, Bombay, 2nd edition 1948).
Mukherjee, R. K., *Ancient Indian Education* (Macmillan, 1947).
Naik, J. P., *Educational Planning in India* (Allied Publishers, Bombay, 1965).
Nurullah, S. and Naik, J. P., *A History of Education in India* (Macmillan, Bombay, 2nd edition 1951).
Oakley, R. (ed.), *New Backgrounds* (O.U.P., 1968), Chapter III by Roger Bell.

Research and Reference Division, *India – A Reference Annual, 1968* (Publications Division, Ministry of Information and Broadcasting, Government of India, 1968).

Sargent, J., *Society, Schools and Progress in India* (Pergamon, 1967).

Sen, B. N., *Development of Education in New India* (New Book Society of India, New Delhi, 1966).

Shrimali, K. L., *Problem of Education in India* (Publications Division, Delhi 1961).

Shrimali, K. L., *Education in Changing India* (Asia Publishing House, 1965).

Thapar, Romila, *A History of India,* Vol. I (Penguin, 1966).

Chapter 10

Culture Contact with the Host Society

We are concerned here with the two main groups of Indians who enter our society as immigrants, namely the Hindus from the border areas of the Punjab State and from the central and southern areas of Gujarat, and the Sikhs who come chiefly from the Eastern Punjab. In Chapter 8 we considered some of the more important features of the social background of Hindus in particular, and we shall now discuss further some of the results of their culture contact with the natives of our own country. In Chapter 7 the religion of the Sikhs was described in somewhat general terms, and in the latter part of the present chapter we shall have a closer look at the Sikh group and at the way in which it differs in its reactions from the Hindus to our society. One thing must be realized from the start, and that is that one cannot abstract the term 'Indian' and begin to generalize about language, customs or behaviour. There are Punjabis who are Sikhs and others who are Hindus; there are both Hindu and Muslim Gujaratis.

Because of their difference in language and religion, even neighbouring groups may have very little in common with one another. Rashmi Desai points out that the migrants from India retain the unity which their language, kinship and their regional culture provide (1). At the same time, the sort of social structure and caste systems to which the Hindu is accustomed is not easily transportable to a foreign soil such as our own, and to a society which has its own industrial, commercial and technological complexities. There is naturally enough a 'conserving' attitude among the first generation of immigrants. This is not the outcome of mere sentiment nor of unthinking conservatism; it derives from an inherited and accustomed sense of community within the framework of the extended family, with its close kinship ties and its quite sophisticated caste culture.

At first there will certainly be a studied attempt to maintain class and caste status, with all the tabus, strictures and sanctions that are attached. Relationships with the village kin-group back home will be maintained as fully and as long as possible; and, indeed, the new community in the foreign society will be regarded simply as an extension of the old community in the village back in the Punjab or Gujarat. There is security in the group, a bond of fellowship which will respond both to individual and community need; and there is a strong sense of identity. In a strange land, with vastly different standards of behaviour and social customs, where the *mores* appear to make right the things and actions which back home were wrong, it becomes essential to maintain a certain solidarity and a common bond.

The Gujarati Hindus, for example, have a very close community and strict rules concerning endogamous marriage. This means, in the terms of the Report on British Race Relations (1969), that they become increasingly 'encapsulated' since their own natural social isolation is heavily reinforced by the difficulties that they encounter with regard to both housing and work (2). Concerning housing, because of the difficulties of obtaining mortgages and because of the prohibitive market prices, they are forced into the position of forming groups in order to purchase houses in common ownership. There is little doubt that this tendency to operate a co-operative buying system, not initially of their own deliberate choice but imposed upon them through economic and social pressures, will produce the sort of ghetto situation which most people would consider it is desirable to avoid.

Gujaratis are more literate and generally more highly educated than most Indians; in fact, the males of Gujarat, with a percentage literacy of 41 at the 1961 Census, come towards the top of the literacy table. A large proportion of them are in possession of university degrees, whilst many of the remainder have at least a high school education. When they come to England the well-educated have a somewhat agonizing choice within the realm of work: either they can take up white-collar employment at a comparatively low rate of pay, or they can work in some form of British transport or take up labouring and earn what, for them, is good pay.

Much of the bitterness and dissatisfaction felt by Indian immigrants with their new position in our society is associated with these two basic problems of housing and work. Even if they successfully overcome the housing situation to the extent of finding somewhere to live, and in addition obtain work that is both amenable and remunerative, there is still the whole question of human relationships within the host society that, for most of them, remains unresolved. In his essay entitled 'The File of Regrets', Syed Ali Baquer somewhat sadly comments:

'But the tragedy of the immigrants, and more particularly of the Asians, is heightened by the fact that the only point of contact between them and the native population is the work situation, and if they fail to strike a relationship here, they never get invited to British houses' (3).

If complete social segregation is to be avoided in a multi-racial and multi-cultural society, one thing is certain: there must be the opportunity and occasion outside work contact for some sort of social intercourse between peoples of very different cultures. We shall consider more fully in a later chapter some of the problems of assimilation and integration, but it should be stated here that in this particular realm far too much is left to chance. It may be true, as some seem to assert, that assimilation by and large is not something that is artificially planned and organized, but rather something that happens in a natural and practical way. But it is equally true that it cannot happen at all if all avenues are closed from the very beginning of the immigrant's experience of our society. This is not, of course, a one-sided affair. Cultures define the areas and levels of participation, and Rashmi Desai, who is nothing if not objective in his judgement, has rightly said that 'where there is a wall, both sides have built it' (4).

It is not always, however, the *fact* of the wall that is of significance, but rather the way in which the wall has been built and the materials of which it is constructed. In matters of race relations it is not enough to talk in some-what airy and general terms of 'prejudice' and 'racial discrimination'. Problems of culture contact are specific and they require some careful analysis; moreover, the bricks from which the wall of division is built are not reducible simply to terms of 'colour', or incompatibility of stereotypes. There is a basic ignorance within the host society, and even amongst some of the most intelligent, of the essential nature of the culture of the Hindu and of all that this culture implies. Prejudice derives from insufficient knowledge or evidence; it is basically unreasonable or irrational, and irrationality very quickly gives rise to fear (5). We all show a reluctance to accept the unfamiliar, if not a great trepidation in relation to such acceptance. Education, the provision and discussion of the fundamental in-formation concerning race, culture, religion, custom and so forth, can all do much in our society to provide a deeper understanding of, for example, the Hindu way of life, which is one of the most ancient in the world.

It is interesting to note how far matters of food and diet provide another brick in the wall that divides the Hindu from his white host. Most Gujaratis are vegetarians and they have established their own grocery supplies, both wholesalers and retailers, for their own peculiar types of food. This sort of business activity has a double advantage in that the Gujaratis are able to receive easily the sort of food they enjoy, and also keep much of the earned wealth of the community within the social group. Indian shops for selling other commodities, such as dress, are also being established. Societies have always tended to be suspicious of and to resent the sub-society within its confines; the group that learns to be self-sufficient within the host society seems, almost inevitably, to become unpopular. The Kenyan Asians have proved to be a case in point. The Jews also – in particular the orthodox – have invariably developed a similar position in whatever society they have found themselves: their religious, social and food tabus have always formed a 'wall' between themselves and their host society. Their earnings have been ploughed back into their own kosher shops and suppliers; and their resultant ghetto communities and their financial success have been resented by their hosts.

No one can pretend, whatever their politics or ideology, that this sort of situation is not a serious or a potentially explosive one; it is a situation which must be faced realistically and honestly, as well as dispassionately and with sensitivity. If one can foresee possibilities of dissension and dangers of division, it is obviously important to describe and diagnose them, and as far as one is able to outline the prognosis. It is equally important to suggest a variety of solutions to the problem without arousing popular animosity or ill-informed and generally ignorant attitudes. Any social or cultural group which becomes isolated or segregated may, in one way, develop a sense of self-sufficiency and security; but, in certain circumstances, such a group may become the object of attack, abuse and persecution until its very identity and existence may be in danger. Immigrant groups invariably suffer the stress of divided or dual loyalties, and the Hindus are no exception to this.

Whilst the practice of the Hindu religion does not require the establishment of ornate temples for its continuance in a foreign country, the Hindus have not neglected their particular forms of worship which may still be pursued in their homes. The continuance of the beliefs and worship is still linked with their general social system and caste structure; but even when the latter begins to grow thin the philosophical concept of *karma* still remains. But possibly even more important is the fact that the Hindu religion has existed in one form or another for over three millennia, and India herself has been subjected to invasions, both political and religious, which have never succeeded in destroying the basic acceptance of Hindu faith and belief. The Hindu abroad retains his identity through the extension of his social system into the new environment, and through his acceptance and pursuance of his own native religion, which he can practise in his own home.

Up to the present time, however, the majority of the Indian immigrants, that is about four-fifths, have been Sikhs from Jullundur and Hoshiarpur in the East Punjab, an area referred to as the Doaba. We have already discussed the religion of the Sikhs in Chapter 7, but it is important here to say a little more about their general background. The report on British Race Relations (1969) holds that

'Of the three main constituents of the coloured immigration from the Commonwealth, the Sikhs are the most homogeneous, the most cohesive, and the best organized' (6).

In the Punjab they live chiefly in villages where local customs and traditions

L

control their lives. They have a great sense of community or 'belonging-ness', which derives from a history of unity in and through persecution.

The Sikhs are remarkable for a number of things, some of them seemingly quite contradictory. Despite the fact that Sikhism has much in common with the Christian concept of love and peace, the Sikhs have been renowned for their relentless and tenacious qualities in war, and they formed the nucleus of the Indian Army. They also have a history of migration and so have formed strong links over the years with our own society; and they have, in addition, had time to make a reasonable evaluation of the British host society, its environment and way of life.

The Sikhs were initially concerned with making an adequate living in Britain, and with amassing sufficient funds in order to improve their own standard of living as well as that of their extended families at home. Every immigrant group has its peculiar problems, but the Sikhs, unlike the Hindus, have no complex or developed caste system (7). Since the inception of the Sikh religion they have strenuously opposed, in principle, the caste division of society. The Sikhs are a brotherhood in which there is a sense of equality, and in which there is considerable respect shown for all human life. Cruelty, greed and sensual excesses are forbidden by their religion and philosophy as well as by individual precept. There is a very strong belief in the importance of the family and of family life; and Sikh attitudes in the context of western culture contact react strongly to those elements which might in any way endanger the stability of the family.

In this latter respect the Sikhs have tended to adopt a policy rather different from that of the Pakistanis, and also the West Indians, in their pattern of migration. As soon as it became apparent that immigration control was inevitable in our society, the Sikhs ensured that their wives, children and other dependants came over to this country. In consequence, whilst there are many married Pakistani males over here without their wives and families, there are very few Sikh males in this situation. This familial unity is generally reinforced by a group unity in which barriers of class and education barely exist (8). It is this close sense of identity which has made it possible for Sikhs to settle in a place like Southall, where a considerable concentration of Indian labour has taken place since the Second World War. G. S. Aurora states that by 1959 nearly 70 per cent of the Indian workers in Southall were employed in a handful of firms; and by 1965, 90 per cent of the unskilled labour at one rubber factory was composed of Sikhs (9).

Such concentrations in the realm of labour led also to concentrations in housing and to all the consequent problems of overcrowding. Only gradually, through purchase and ownership, whether personal or com-munal, have the Sikhs been able to establish a life-style which is essentially their own. Many young Sikhs came to this country holding the pragmatic view that when one is in Rome one should do as Rome does. In conse-quence they began to discard some of the more outward signs of their faith and culture, in particular their turbans, their long hair and their beards. Many have adopted completely western modes of dress. But to many others all this accommodation to the way of life of the host society has seemed traitorous and a rejection of their social and religious identity. Internal strictures may have very little effect on some of the younger generation; when, however, the group or some symbol of the group is attacked from outside a new solidarity begins to arise. Thus, for example, when Sikhs have been forbidden to wear their turbans, particularly in conjunction with the uniform of some public service, they have frequently displayed their unity by reverting to their traditional dress, thus presenting a common front to the enemy until they have fully established their rights.

There is what might be termed a 'theoretical equality' between men and women within Sikhism. There is, however, a clear recognition of the difference in function between men and women, based almost entirely upon the biological fact of child-bearing. It is the woman's job to produce children, to care for them and her husband, and to look after the home. In so far as the wife fulfils these functions, and is conscientious in the main-tenance of the household, she is held in respect. But there is always a dis-tance between men and women prescribed by social tabus and traditions. Sex is not generally discussed in any open or light-hearted way; men and women do not demonstrate their affection in public; and extra-marital intercourse is both heavily frowned upon and uncommon. It is important for a woman to dress modestly and to behave modestly; moreover, she will join groups of women, and not of men, on public occasions, whether marriages, cremations or religious festivals.

Wherever they live the Sikhs establish centres for their religious practices and for the perpetuation of their social culture and their customs. These centres, or *gurdwaras*, are more than temples or churches; they are halls where Sikhs may meet to discuss their problems, or where the homeless may shelter, or where children who are unable to read their holy scriptures, the *Adi Granth*, in the Gurmukhi script, may be taught by the local *guru*. The *gurdwara* is a sort of social centre where meals may be served to the hungry, the poor and the unemployed; and it is a place, without furnishings, religious images or elaborate symbols, where Sikh worshippers may just relax and meditate. E. J. B. Rose points out that the arrival of the women dependants of the Sikhs has greatly increased the strength of the *gurdwaras*, since the women

'tend to keep all the religious fasts and they maintain religious observance in the home. Moreover, no institutionalized form of social seclusion prevents Sikh women from attending any kind of public gatherings' (10).

The very forces which make for Sikh solidarity are at the same time the forces which prevent assimilation or integration. Where a group desires to preserve its native culture at all costs there is an inevitable tendency to close the ranks and raise the wall of division. Special schools are initiated to ensure that the next generation will learn their native language as well as archaic scripts in which their holy scriptures are written. This is not peculiar to such immigrants as the Gujaratis and Bengalis; it is equally true of such groups as the Jews and, of course, the Pakistanis. It is all somewhat redolent of the ancient Israelite in exile who could plan, think and dream of one thing only – his return to the land of Yahweh and the home of his religion and language; or, failing that, the re-creation of his culture and belief in the land of his exile. It was in exile that the Jewish synagogue was born; it is in the land of Indian dispersion that the real value of the *gurdwara* and the *ashram* has been discovered.

It has been said by a Sikh anthropologist that whilst it is true that the Sikh needs to know English ways in order to learn them, it is equally true that the Englishman needs to know Sikh ways in order to teach them. This is a gentle reminder that integration and assimilation represent a two-way process. It is foolish to point at others and say that they do not integrate if the host society, in terms of both organizations and individuals, fails to educate its own members to integrate with others. The dangers of developing a cultureless group of young people as a result of their contact with alien societies have been fully discussed and exploited. The dangers are there and only the biased or ignorant would deny or underestimate them. Alienation is always a sad thing, whether within the family, or within the larger peer group, or within the total indigenous culture; it is doubly sad when the alienation leaves a void without any attachment or possibility of further identity. The creation of a new culture demands deep thought as well as sympathetic understanding, and 'Positive efforts by the Government and by local authorities will be needed to help adolescents to remain within their own culture while feeling at home in the culture of their adopted country' (11).

REFERENCES

1 Desai, Rashmi, *Indian Immigrants in Britain* (O.U.P., 1963), p. 1.
2 Rose, E. J. B. (ed.), *Colour and Citizenship: A Report on British Race Relations* (O.U.P., 1969), p. 471.
3 Baquer, S. A., 'The File of Regrets' in Tajfel, H. and Dawson, J. L., *Disappointed Guests* (O.U.P., 1965), p. 112.
4 Desai, R., op. cit., p. 87.
5 *Vide* Stafford-Clark, D., *Prejudice in the Community* (National Committee for Commonwealth Immigrants, 1967), pp. 3–4.
6 Rose, E. J. B. (ed.), op. cit., p. 452.

7 Caste does survive among the Sikhs in the Punjab in a residual form. It represents the relics of an occupational hierarchy, and a remnant of the Hindu caste system retained by some groups after conversion to the Sikh religion. The most numerous groups are the Jats. (*Vide* Rose, E. J. B. (ed.), op. cit., pp. 55–6.) J. H. Hutton cites the examples of the Mazhbi Sikhs who are looked down upon by Sikhs who are not Mazhbi. For fuller details *vide* Hutton, J. H., *Caste in India* (O.U.P., 4th edition 1963), pp. 37, 117–8, 123, 204.

8 See reference 7.

9 *Vide* Aurora, G. S., *The Frontiersmen* (Popular Prakashan, Bombay, 1967), pp. 18, 30 and 77; and Marsh, P., *The Anatomy of a Strike* (Institute of Race Relations Special Series, 1967), p. 16. Both quoted in Rose, E. J. B. (ed.), op. cit., pp. 453–4.

10 Rose, E. J. B. (ed.), op. cit., p. 460.

11 Ibid., p. 468.

BIBLIOGRAPHY

Arthur, J. *et al.*, *Integration of Children of Immigrants into Schools* (MacGibbon & Kee, 1966).

Aurora, G. S., *The Frontiersmen* (Popular Prakashan, Bombay, 1967).

Banton, M., *White and Coloured: the Behaviour of British People towards Coloured Immigrants* (Cape, 1959).

Borrie, W. *et al.*, *The Cultural Integration of Immigrants* (UNESCO, 1959).

Bowker, G., *Education of Coloured Immigrants* (Longmans, 1968).

Burgin, T. *et al.*, *Spring Grove: The Education of Immigrant Children* (O.U.P., 1967).

Burney, E., *Housing on Trial: a Study of Immigrants and Local Government* (O.U.P., 1967).

Carey, A. T., *The Colonial Students* (Secker & Warburg, 1956).

Chater, A., *Race Relations in Britain* (Lawrence & Wishart, 1966).

Collins, S., *Coloured Minorities in Britain* (Lutterworth Press, 1957).

Davison, R. B., *Black British: Immigrants to England* (O.U.P., 1966).

Desai, R., *Indian Immigrants in Britain* (O.U.P., 1963).

Eisenstadt, S. N., *The Absorption of Immigrants* (Routledge, 1954).

Griffith, J. A. G., *et al.*, *Coloured Immigrants in Britain* (O.U.P., 1960).

Hawkes, N., *Immigrant Children in British Schools* (Pall Mall Press, 1966).

Hepple, B., *The Position of Coloured Workers in British Industry* (N.C.C.I., 1967).

Hiro, D., *The Indian Family in Britain* (Community Relations Commission, 1967).

Hooper, R. (ed.), *Colour in Britain* (B.B.C., 1965).

Huxley, E., *Back Street New Worlds: A Look at Immigrants in Britain* (Chatto & Windus, 1964).

John, De Witt, *Indian Workers' Associations in Britain* (O.U.P., 1969).

Jordan, R. R., *The Integration of Coloured Commonwealth Immigrants within the English Educational System* (Univ. of London Press, 1965).

McCowan, A., *Coloured Peoples in Britain* (Bow Group, London, 1952).

Oakley, R. (ed.), *New Backgrounds* (O.U.P., 1968), Chapter III by Roger Bell.

Patterson, S., *Immigrants in Industry* (O.U.P., 1968).

Patterson, S., *Immigration and Race Relations in Britain: 1960–1967* (O.U.P., 1969).

P.E.P., *Report on Racial Discrimination* (Community Relations Commission, 1967).

Rex, J. *et al.*, *Race, Community and Conflict: A Study of Sparkbrook* (O.U.P., 1967).

Richmond, A. H., *The Colour Problem* (Penguin, revised edition 1961).

Rose, E. J. B. *et al.*, *Colour and Citizenship: A Report on British Race Relations* (O.U.P., 1969).

Singh, A. K., *Indian Students in Britain* (Asia Publishing House, 1963).

Skone, J. F., *Public Health Aspects of Immigration* (Community Relations Commission, 1968).

Tajfel, H. (ed.), *Disappointed Guests* (O.U.P., 1965).

Wickenden, J., *Colour in Britain* (O.U.P., 1958).

Wright, P. L., *The Coloured Worker in British Industry* (O.U.P., 1968).

Yudkin S., *The Health and Welfare of the Immigrant Child* (Community Relations Commission, 1968).

Part Three
The Pakistanis

Chapter 11

General Background
of Pakistan

A THE LAND

When Pakistan became a separate state from India in 1947 it was formed in such a way that it comprised two areas divorced from each other by a distance of about 1,000 miles of land and 2,500 miles of sea. No one can pretend that this partition from the State of India is, in its present form, a really successful one since, although Pakistan is a sovereign state, there is a minimum of communication between its two 'wings' except at the more official levels.

West Pakistan is nearly six times as large as East Pakistan in land area, and at the Census of 1961 it was estimated as 310,403 square miles. It is a land of mountains, plains and plateaux, watered by the great Indus, Chenab and Sutlej river systems. Although West Pakistan has, generally speaking, a continental type of climate and the rainfall is not excessive, during the rainy season the large rivers are forced to carry considerable quantities of water which frequently flood the surrounding country. The Punjab plain is divided up into a number of *doabs*, or stretches of land lying between two rivers or tributaries. The elevated land in the centre of the doab is referred to as the *bar*, which consists of old alluvial soil and is the oldest level of deposition of the existing drainage system.

It is these doab areas which the present government is seeking to irrigate and to convert into prosperous agricultural lands, and in this project it has had some considerable success. The largest of the doabs, however, referred to as the Thal or the Sind Sagar Doab, which lies between the Indus and the Chenab rivers, presents 'greater physical obstacles to irrigation than were found in the central doabs' (1). Professor O. H. K. Spate maintains that the large-scale irrigation of the Thal area should provide land for about a million people. This would be no inconsiderable achievement when one considers that the present estimated population of Pakistan as a whole is around one hundred million.

East Pakistan has an area of some 55,126 square miles and it comprises the two main physical regions of the lower Gangetic Plain and the Chittagong Hill Tracts. These hill tracts lie in a zone of heavy rainfall in the extreme south-east of the province and close to the coast. Chittagong itself is an area of considerable expansion, and it forms a natural outlet for

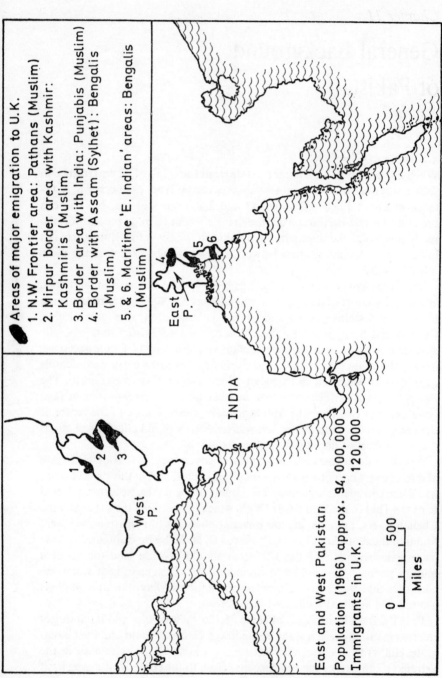

Areas of major emigration to U.K.
1. N.W. Frontier area: Pathans (Muslim)
2. Mirpur border area with Kashmir: Kashmiris (Muslim)
3. Border area with India: Punjabis (Muslim)
4. Border with Assam (Sylhet): Bengalis (Muslim)
5. & 6. Maritime 'E. Indian' areas: Bengalis (Muslim)

INDIA

West P.

East P.

Miles
0   500

East and West Pakistan
Population (1966) approx. 94,000,000
Immigrants in U.K.   120,000

Pakistan: areas from which Pakistanis have emigrated to the U.K.

Assam, seeking for many years to rival Calcutta in its importance as a port. The Lower Gangetic Plain extends from the Himalayas (the 'abodes of snow') in the north to the Bay of Bengal in the south. The plain is very flat, most of it being less than 30 feet above sea-level, but here and there rising to above 100 feet. Throughout the plain there is a network of rivers, lakes, marshes and swamps; and the chief rivers in the network are the Ganges (Ganga), flowing from the west, and the Jamuna which flows from the north. The delta formed by these two great rivers and the Meghna, flowing from the north-east, is the biggest in the world.

East Pakistan has a humid, hot climate, with a very heavy rainfall which causes the rivers to flood and saturate hundreds of square miles of surrounding land. The soil is kept fertile by the silt which is deposited each year; and the fresh land areas, formed by the deposits of silt and sand in the river beds, are called *chars* or *diaras*, or flood-plain islands.

It is estimated that about 4·5 per cent of the total area of Pakistan, or 10·5 million acres, is composed of forest land. The amount in acreage is roughly the same in both East and West Pakistan; but whilst it represents about 16 per cent of the total area in the East province, it is only about 2·5 per cent in the West. According to Professor Kazi S. Ahmad these percentages are far too small to meet the needs of the country, since the area under forests should be in the region of 20 to 25 per cent. This is necessary so as to reduce the dangers of soil erosion, and in order to provide timber for building, furniture, fuel, raw materials for an increasing variety of new industries, and wood-pulp for paper-making (2).

In West Pakistan the chief products include maize, millets, rice, sugar-cane and cotton, which are all sown between April and June; and barley, wheat, grain and oil-seeds, which are sown after the rains of October and November. In East Pakistan rice, jute, tea, wheat, tobacco, pulses, sugar-cane and oil-seeds are all produced. Of all these products rice is by far the most important crop in the whole of Pakistan; and although the western province helps to supply the eastern province, Pakistan still does not produce enough rice to supply its own people with what is their staple diet. In consequence large quantities have to be imported from Burma and other eastern countries.

The oils obtained from the great variety of oil-seeds which are grown are used for various purposes, from fuel in lamps to essential ingredients in cooking and in the manufacture of sweets. The production of tea is second in importance in East Pakistan as a cash crop, and over 90 per cent of that crop comes from Sylhet. So successful is this production that there is a Tea Development Committee whose object it is to find ways of extending tea cultivation to new areas, since tea obviously has a great export market. Before the year 1960 up to thirty million pounds of tea were exported by East Pakistan every year.

The chief cash crop of East Pakistan, however, is jute and about 55 per cent of the world's supply is grown here. The problems of jute production – agricultural, technological and marketing – are regarded as of such considerable importance that a Central Jute Committee has been established in order to investigate and provide solutions to those problems. In 1957 the Committee founded a Jute Research Institute at Dacca, and then proceeded to establish farms at Chitla and Dinajpur. Professor Spate makes the point that

'if E. Pakistan has a quasi-monopoly of the jute trade, the jute trade has a monopoly of E. Pakistan: apart from tea there is no other significant cash crop. As for *India*, the importance of the commodity may be judged from the fact that in 1948 about one-third of all her foreign exchange earnings – and two-thirds of hard currency – came from jute' (3).

And Spate goes on to emphasize that the 'cut-throat attitude' on both sides might well expose the jute trade to either a complete dislocation of the manufacturing industry, or a frantic over-exporting of large quantities of raw jute from Pakistan leading to a collapse in prices.

It is clearly not our purpose here to discuss all the geographical features or natural resources of Pakistan, but merely to set the stage as it were for a consideration of the culture and problems that are the inheritance of some of the immigrants to this country. We can do little more here than to indicate that, given the good-will, the capital, the expertise and power to organize and analyse critically their economic position, the Pakistani people have considerable potential for development within their frontiers. One of the biggest drawbacks is the territorial division of Pakistan into two widely-separated land areas. This makes unity difficult and the possibilities of political divorce and isolation considerably greater. But there are certain spiritual and impalpable forces at work in a society which finds its ultimate unity in a religious faith, however widely separated it may be in other respects.

In 1948 Pakistan became a member of the United Nations Organization, and she is in consequence in receipt of both financial and technical help. In addition, as a member of the South-East Asia Treaty Organization (SEATO), Pakistan feels confident that she has a very important part to play in 'maintaining the vital political stability and economic progress of South-East Asia' (4). Pakistan has sought, and received, the help of such countries as the United States, West Germany and Japan from whom she has received advice, economic and technical assistance, educational help and – not least important – the necessary markets for her exports.

B THE PEOPLE

One cannot generalize about the people of Pakistan any more than one can about the people of the sub-continent of India generally. It is, for example, not very enlightening to say that people in any particular area are 'of mixed race' since this statement can be applied to most groups. And it must be always remembered that when speaking of 'Pakistanis' we are certainly not referring to a homogeneous group. Just as there are considerable racial differences between the peoples of East Pakistan and those of West Pakistan, so there are also differences among the peoples of each province.

In East Pakistan the people are a mixture of Mongolian and Dravidian: they are short or medium in height, dark in complexion, and have broad noses and broad foreheads. In West Pakistan there are a larger number of relatively isolated tribes and groups with very different racial origins. Those peoples who live in the region of the North-West Frontier and Baluchistan, the Pathans and the Baluchis, are a mixture of Turks and Iranians. They have fair complexions, long and pointed noses and usually dark, piercing eyes. Whilst the Pathans are tall and heavy, the Baluchis are comparatively short, with curly hair and oval faces. In the south of Baluchistan there is a group of people called the Brahuis, who are considered to be descendants of the Dravidians, a race who migrated from the Mediterranean into India. Entering from the north-west they made their way south and also east. There is, therefore, a link racially between some of the Dravidian elements in the west province and the Mongolo-Dravidians in the east province.

East of the Indus river the people of the plains in West Pakistan are Indo-Aryans. Their history, as we have already seen, goes back to the invasion of the sub-continent by the Aryans (or *aryas*) about 1500 BC or before; and the Jats and the Rajputs are their present descendants. The Indo-Aryan types are tall or medium in height; they have long heads, prominent noses, black and wavy hair, black or very dark eyes, and brown or fair complexions. Although there has been considerable migration and inevitable intermixture over the centuries, the rules of endogamous marriage among various castes, tribes and groups have helped to keep certain racial elements relatively pure.

The distribution of the population in Pakistan depends, as in most countries, upon such factors as the agricultural and economic resources available. These in turn are relative to such variables as climate, soil fertility, water-supply, cultivable land, forest area and so forth. Foreign investment in Pakistan will decide to a considerable extent the amount of capital available, and also how and where it will be invested (5). In view of these facts it is not surprising that the density of population in East Pakistan is far greater than in West Pakistan; but economic factors are, of course, not the only ones – political disturbances and exchanges have resulted in large numbers of Muslims entering East Pakistan.

The only area in East Pakistan which has a density lower than 526 persons per square mile is the Chittagong Hill Tract area. Here the communications are difficult; there is very little arable land and a considerable amount of forest; in consequence the population density is about 76 persons per square mile. The average density in East Pakistan as a whole is 922 people per square mile; in West Pakistan it is 138 per square mile. The western province, it must be remembered, has a great deal of dry, sterile, unproductive land, and the population in the hill country and sandy waste lands of Baluchistan and Sind is sparse.

Population of Pakistan – Census of 1961

	Population	Density per square mile
Pakistan	93,720,613	652
East Pakistan	50,840,235	922
West Pakistan	42,880,378	138

According to the 1961 Census 60 per cent of the working population in West Pakistan are employed in agriculture, whilst in East Pakistan the percentage is over 80.

One of the biggest problems experienced by Pakistanis in their concern for unity is that of verbal communication. The two national languages of Pakistan are Urdu and Bengali, the latter of which is spoken by 98 per cent of the people in East Pakistan. Urdu is spoken in Karachi and in other places in West Pakistan, with a variety of regional languages, especially in the Punjab. Urdu is also the normal medium of instruction in West Pakistan, except where instruction is given in one of the regional languages, such as Sindhi, Pushto or Punjabi. English is important as a second language throughout Pakistan, particularly among businessmen and government officials, and is used as the chief medium of higher education.

Most of the Pakistanis who have left their country to migrate to Britain have come from the hill districts of Mirpur in the western province and of Sylhet in the eastern province. Because of the infertility of the soil in these areas, and the fact that everyone lives at almost famine level, the sons of farmers in these lands have left home to seek employment in the towns, or in the ports, or abroad. They tend, therefore, to be simple, poor and uneducated, if not illiterate. The only exception to this appears to be the emigrant from East Bengal, where there has been a long tradition of literacy (6).

C THEIR HISTORY

In considering the history of Pakistan and the Pakistanis we are concerned with a people who have existed as an independent Islamic state only since 1947. The Muslim peoples of India, however, had a unity and a somewhat nebulous identity long before the occasion of partition itself; and for many years they had dreamed of their own society or state in which all its members were linked by a religious faith and a specific social order.

The Muslims first appeared in India during the latter part of the seventh century. After the death of the prophet Muhammad in AD 632, his Muslim followers and converts very quickly developed the concept of the *jihad*, or holy war; and many of them sought by every means to make converts to the religion of Islam. It is clear, however, that there were always those who rejected any form of persecution or conversion by force.

In AD 712 the Arab leader, Muhammad bin Qasim, conquered Sind and set up Muslim rule; the earliest converts were usually Hindus of low caste who left Hinduism believing that the Muslim faith offered them equality. When Muhammad bin Qasim wrote to his uncle requesting guidance regarding the natives of Sind, this is the reply he received:

'It appears that the chief inhabitants of Brahmanabad had petitioned to be allowed to repair the temple of Budh and pursue their religion. As they have made submission and agreed to pay taxes to the Caliph, nothing more can be properly required from them. They have been taken under our protection, and we cannot in any way stretch out our hands upon their lives or property. Permission is given them to worship their gods. Nobody must be forbidden or prevented from following his own religion' (7).

The early rule of the Muslims in India was unquestionably tolerant once conquest had been made.

Towards the end of the tenth century Mahmud of Ghazni, a principality of Afghanistan, decided to make expeditions or raids into the fertile Punjab plains in order to fill the coffers of the depleted Ghazni treasury. The greed for gold was excused by the fact that in their excursions into the Punjab the Muslims under Mahmud were motivated by iconoclasm. In sacking the Hindu temples they were conscious of doing Allah a service. There is no doubt, however, that the terrible destruction of Hindu centres of culture, such as the seashore city of Somnath in AD 1025, remained burnt into the memory of the Hindus for a very long time. A thirteenth-century account of the event, from an Arab source, claims that 50,000 Hindus were killed during the pillaging of the temple erected to the god Somnat (8). Out of his ill-gotten gains Mahmud founded a library, a museum, and a fine mosque at Ghazni.

In 1185 Muhammad Ghuri, who had invaded India through the Gomal

Pass, conquered Lahore and began to attack the Rajputs who controlled the Gangetic plain. After a number of battles he conquered the kingdom of Delhi and Ajmer in 1192; but he was assassinated in 1206. After his death the Ghuri kingdom of Afghanistan did not survive; but the Indian part of the kingdom soon became the basis for a new political element in India, namely the Delhi Sultanate. This was the rule of the Afghan or Turkish Sultans.

The last and one of the greatest of the Moguls was Aurangzeb who ruled almost the entire sub-continent of India; but when he died in 1707 Islamic power began to decline. As this power declined so British influence increased, and after the exile of the Mogul emperor in 1858 relationships between the British and the Muslims deteriorated. There was considerable suspicion on both sides and Dr Kazi Ahmad is certainly not guilty of partisanship when he states that,

'The British suspected the Muslims of being hostile to the British rule in India. The Hindus naturally enjoyed British patronage. The Muslims were left far behind them in education and economic welfare. All this led to a reaction against resurgent Hindu nationalism' (9).

Eventually the leadership which the Muslims lacked was provided by Sir Syed Ahmed Khan, who in 1875 founded Aligarh College which became the Aligarh Muslim University in 1921, and which today has over 5,000 students.

When the Hindus formed the Indian National Congress in 1885 the Muslims at first joined in support; but when they realized that a liberated and free India would be dominated by Hindus they withdrew their support, and in 1906 they founded the Muslim League. In 1930 the possibility of a separate Muslim state was being discussed, and it was adopted as a definite aim at a meeting of the League in 1940. At that time Mohammed Ali Jinnah was the President of the League. Eventually, on June 3, 1947, India was partitioned between the Hindus and the Muslims. The old provinces of the Punjab, Bengal and the Sylhet district of Assam were split up, and in August 1947 Pakistan became a separate and independent nation with its capital at Karachi. Ali Jinnah was elected its first President by the Constituent Assembly.

In 1956 Pakistan became the Islamic Republic of Pakistan and remained within the British Commonwealth of Nations; but in October 1958 General Mohammed Ayub Khan, after a military coup, became head of the new state, now referred to simply as Pakistan. A new constitution was formulated in 1962 and the new nation was renamed the Republic of Pakistan. The capital was removed from Karachi to Rawalpindi in 1959, until the newly-built capital at Islamabad could be completed. Although all these

9. *Top:* The Market Square at Peshawar, Khyber Pass, Pakistan, (*bottom*) The horse-drawn Tonga taxi of the Pakistani village and town.

10. *Top:* The roofs of Lahore, Pakistan, (*right*) A bazaar in Lahore.

capitals were in West Pakistan it was not intended that East Pakistan should be left out in the cold, and Dacca was nominated as the second seat of the Government and the main seat of the National Assembly. The provincial capital of West Pakistan is at Lahore and it controls twelve administrative divisions, which in turn are subdivided into forty-four districts and six agencies. The provincial capital of East Pakistan is at Dacca, controlling four administrative divisions which are subdivided into seventeen districts.

After the partition in 1947 there occurred considerable transfers of population between India and Pakistan. There was, for example, an exchange of people between East and West Punjab. Many Muslims sought refuge in Pakistan from every part of India; and these refugees (*muhajirs*) have helped to enrich the Pakistan society with the great variety of culture which is to be found scattered throughout the sub-continent.

Professor Ahmad speaks of Pakistan as a new state with an old civilization, and somewhat wistfully adds that the inhabitants of the Indus valley of about five thousand years ago had an advanced culture and, in fact, lived a better life than villagers in the same area do today.

'Their towns were well laid out with wide streets, two-storey houses and very big public baths. The people wore fine muslin clothes and polished ornaments. The vessels that they used for their cooking and eating were well made and of a pleasing design' (10).

Pakistan is moving towards something new; a young nation with a new vision of national identity. It is an identity that has in a sense to be created because of the multiplicity of races, origins, languages, cultures and customs that all go to make up two wings of a nation divided by a thousand miles of land.

REFERENCES

1 Spate, O. H. K., *India and Pakistan* (Methuen, 2nd edition 1957), p. 478.
2 Ahmad, K. S., *A Geography of Pakistan* (O.U.P., 1964), p. 43.
3 Spate, O. H. K., op. cit., pp. 283–4. Professor Spate italicizes 'India' to distinguish the political entity of the Union or Republic of India from the Indian subcontinent.
4 Ahmad, K. S., op. cit., p. 179.
5 Ibid., pp. 146–9.
6 *Vide* Rose, E. J. B., *et al.*, *Colour and Citizenship: A Report on British Race Relations* (O.U.P., 1969), pp. 58–62.
7 Eliot, H. M. and Dowson, J., *The History of India as Told by its Own Historians* (C.U.P., 1931), Vol. I, p. 185.
8 *Vide* Thapar, Romila, *A History of India* (Penguin, 1966), Vol. I, pp. 233–4.
9 Ahmad, K. S., op. cit., pp. 4–5.
10 Ibid., p. 145.

M

BIBLIOGRAPHY

Ahmad, K. S., *A Geography of Pakistan* (O.U.P., 1964).

Davis, K., *The Population of India and Pakistan* (Princeton Univ. Press., 1950).

Eglar, Z., *A Punjab Village in Pakistan* (Columbia Univ. Press, 1960).

Lewis, S. R., *Economic Policy and Industrial Growth in Pakistan* (Allen & Unwin, 1969).

Sayeed, K., *The Political System of Pakistan* (Allen & Unwin, 1967).

Sayeed, K. B., *Pakistan: The Formative Phase 1857–1948* (O.U.P., 2nd edition 1968).

Spate, O. H. K., *India and Pakistan: A General and Regional Geography* (Methuen, 2nd edition 1957).

Stephens, I., *Pakistan: Old Country, New Nation* (Penguin, 1964).

Tayyeb, A., *Pakistan: A Political Geography* (O.U.P., 1966).

Weeks, R. V., *Pakistan: Birth and Growth of a Muslim Nation* (Van Nostrand, 1964).

Wilber, D. N., *Pakistan: Its People, Its Society, Its Culture* (H.R.A.F. Press, New Haven, 1964).

Wilber, D. N., *Pakistan, Yesterday and Today* (Holt, Rinehart & Winston, 1964).

Williams, L. F. R., *The State of Pakistan* (Faber, 1962).

Chapter 12

The Religion
of Pakistan

A THE HISTORICAL BACKGROUND OF ISLAM

> God, there is no god but He, the Living, the Everlasting. . . .
> His Throne comprises the heavens and earth;
> He is the All-high, the All-glorious.
>
> (From The Koran, Sura 2.)

Since most Pakistanis are Muslims of one sort or another we are confining our attention in this chapter to the origin, development and doctrines of Islam. In order to understand the fundamental tenets of the Muslim faith it is necessary to trace its origin in Arabia during the sixth century AD. Professor Guillaume maintains that the ancient Habiru 'are almost certainly to be identified with the Arabs' (1), and that the Hebrews of the Old Testament were Arabs and part of the inhabitants of the Arabian peninsula. He also considers that the most likely meaning of the word 'Arab' is 'nomad' or 'wanderer', which is precisely what most of the Arabs were. They wandered perpetually throughout the peninsula and raided wherever they could.

At this time the Arabs worshipped a number of gods, including Al Ilah (Allah) or 'the god', Al Lat or 'the sun', Al Uzza or Venus, and Manat or Fortune. Allah was regarded as the father of the other three who were female; and, whilst there were certainly many other deities worshipped both at Mecca and elsewhere in Arabia, these were at the head of the hierarchy. Al Lat was the great mother goddess who was represented in so many ancient religions, and who reappeared in a variety of different guises in more modern ones. In connection with the worship of the three daughters of Al Ilah there occurred a considerable amount of sacrifice, both human and animal, as well as fertility ritual. Coupled with this typical polytheism there were also various animistic beliefs, largely involving stones, trees and wells, and spirits or *djinns*, which were believed to inhabit both natural objects and places, and to need placating.

There were, however, other currents of belief in Arabia including both Judaism and Christianity. How and when the Jews entered the peninsula is disputed by scholars, some of whom argue for a date as early as the eighth century BC, and others for one as late as the first and second centuries

AD. It seems highly probable that from the time of the fall of Samaria in 721 BC there were fugitives from Palestine moving into Arabia under pressure from surrounding countries, down to the ruthless repression and persecution by the Romans in the first two centuries after the death of Christ. The Jews who entered Arabia sought to proselytize wherever they went; and they were not without success both in religion and business. It is clear that many of them became large landowners, traders, organizers of large marts for the barter of iron goods, including arms and armaments, and woven articles. As Professor Guillaume remarks:

'Thus it can readily be seen that Jewish prosperity was a challenge to the Arabs, particularly the Quraysh at Mecca and the Aus and Khazraj at Medina' (2).

And it was a challenge which the Arabs, in the long run, resented and which led to some harsh treatment when the Muslims eventually took up arms in order to establish their Islamic empire.

Christians in Arabia belonged to three different sects: the Greek Orthodox, the Nestorians and the Monophysites. Each of these sects was active in making converts among the Arabs, and both monasteries and churches were established close to the major caravan routes. Perhaps the most important link with Islam itself as it developed through the teaching of Muhammad was the doctrine of the Monophysite sect that there was only one nature in Christ, and that 'the Trinity is one Divinity, one Nature, one Essence'. This belief led to a great deal of intolerance and persecution among the Christians themselves – orthodox against heretics and vice versa; but it also established a link with the unrelenting monotheism of Islam, and in consequence Christians found themselves, for some years, rather better treated than the Jews.

B MUHAMMAD (AD 570–632)

Mecca had for hundreds of years been a place of pilgrimage for visitors from all over Arabia, and it contained a sanctuary, the Kaaba or 'cube', which was the centre of polytheism, idolatry and superstition. There was a tradition that Al Ilah had thrown down a black stone as a sign of his presence among the Arab people; and this stone or aerolite was embedded in the wall of the Kaaba in order that it might be touched or kissed by the visiting pilgrims. There were other holy objects and places in Mecca, such as Zamzum, traditionally the sacred well which was revealed by Yahweh to Hagar and Ishmael when they were dying of thirst in the hot and dusty desert.

Muhammad was born in Mecca in AD 570, the year in which, according to tradition, an expedition by an Ethiopian army against the Arabian city was miraculously routed. Apparently there were elephants in the ranks of the invading army, and, according to Sura 105 of the Koran, the strong attack was eventually stayed by the intervention of Al Ilah who sent flocks of birds against the enemy. The birds dropped stones on them and killed them outright. Some scholars more soberly suggest that the Ethiopians were in fact destroyed by a virulent attack of smallpox.

Muhammad's father had died before the prophet's birth, and his mother died when he was only six, so that he was brought up mainly by his grandfather and then a foster-mother. There are the usual late legends surrounding his birth with which we will not concern ourselves here except simply to say, without prejudice, that in all religions there are those elements of legend, portent, myth and magic which may be received at varying levels by different devotees. It is, of course, important to be rational and enlightened; it is equally important to respect the beliefs of others, whether it be the story of the Three Magi, the supernatural conception of the Buddha, or the ascension into Heaven on a cloud of Lao-Tzu. These things are but the trimmings of religious acceptance and belief, and as Guillaume pointedly remarks:

'A prophet's personality should be able to stand on its own merits. If it can, it needs no portent; if it cannot, a portent merely compromises the credibility of the whole narrative by importing the incredible' (3).

Muhammad was a member of the Quraysh tribe, and as soon as he was old enough he began to travel with the caravans trading between Mecca and the capitals and marts of the Middle East. At the age of twenty-five he was employed by a rich widow of forty, named Khadija, who successfully ran a trading business. Khadija appears to have been impressed both by Muhammad's trading acumen and by his personality and appearance, for, according to tradition, she proposed to him and they were married. Khadija gave Muhammad seven children although none of the males survived; and as long as she lived Muhammad remained faithful to her. After her death he appears to have had at least eight more wives and a number of concubines. Muhammad's great anxiety was to obtain a male heir, but this he eventually failed to do since all his sons died in infancy.

His many journeys must have brought Muhammad into contact with Jews, various sects of Christians, and Zoroastrians from Persia. Although it is usually claimed that Muhammad could neither read nor write, it seems reasonable to suppose that he had considerable conversation with members of other religions; and that wherever he found an acceptance of monotheism and dualism (God-Devil) he discovered a response within himself. He was personally disgusted with the moral laxity of the city of Mecca, and strongly opposed to its polytheistic and idolatrous practices. He saw the struggle of right and wrong, good and evil, as a dramatized battle between Al Ilah (or Allah) and Iblis (or Shaytan), between God and the Devil. And as he listened to the accounts of Yahweh, Jesus and Ahura Mazda and their struggles with the powers of darkness, Muhammad must have felt his inner being responding to the truth as he saw it in other great religions.

When he was about forty years old, Muhammad became increasingly contemplative, and he would repeatedly retire to the hills surrounding Mecca, particularly during the holy month of Ramadan, and there sit in meditation in a cave. It was during one of these periods of retirement and contemplation that, according to the prophet, he felt very strongly the presence of some strange supernatural power which eventually materialized before him in the form of the Archangel Gabriel. The latter said to him, 'Thou art the apostle of God,' held out a piece of silken brocade and asked him to read or recite what was written upon the silk. This, quite naturally, is the point of emphasizing Muhammad's illiteracy – he obviously could not read or recite what was written there if he had never been taught to read. But three times the voice demanded that he should cry out the words that he saw. Some eleven centuries before, a similar demand had been made of the Hebrew prophet now referred to as Deutero-Isaiah:

> The voice said, Cry. And he said,
> What shall I cry?
> All flesh is grass. . . . (4).

Now to Muhammad the voice comes back:

> Cry, in the name of the Lord!
> He who created man from clots of blood.
> Cry, the Lord is wondrous kind,
> Who, by the pen, has taught mankind
> Things they knew not – being blind (5).

At first Muhammad was considerably disturbed, both mentally and spiritually. He felt that he must be possessed by a *djinn* which had transformed him into a *sha'ir* or soothsayer, and that the only solution for him was to hurl himself over a precipice. This was undoubtedly for Muhammad a period of considerable darkness and distress, but there was nothing novel about such an experience for a great religious leader and prophet. And the only immediate comfort that such a person could derive was to be found in the Buddha's reply to the nagging temptation presented to himself, namely, to keep quiet about his revelation because it was too profound for others to comprehend. The Buddha's answer was, 'There will always be some who will understand.' Muhammad found the immediate understanding that he required in his wife Khadija; she believed in her husband and in his visions, and encouraged him to go on seeking the truth.

Throughout his life the voice and the visions came repeatedly to Muhammad, revealing to him Al Ilah, or Allah, as the one and only God; all other gods were simply idols; and the struggle between good and evil, between God and the Devil, would soon result in the judgement of God and the supremacy of the good. As he became convinced of the supernatural origin of these phenomena, of the things he saw and the words he heard, Muhammad began to preach amongst his relatives and friends: and his wife was one of his first converts.

The immediate reaction was hostile: a hostility directed against Muhammad himself because of the presumption of his claims to be a prophet, indeed the chief of the prophets, and an apostle sent by God. But it was also a hostility directed against his uncompromising message. Muhammad had attacked the worshippers because of their idolatry and polytheism; it was said that at this time there existed three hundred and sixty shrines in Mecca, one for each day of the lunar year, providing a considerable revenue for the Meccan traffickers in idols, images and prayers for pilgrims. In a period of moral laxity he taught that man was responsible for his own sin and evil; and in a society in which there were the very rich and the very poor, Muhammad, in typical prophetic fashion, attacked those who were grinding the faces of the poor – just as the Hebrew prophet Amos had done nearly fourteen hundred years before. Muhammad believed that in Allah's eyes all men were equal, and that in consequence there should be no distinctions of class, whether on the basis of inheritance or of acquired wealth.

Ridicule, threats and open persecution could not prevail upon Muhammad to cease his preaching and his attempts to convert Arabs to his monotheistic and ethical teaching. He was repeatedly stoned, imprisoned, beaten and even on occasion left for dead; but during his first three years of proselytizing he made only forty or so converts. Muhammad was not the first debunker of the gods to find himself suffering as a result of his temerity; Socrates was also persecuted for seeking to drive the lower deities from the heavens.

Despite, however, all the attempts to undermine and destroy him Muhammad not only survived but began to receive increasing support. Gradually pilgrims began to come from a small desert oasis about two hundred miles north of Mecca called Yathrib, later to be known as Al Medinat, 'the City', that is, the City of the Prophet. They listened to the prophet and were so impressed that they returned to Yathrib full of his message and of his dynamic personality. Eventually, in AD 622, seventy-five leading citizens came as a delegation to Mecca to ask Muhammad to go to Yathrib as their leader and ruler. Muhammad agreed to accompany them, and that year is regarded by Muslims as the beginning of the era of Islam. The word *hijra*, or hegira, is used to describe this great event which Guillaume insists means neither 'flight' not even 'migration', but rather

'the breaking of old ties, and so marks the fact that Muhammad now belonged to Medina and not to Mecca, with all the consequences that were to follow' (6).

It is, however, difficult to find a word which provides, in shorthand, this connotation of 'separateness', and even Guillaume reveals something of this problem in his glossary where he defines the *hijra* as 'the prophet's flight to Medina from Mecca' (7). Muhammad developed into a powerful politician and statesman, and was appointed the supreme magistrate of the Arab courts in Medina. In doing all this Muhammad accomplished a task that only the most competent and diplomatic could possibly achieve. In fact, during his rule at Medina he welded together five tribes, including two Jewish, into an orderly confederation agreeing to accept himself, the prophet of God, as the final arbiter in all their problems, social, legal and political.

After several battles and skirmishes between the Medinans and Meccans, and the subjugation of the Jews in the Hejaz, Muhammad descended upon Mecca in AD 630 with a force of his followers. He entered as conqueror and performed a ritual 'cleansing' of the Kaaba by destroying all the images of the gods and all traces of idolatry. In victory he showed mercy, forgiving all his enemies save only four who were put to death. He then returned to Medina from where he continued the subjugation of his enemies, and gradually succeeded in uniting all Arabia and its many differing tribes and beliefs under the banner of Islam.

When he died in AD 632 he had established a new religion with a completely monotheist creed having universal application. The concept of the *jihad*, or holy wars, was already impressed upon the minds of believers as a sacred duty in the battle against the heretics, amongst whom were by now classed both Jews and Christians who were regarded as *mushrik*, or polytheists. The justification for this view is undoubtedly derived from a passage in the Koran which virtually accuses the Jews of worshipping Ezra as the son of God, and the Christians of similarly worshipping Jesus Christ (8). The reference to Ezra does not appear to have any sort of basis in fact, but is one of the many misconceptions in the Koran concerning both Old Testament and New Testament characters. Muhammad also left the framework of a social system which has remained virtually unchanged in Arabia during the intervening thirteen hundred years. And although Muhammad may certainly not have written or compiled the Koran, any more than Jesus wrote the Christian gospels, there seems little doubt that in the main the book represents a collection of the teachings of Muhammad as revealed – so he believed – by Gabriel, the Archangel of Allah.

C THE KORAN (OR QURAN)

It is important for anyone seeking to find common ground with immigrants of whatever race or creed, to understand accurately their prejudices as well as our own. Part of this understanding involves the correct comprehension and usage of their terms for their religion and religious beliefs. This was the point in Guillaume's insistence that the *hijra* really reflected the spiritual separation of Muhammad from his own folk rather than a mere physical flight to Medina. Similarly, Christ's movement from Nazareth to Jerusalem might be regarded as a migration from his home and a flight from his immediate enemies amongst whom there was no honour for a parvenu prophet. In fact, it was more than a physical movement, it was a spiritual separation from his family and immediate friends who failed to understand the message that he brought.

'Islam' means submission, and Muslims (or Moslems) are those who have submitted to the will of Allah. The term 'Muhammadan', or 'Mohammedan', is objectionable to most Muslims on the grounds that they do not worship Muhammad, nor do they regard him as divine, nor indeed is he central in their religious beliefs. Allah is first and last, and Muhammad is his prophet and apostle. It is, of course, inevitable that Muhammad should be regarded with considerable reverence by his followers, if on this side of idolatry; but such reverence rarely reaches the level of idolatry. Muhammad was and remains, for the majority of the Muslims, a man.

'The Prophet Muhammad was but a man; of a purely human nature. He was neither a great God, nor a small God, nor a sub-God, nor even an auxiliary of God. . . . The Prophet led us into the light of truth, but however great our respect for him may be, he is not raised above the level of man . . . he was God's Apostle and servant' (9).

The *Koran* means, literally, a 'reading' or 'that which ought to be read'. Muhammad considered that this book was the only miracle that God had worked through him. It is claimed that the original was inscribed on pieces of bark, leaves, scraps of parchment and bones, and that Allah had preserved the literal accuracy of everything written. Thus the general view of Muslims towards their scriptures is a fundamentalist one; Allah had dictated it all to Muhammad over a period of about twenty-one years through the Archangel Gabriel, and its truth must be accepted by converts to Islam in a literal fashion. The Koran in its totality is about the length of the New Testament and comprises one hundred and fourteen *suras*, or chapters, arranged in a very artificial order of decreasing length.

In the Koran, Allah is represented throughout as a single God, who is immaterial and invisible, and who adumbrates the entire cosmos with his grace and power. This monotheism is a denial of the Christian concept of the Trinity, which to the Muslim is at best a tritheism, at worst simply another form of polytheism. Allah is without division and without equal; he is omnipotent, creator of heaven, earth, life and death, and in his hands reside dominion and indomitable power. Being an absolutely just god he will wreak vengeance upon all heretics on the Day of Judgement; nevertheless, he is living and compassionate towards those who repent.

Between his God and himself nothing intervenes for the Muslim; nothing stands in the way of his communication with the divine. There is no need for any priest or intermediary, for Allah is omnipresent as well as transcendent. Indeed, Allah

'knows what is in the land and in the sea; no leaf falleth but He knoweth it; nor is there a grain in the darkness under the earth, nor a thing, green or yellow, but it is recorded in His glorious Book' (10).

Allah created man as the crown of his creativity, and one of the impressive facts about the Koran is its emphasis upon the value of the individual. The individual soul is eternal, and the ultimate salvation or damnation of each person is ultimately his own responsibility.

'Whoever goes astray, he himself bears the whole responsibility of wandering . . . whoever gets to himself a sin, gets it solely on his own responsibility' (11).

And yet there is the same sort of adherence to predestination and divine election as one may find in the *Articles of Religion*, Numbers X and XVII, of the Anglican Church. For the Muslim the will of Allah is supreme, to the extent that one cannot even will to take the right path to his Lord except by the will of Allah (12); no one takes heed to the message of Muhammad and the Koran except by God's will (13), but 'let him who will, take heed'. One must have faith in God, yet 'none can have faith except by the will of Allah' (14). We cannot question God's choice or his will: it is supreme, and we can only accept, obey, and in the direst of our troubles shrug it all off and say 'It is *quismat* (kismet, destiny)', or 'It is Allah's will (*inshillah*)'.

The reconciliation of man's freedom with God's absolute will has always presented problems to monotheistic religions. In the Jewish Old Testament, Yahweh was responsible for evil as well as good (15); and in the Christian

New Testament, God has decreed from of old those whom he has pre-destined for salvation (16). Individual freedom appears to have something of a vague unreality about it, even where it is affirmed.

Muhammad is regarded in the Koran as the servant, apostle and prophet of God, who was promised to Adam and foretold by Christ. These ideas appear to be developed from references to the 'seed of the woman' who should 'bruise the head' of the serpent, and in John's Gospel to the advent of 'another Comforter' whom Jesus promised to his disciples, 'that he may abide with you for ever' (17). It is also stated that Muhammad was carried in trance state into the presence of Allah, through seven heavens, and that there he received the revelation of God. St Paul seems to have had quite similar experiences (18). Although Muhammad spoke by revelation, as many of the Old Testament prophets also claimed for themselves (19), he at no time made greater claims than this. Indeed, it is true that in the Koran the same sort of reverence is accorded to Jesus as to Muhammad. The invocation, 'Peace be on him', is always accorded to both when their names are mentioned.

Jesus the Christ (*Aissa al Masih*) is somewhat strangely regarded as the son of the Virgin Mary, and yet as no more than a prophet and apostle like Muhammad himself. He was certainly not, in the Muslim view, the son of God or divine, or more than a human being elevated to the position of a revealer of God's truth. It is certain that Muhammad at no time read any of the Jewish or Christian scriptures, but that he obtained his information through discourse with Jewish and Christian traders. We have already mentioned something of the variety of the sects of the latter, and there must have arisen a considerable amount of confusion in the minds of the Arabs concerning Christian theology. The Koran states that Jesus was not crucified, but that Judas took his place; and, therefore, any question of a supernatural resurrection is by-passed.

There is, however, a belief in personal resurrection on the Day of Judgement, or Day of Separation, when the trumpet shall sound, and the dead will stand up upon the earth. On that day,

'When the sun shall be folded up, and the stars shall fall, and when the mountains shall be set in motion . . . and the seas shall boil . . . then shall every soul know what it has done' (20).

Every individual will have to give an account of the way he has lived, and the good will go to Heaven, or Paradise, which abounds in delightful, deep rivers of cooling water with unendingly fruitful and fertile valleys, with lovely mansions, beautiful youths and maidens. The evil will go to Hell, a place of boiling liquids, molten metal, fire and torture where the individual will suffer eternal torment. It is possible, as with Christianity, to take these things literally; and some Muslims do. But the more sophisticated today would interpret these pictures of Heaven and Hell as allegorical, since the after-life would for them involve a spiritual rather than a physical state. Heaven is, ultimately, the beatific vision of God which is as inexpressible in Muslim terms as it is in Christian or Judaistic.

D THE FIVE PILLARS OF ISLAM

The path of Islam is the 'straight path' – one that begins with the revelation of Allah (or Yahweh) to Abraham, then to Moses in the ten command-ments, followed by the Golden Rule of Jesus and, finally, the inspired *suras* of Muhammad in the Koran. Abraham, Moses, Jesus and Muhammad were all authentic prophets producing between them, directly through the revelation of God, the 'straight path' which reached completion in Muhammad himself.

The five pillars of Islam represent the essential supports of the Muslim belief and faith: they are the creed (*kalima*), prayer (*salat*), charity and almsgiving (*zakat*), fasting (*saum*) and pilgrimage (*hajj*). The creed of Islam is simple, straightforward, and memorable – 'There is no god but Allah, and Muhammad is his prophet'. Compared with the intricacies and complexities of some of the formulated Christian creeds, such a simple statement of belief must inevitably prove attractive to societies which are themselves, for the most part, uncomplicated in thought and structure.

The Koran admonishes the faithful to 'be constant in prayer' (21), in order that he may submit himself perpetually to Allah's will, and that he may keep the whole of his life in a proper perspective. The Muslim must pray five times a day – on rising, at noon, in the mid-afternoon, at sunset and before retiring. These acts of devotion and worship may take place anywhere, although the devotee is required, if possible, to wash first and then kneel (usually on a small prayer-mat) facing Mecca, and with his forehead touching the ground. It is clear that this demand can create problems in a society which is foreign to the worshipper, upon whom there are other pressures of study or work in community with non-Muslims. This is largely a question of accommodation on both sides, and where there are groups of Muslims working or studying together special arrange-ments can usually be made so that prayers may go on uninterrupted. Nevil Shute has provided us with a picture of some of the problems that may arise in a multi-racial community, and also some of the possible means of adaptation and integration; for prayer is not just an isolated ritual but a full participation in life's activity (22). Wherever possible noon prayers are held collectively in a mosque on the holy day of Islam, which is Friday; the Koran is also recited corporately by the congregation. A sermon is usually provided by an *imam*, who is the leader of the mosque and responsible for the organization of both worship and religious teaching, but who is in no sense regarded as a priest or intermediary between Allah and mortal man. Muslims are called to prayer by the *muezzin*, or proclaimer, who climbs the slender turret of the mosque, and cries out:

> God is most great!
> God is most great!
> I witness that there is no god but Allah.
> I witness that Muhammad is the apostle of Allah.
> Arise and pray; arise and pray.
> God is great;
> There is no god but Allah!

Charity and almsgiving are a very strong feature of the Muslim religion, and to some extent obligatory upon all believers. This compulsory form of almsgiving is assessed by Islamic canon law as being $2\frac{1}{2}$ per cent of a man's annual income in money or in kind. Like everything else in religion, or in life generally, almsgiving is open to abuse. If it is more blessed to give than to receive there will always be those beggars and scroungers only too willing to assist others to be 'blessed' by the simple acceptance of their offerings. But the sometimes wearing and wearying cult of *baksheesh*, whereby the beggar seeks by persistent importuning and harassment to cajole others into giving him alms 'for the love of Allah', is a complete perversion of the Koranic desire to assist those in need; and certainly the Muslim pillar of *zakat* should not be judged by those who abuse it.

The fourth pillar is that of fasting which is obligatory on all Muslims during the holy month of Ramadan, the month during which, so it is said, the Koran was revealed to Muhammad. All devotees must, during the hours between sunrise and sunset of every day of Ramadan, abstain from all forms of food and drink. The only exceptions to this are those Muslims who are ill or on a journey; they are excused but must still make up the time later on with fasting. Again, there will always be those who will abuse a religious injunction: some will inevitably turn the night into day, and during the hours of darkness feast and make merry and be unfit for work during the daytime. No one would suggest, however, that such people are the norm; and when one reflects upon the incredible heat and aridity of most Muslim countries one can only marvel at the self-restraint and self-sacrifice during the hours of light.

Once in a lifetime the devout Muslim is expected to perform a pilgrimage to Mecca. Some followers save up for this experience during the whole of their life; others walk hundreds of miles in order to fulfil what is not merely a religious requirement but also a heart's desire. The richer Muslims may, however, travel by bus, car, plane or ship in order to get as close as possible to their final destination. Some of the poorer Muslims may sell themselves into slavery for the rest of their lives in order to see the birthplace of their prophet, and to touch and kiss the Black Stone in the wall of the Kaaba. As he reaches Mecca each pilgrim has to change into two simple robes so that all worshippers appear equal before Allah. Many pilgrims also visit the tomb of Muhammad at Medina, and some go on to the Dome of the Rock on the site of the old Jewish temple in Jerusalem.

E SOME GENERAL IDEAS AND DEVELOPMENTS IN ISLAM
Before the time of Muhammad there was considerable intertribal warfare and violence; Muhammad brought unification and peace to the Arab peoples. It is true to say that, before Muhammad became the founder and leader of the Islamic faith, women were regarded as mere chattels and baby girls were frequently buried alive as sacrifices to the *djinns* that terrified the superstitious Arabs. The reforms which Muhammad introduced considerably improved the general social and legal status of women, and the sacrifice of baby girls was forbidden. There has been a great deal of misunderstanding about the Muslim attitude to women, and it must be emphasized that Muhammad sought to protect both the institution of marriage and also the position of women. Anyone who is in doubt about his official attitude, at least, should carefully read *sura* 4 of the Koran, entitled 'Women'.

Muhammad lived in the midst of a polygamous society, and the reforms he introduced were not calculated to transform that society completely, but rather to stabilize it and to mitigate its worst evils. The rich sheiks bought up as many women as they could for wives, concubines and slaves; many poor men were unable to find a wife. Certainly there was a considerable anxiety among men to produce male heirs, and Muhammad himself experienced something of this anxiety; male children were delicate and frequently died in infancy, leaving a surplus of women. Muhammad accepted polygamy, but he prescribed a limitation to it; a man might have up to four wives at any one time, but no more (23). He himself was an exception to this rule, and eventually he had nine wives before he died, but no male heir survived him. He gave, however, a certain dignity to marriage and a regulation to divorce and female inheritance. In a time of considerable moral laxity he made adultery an offence punishable by death. The state of *purdah*, or separation, was introduced into the Muslim homes not in order to demean the position of women, but rather in order to elevate it and to protect them from the lecherous advances of men and the widespread promiscuity of his day. Similarly the *yashmak*, or veil worn by Muslim women in public, was conceived largely as a protection for women from the lustful eyes of men. Today, where eastern societies have had the full impact of culture-contact with the West, both *purdah* and the veil are increasingly regarded as male instruments of domination and subjugation: and many Muslim societies are slowly emancipating themselves from these customs.

Muhammad, who must have acquired considerable wealth during his lifetime, felt that acquisitiveness should be balanced by compassion for the failure and poverty of others. He had been brought up in a world of extremes – extreme wealth and extreme poverty. He taught that every Muslim was a brother to every other Muslim, and that one should help another within the Faith in every way possible. Where there was obvious need, any required capital should be loaned to a brother, whilst any interest taken should be reasonable and on business loans only. It is perhaps noteworthy that each of the hundred and fourteen *suras* of the Koran, save only the ninth, begins with the statement, 'In the Name of Allah, the Compassionate, the Merciful'; and even the ninth, which is preoccupied with repentance, making war on unbelievers, and the punishments of hell-fire, even the ninth states that 'Allah is the Forgiving One, the Merciful'. It is this compassion and mercy that the Muslim is enjoined to show towards all members of the Islamic brotherhood.

Much has been made of the concept of the *jihad*, or holy war, in the religion of Islam, particularly, it need hardly be said, by the enemies of this religion. Certainly a holy war is enjoined by the Koran, which says

'Fight for the sake of Allah those that fight against you, but do not attack them first. Allah does not love the aggressors' (24).

This would seem to regard the *jihad* as a purely defensive measure, and to some extent this view is supported by other passages which appear to suggest that there should be no compulsion in religion (25), and even that there may be room for more than one religion (26). But other passages equally seem to support more aggressive opposition (27). Muslim scholars themselves have denied that their record of intolerance is in any degree greater than that of other major world religions. It is certainly not a very profitable exercise to attempt to weigh the atrocities of one religion against another. If we were writing at the moment an account of the main principles of Christianity instead of those of Islam, we would certainly not elaborate on such things as the pogroms against the Jews by 'Christian' societies, or the activities of the Spanish Inquisition against heretics. The *jihad* was undoubtedly originally conceived as a means of self-defence against those who would destroy the disciples of revealed truth; that it has since been used for territorial conquest or as a political weapon in no way nullifies the original truths of the religion defended or propagated by such means. And if it should be used in the future in such a way, it could no more claim the sanction of Muhammad than the thumb-screw, rack or Crusader's sword could claim the *imprimatur* of Christ.

There are some general teachings of interest which must receive mention here. Muslims are buried in an upright position, which certainly proves economical of space in the crowded Muslim burial grounds. There is a strong belief that the resurrection is a physical event which will take place in the future, and that each individual will literally rise up and stand upon the earth (28). The belief in the resurrection of the body was not accepted by the early Hebrews, but it seems to have been a somewhat late development during the Diaspora or Jewish Dispersion. Certainly the influence of Persian Zoroastrian belief can be detected here, and it was a tenet of the Pharisaic belief in the time of Jesus, although the Sadducees strongly rejected it. Muhammad's own acceptance of it was initially ridiculed.

The doctrine of the Holy Spirit in Islam is somewhat difficult to delineate. The Koran implies that the Spirit of God was breathed into Mary in order that the virgin might conceive Jesus (29). This was an inbreathing of God similar to that whereby Adam was produced (30). Indeed, the Hebrew word used in the Old Testament for the Spirit of God is *ruach*, which means 'breath' or 'wind'. There is certainly no belief among the Muslims of a separate person or being involved in the concept of God's Spirit or the Holy Spirit; it is simply a dynamic emanation of God in his act of creation, for Allah is always and only one God. Guillaume argues that the Muslim doctrine of God in philosophical theology is not so far removed from the Christian system until the crucial dogma of the Trinity is broached. He says:

'The day may come when Muslims and Christians will realize that they have so much in common that they need no longer regard one another with suspicion and dislike' (31).

No doubt if one looks for common ground there is much in the basic principles of Islam and Christianity that can form the foundation of both agreement and further dialogue – if only the spirit is willing.

F THE SPREAD OF ISLAM

It is, of course, impossible here to tell the full story of the growth and spread of the Muslim faith, and this is not in any case the purpose of this section. We are concerned ultimately with Islam as a part of the religio-cultural background of the Pakistanis. After his death, in AD 632, Muhammad was succeeded by his faithful friend and father-in-law, Abu Bakr, who had also been one of his first converts. Abu Bakr was elected *khalifa* (caliph), which means a lieutenant, deputy or successor. He immediately made his position felt by participating in punitive campaigns

11. *Top:* The Pakistani Secretariat, Rawalpindi, (*bottom*) Medical College for Women, Lahore.

12. The Badshahi Mosque, Lahore, built by the Emperor Aurangzeb Alangir in 1672.

against those tribes which refused to pay their taxes. Once Arabia had been firmly reunited under the flag of Islam, the trained and drilled Muslim troops looked farther afield, and gradually Babylonia, Syria, Palestine, Byzantium and Persia became subject to the Arab peoples. Then when Egypt and North Africa fell into Muslim hands, many more converts to Islam were made, although it is important here to emphasize that no great intolerance was expressed towards those who were members of Judaism or Christianity, that is, the 'peoples of the Book'.

Despite their own internal rifts and religious divisions, the Arab armies very soon crossed into Spain in AD 711, and then entered France where, in AD 732, they were driven back from Tours by Charles Martel who defeated them at Poitiers. This has always been regarded as one of the most decisive battles of history in that the proselytizing powers of Islam, which might well have converted the whole of Europe to the Muslim faith, were frustrated. This, however, seems a somewhat unlikely possibility when one views in perspective the actual attitude of the Arabs to the Jews and Christians they had conquered elsewhere. In the event, the Arab armies retired into Spain where they had a considerable cultural influence until the fifteenth century. Scholars from all over Europe migrated to Spain in order to study philosophy, medicine, mathematics and astronomy.

At the time when the Muslims were being driven back by Martel in France, other Muslim armies were successfully moving eastwards into India and even as far as China. Later, during the sixteenth century, the Moguls drove south into the sub-continent of India through the Afghan passes, and were successful in subjugating the Indian population in some of the most fertile land of the peninsula. There was some strife between the Muslim and Hindu religions from this time, but the Emperor Akbar (who ruled from 1556 to 1605) made a personal study of all the great religions and, although a Muslim himself, he declared an open policy of toleration. To some extent he attempted to do at the more political level what Kabir (1440–1518) and Nanak (1469–1539) had sought to accomplish at the purely religious level. After the reign of Akbar there was some degeneration in the Mogul court, and what began very reasonably as religious tolerance ended in a toleration of incredibly loose moral behaviour. During the later reign of the Emperor Aurangzeb (1658–1707) manpower and wealth were wantonly wasted on grandiose schemes for the conquest of the whole of southern India.

Eventually India was taken over by the British, who first obtained a foothold there through the activities of the East India Company which was formed in 1600. From the year 1784 the British Government supervised all the political activities which the East India Company undertook, and men who had been selected from outside the company's service were appointed as governors-general. After the Indian Mutiny, which broke out in 1857,

N

and after order had been restored by the middle of 1858, British rule was at last accepted by the population. The East India Company now came to an end and the British Government took over direct administration. In 1879 Queen Victoria was proclaimed Empress of India.

It was in the 1930s in the midst of considerable political argument, aggravated by mutual Muslim and Hindu jealousy, and mildly accompanied by the sweet reasonableness of Mahatma Gandhi's principle of *satyagraha*, the force of spiritual love or 'passive resistance', that Jinnah, leader of the Muslims, first proposed a scheme to protect those provinces which were predominantly Muslim. This was the concept of Pakistan, a word meaning the 'Land of the Pure'. When the partition of India was eventually effected in 1947 the 'Land of the Pure' was established; and it consisted of two widely separated areas of land: West Pakistan in which Urdu is spoken, and East Pakistan whose language is mainly Bengali. The force which binds two such distant lands together is a common acceptance of monotheistic, Islamic faith.

G SOME ASPECTS OF ISLAM

One of the outstanding features of the Koran is its continual insistence upon not only the unity of Allah but also the essential unity of true religion.

'Therefore stand firm in your devotion to the true faith, which Allah himself has made, and for which He has made man. Allah's creation cannot be changed. This is surely the true religion, although most men do not know it. Turn to Allah and fear Him. Be steadfast in prayer and serve no other god besides Him. Do not split up your religion into sects, each exulting in its own beliefs' (32).

But it is unrealistic to expect any religion to have absolute unity, for it is not in man's nature to accept everything of a spiritual character without criticism or personal interpretation. Islam is no exception to this. We cannot describe here all the sects that have developed in Islam; but the main division is that between the Sunnis, who represent something like 80 per cent of the Muslims, and the Shias.

The Sunnis are the orthodox who follow the path or tradition recording the practice of the prophet Muhammad. These followers accept the first four caliphs as rightly guided, and Ali is regarded by them as the last of their legitimate caliphs. On the other hand, the Shias are the partisans of Ali and regard him as the first of the *imams*, or leaders. From Ali to Al Mahdi, who was born in Samarra in AD 880, there were altogether twelve imams. Al Mahdi, the twelfth, is said to have disappeared in his youth but did not die, and he remains as the 'hidden imam' who will return at the appointed time to establish a reign of purity and righteousness. These

Shias are known as the 'Twelvers' because of their belief in twelve imams. There are also, however, the 'Seveners' who believe that seven imams have existed and that the last was called Ismail. The latter is also believed to have disappeared, but he will eventually return and rule over the earth. The Twelvers are today a strong group in Iran, Yemen, Iraq, Syria and Pakistan; the Seveners, or Ismailis, are found in parts of Africa, Asia and the sub-continent of India where they are referred to as Khojas. The latter sub-group of the Ismailis, in particular, pay tithes to the Aga Khan who is their spiritual head, and who makes good use of the money in providing his people with schools and other social amenities. The disappearing, 'hidden' imams and their ultimate self-revelation or return underline the fundamental yearning of man for some supernatural or extra-natural means of redemption from his present unhappy or unfulfilled state. There is hardly any major religion which does not, in one of its forms or sects, anticipate the return of a messiah, imam, avatar or buddha.

The Assassins (*Hashishis*) were an offshoot of the Ismailis, and some are still to be found in small numbers in East Africa, India and Pakistan. At the time of the Crusades they used to drug themselves with hashish and then, in a completely abandoned manner, would set upon their enemies and destroy them. Their leader was referred to as the Old Man of the Mountains. Another sub-sect were the Druzes, who derived their name from their leader, Darazi, during the eleventh century. Darazi supported the claims of a certain Al Hakim to divinity, and when the latter mysteriously disappeared it was held that he would eventually return in some future age. Today the Druzes are little more than a minor secret society with an esoteric teaching which, according to Guillaume, makes their connection with Islam 'little more than nominal' (33).

The most recently formed sect of Muslims is that represented by the Ahmadiyya movement. In 1890 a Punjabi called Ghulam Ahmad made a claim to be the Islamic Mahdi, the Christian Messiah, and the Hindu Avatar, Krishna. Not surprisingly the Ahmadiyyans are not regarded as orthodox Muslims. When Ghulam Ahmad died in 1908 the sect split into two groups, one with its headquarters at Qadian in India, and the other at Lahore in Pakistan. The Ahmadiyyans are thus today represented by the Qadianis, who regard Ahmad as a prophet, and who have founded a mosque in this country at Southfields in London; and by the Seceders, to whom Ahmad is merely a reformer, and who have established a mosque at Woking in Surrey.

It is interesting to note that out of Islam, one of the most transcendent of religions, there has arisen one of the most absolute and profound forms of mysticism that the world has ever produced. The devotees of this mysticism derived their name from the cloak or habit of white wool (*suf*) which they wore.

'Because of their clothes and manner of life they are called Sufis, for they did not put on raiment soft to touch or beautiful to behold; they only clothed themselves in order to hide their nakedness, contenting themselves with rough haircloth and coarse wool' (34).

The Sufis lived an ascetic life of meditation, prayer and poverty. They believed in the unity of Allah, but Allah comprised all beings, all existence; and at least one of their members, Al Hallaj, was put to death for blasphemy when, in AD 922, he was crucified for saying, 'I am the Truth.' The Sufis, however, have always claimed that their view of God, and of his immanence and omnipresence, is well represented in the Koran where God reveals that

'*We* created man. We knew the promptings of his soul, and are closer to him than the vein of his neck' (35).

Man has already a union with God in which his immortality is assured, and in which all the souls, emanations and incarnations from God are finally one. And although his origin may be found in Islam, the Sufi himself is at home in all religions where the individual is permitted to develop a personal relationship with God. That personal relationship has been expressed by such mystics as Jalalud-din Rumi (1207–73), Farid al-din 'Attar (born 1119), Muhammad al-Ghazali (1059–1111) and Muhammad Iqbal of Lahore (1876–1938). 'Attar concluded his great poem entitled 'The Conference of the Birds' with an expression of the ultimate unification of the individual soul and Allah:

> Come you lost atoms, to your Centre draw,
> And *be* the Eternal Mirror that you saw;
> Rays that have wandered into darkness wide,
> Return, and back into your Sun subside (36).

REFERENCES

1 Guillaume, A., *Islam* (Penguin, 2nd edition 1956), p. 2.
2 Ibid., p. 12.
3 Ibid., p. 23.
4 *Vide* Isaiah 40, verses 6–8 (A.V.).
5 The Koran, *sura* 96.
6 Guillaume, A., op. cit., p. 40.
7 Ibid., p. 201.
8 The Koran, *sura* 9. The passage reads: 'Fight those who do not believe in Allah, and do not forbid what God and his apostle have forbidden, and do not follow the true religion of those to whom scriptures were given, until

they pay tribute out of hand, and are utterly subdued. The Jews say that Ezra is the son of Allah, while the Christians say that the Christ is the son of Allah. . . . May Allah confound them; how perverse they are!'

9 Morgan, K. W. (ed.), *Islam – The Straight Path: Islam Interpreted by Muslims*, article by Mohammed Abd Allah (Ronald Press, N.Y., 1958), p. 40.

10 The Koran, *sura* 6.

11 Ibid., *sura* 4.

12 Ibid., *sura* 76.

13 Ibid., *sura* 74.

14 Ibid., *sura* 10.

15 *Vide* Numbers 22, v. 22; Judges 9, v. 23; I Samuel 16, verses 14, 15, 23; II Samuel 24, verses 1 ff; I Kings 22, verses 19 ff; Isaiah 45, v. 7 ('I form light and I make darkness; I make peace and I create evil.' – Moffatt's translation).

16 *Vide* Romans, 8, verses 28–30.

17 *Vide* Genesis 3, v. 15; John 14, v. 16.

18 *Vide* II Corinthians 12, v. 2.

19 *Vide* Isaiah 1, v. 2.

20 The Koran, *sura* 81.

21 Ibid., *sura* 29.

22 *Vide* Shute, Nevil, *Round the Bend* (Pan Books Ltd, 1968), pp. 63, 107–14 *et passim*.

23 *Vide* the Koran, *sura* 4.

24 Ibid., *sura* 2.

25 Ibid., *sura* 2 ('There shall be no compulsion in religion').

26 Ibid., *sura* 109 ('Unto you your religion, and unto me my religion').

27 Ibid., *sura* 9 ('Will you not fight against those who have broken their oaths and conspired to banish the apostle?').

28 Ibid., *sura* 75.

29 Ibid., *sura* 21 ('We breathed into her who was chaste Our Spirit, and we made both her and her son a sign to all men').

30 Ibid., *sura* 15 ('And when I have made him a complete man and breathed into him my spirit, fall down prostrating yourselves before him').

31 Guillaume, A., op. cit., p. 199.

32 The Koran, *sura* 30.

33 Guillaume, A., op. cit., p. 125.

34 Abu Bakr al-Kalabadhi, *The Doctrine of the Sufis*, translated by A. J. Arberry (C.U.P., 1935), p. 6. (The writer lived in the tenth century AD.)

35 The Koran, *sura* 50.

36 Happold, F. C., *Mysticism* (Penguin, 1963), p. 232.

BIBLIOGRAPHY

Ali, Ameer, *The Spirit of Islam* (Christophers, 1922).

Andrae, Tor, *Mohammed: The Man and his Faith* (Scribner's Sons, 1936).

Arberry, A. J., *Doctrine of the Sufis* (C.U.P., 1935).

Arberry, A. J., *Sufism* (Allen & Unwin, 1950).

Arberry, A. J., *The Koran Interpreted* (Allen & Unwin, 1955).

Arberry, A. J. *et al.*, *Islam Today* (Faber, 1943).

Arnold, T. W. and Guillaume, A. (eds.), *The Legacy of Islam* (O.U.P., 1931).

Cragg, K., *The Call of the Minaret* (O.U.P., 1956).

Cragg, K., *Sandals at the Mosque* (S.C.M., 1959).

Dawood, N. J. (tr.), *The Koran* (Penguin, 3rd revised edition 1968).

Gibb, H. A. R., *Mohammedanism* (O.U.P., 1964).

Guillaume, A., *The Life of Muhammad* (O.U.P., 1955).

Guillaume, A., *Islam* (Penguin, 2nd edition 1956).

Happold, F. C., *Mysticism* (Penguin, 1963).

Iqbal, Mohammed, *The Reconstruction of Religious Thought in Islam* (O.U.P., 1934).

Jurji, E. J., *Illumination in Islamic Mysticism* (Princeton Univ. Press, 1938).

Mahmud, S. F., *The Story of Islam* (O.U.P., 1965).

Margoliouth, D. S., *The Early Development of Mohammedanism* (O.U.P., 1914).

Nicholson, R. A., *The Mystics of Islam* (Routledge, 1963).

Parrinder, G., *Jesus in the Qur'an* (Faber, 1965).

Pickthall, M., *The Meaning of the Glorious Koran* (Allen & Unwin, 1930).

Rodwell, J. M. (tr.), *The Koran* (Everyman Library, J. M. Dent, 1909).

Smith, W. Cantwell, *Islam in Modern History* (Princeton Univ. Press, 1957).

Spencer, S., *Mysticism in World Religion* (Penguin, 1963).

Tritton, A. S., *Islam* (Hutchinson's Univ. Lib., 1966).

Verhoeven, F. R. J., *Islam, its Origin and Spread* (Routledge, 1962).

Watt, W. M., *Muhammad at Mecca* (Clarendon Press, Oxford, 1926).

Chapter 13

Social Background
of the Pakistanis

A THE MUSLIM WAY OF LIFE

In speaking of the social background of the Pakistanis it must be re-membered that we are not dealing with a homogeneous group of people living in the same general area and all speaking precisely the same language. We are concerned with two main groups of people living about a thousand miles apart. As far as immigrants to our own society are concerned, in West Pakistan we are thinking in terms of the refugee areas of the Punjab and Kashmir, and also of the North-West Frontier and Mirpur. In East Pakistan we are specifically considering groups in the Sylhet region bordering on Assam, and some of the maritime areas of East Pakistan. Thus we are, in fact, thinking of a variety of people including Pathans, Kashmiris, Punjabis and Bengalis whose only common denominator is that they are Muslims.

In Chapter 12 we described, in somewhat general terms, the main religion of Pakistan, namely Islam; and we are now concerned to discuss some of the implications of that religion for the Pakistani way of life. The social customs and structure of Pakistan derive from its religion and spiritual aspirations just as much as the Indian social format is ultimately based upon Hindu belief and culture. Islam is essentially the religion of submission and acceptance; and the submission of the Muslim Pakistanis is primarily to Allah, and to the teaching of Allah as mediated through Muhammad in the Koran.

This Islamic teaching involves an entire way of life and code of be-haviour that has, in many respects, remained virtually unchanged for centuries. The social aspects and ideals of the Koran are regarded by the great majority as still binding upon strict Muslims. Indeed, in their schools the Muslims are so imbued with their 'Holy Writ' from a very early age that the possibility of opposing its code scarcely occurs to them. Its very sounds, syllables and cadences have been beaten into their bodies by their mentors until its every letter has been seared into their memories, if not into their souls. The words of Allah are not merely 'religious' words in some remote spiritual sense; they are words that apply to the whole of life, to both the social and domestic economy, to eating and drinking habits as well as articles of dress.

There is always, inevitably, a hiatus between the ideal and the actual, between what is believed and required and what is, in fact, done. There is nothing unique about the Pakistani society in this respect; in our own society, for example, we believe very firmly (we say) in the equality of men and women, but we are still slow to accept that principle of equality in every aspect of our professional, economic and domestic life.

There can be no doubt that Muhammad's teaching did a great deal to improve the lot of women in Arab society, as indeed he intended it should do. But one cannot help wondering about the 'liberal teachings of Islam' to which Dr Farrukh Hashmi refers in the following passage:

'The position of women in the Moslem home has been a source of great confusion and controversy because the liberal teachings of Islam have at times been misinterpreted or ignored by the cultural patterns of the Middle East tradition and Arab tribal customs' (1).

And Dr Hashmi goes on further to assert that according to Islam a woman should not be ill-treated, and that in Muslim law men and women are accepted as equal.

The Koran, however, does not altogether support this judgement of a liberal Islamic attitude, to the extent of equality between men and women. In the *sura* entitled 'The Cow' in the Koran, it states quite explicitly that women shall with justice possess rights similar to those exercised against them, but that men, nevertheless, 'have a status above women' (2). In another *sura*, entitled 'Women', there is quite clearly a much more forgiving attitude towards men who 'commit indecency' than towards women who 'commit fornication'. In the case of the men, if they repent and 'mend their ways' they are allowed to go because 'Allah is forgiving and merciful'. But in the case of the women, on the testimony of four witnesses, they are to be confined to their houses 'till death overtakes them or till Allah finds another way for them' (3).

The relative position of men and women is, however, expressed quite explicitly in the following statement from the same *sura*:

'Men have authority over women because Allah has made the one superior to the other, and because they spend their wealth to maintain them. Good women are obedient. They guard their unseen parts because Allah has guarded them. As for those from whom you fear disobedience, admonish them and send them to beds apart and beat them. Then if they obey you, take no further action against them' (4).

Women are thus regarded by the Koran as inferior to men, and the one virtue demanded of them is that of obedience, failing which there is divine sanction for beating them. Indeed, the above Koranic statement is about as 'liberal' as that of St Paul in his 'Letter to the Ephesians', where he admonishes wives to be subject to their husbands, since the husband is the head of the wife just as Christ is the head of the church; 'so wives are to be subject to their husbands in every respect' (5). It must be admitted, however, that despite this general acceptance of man's superiority, there is throughout the Koran a protective attitude towards women and a rejection of their exploitation.

There is also in the Koran an implicit acceptance of the owning of slaves, and nowhere is it suggested that such ownership is wrong. There is, however, no justification in the Koranic code for the maltreatment of slaves; in fact all its admonitions are to the contrary. Kindness – the same sort of kindness – is to be shown towards parents, kindred, orphans, the needy, near and distant neighbours, fellow-travellers, wayfarers, 'and to the slaves whom you own' (6). This fact is mentioned in this section, not because it is suggested that there is any form of slavery in Pakistan, but to emphasize the liberal extension of the concept of 'kindness' within the Koran. Indeed, the whole passage referred to suggests that the bounty which Allah has bestowed upon his children is something that must be shared with all men, whatever their class, colour or station in life. Almsgiving, or *zakat*, is due from every Muslim, and all are exhorted to 'give generously for the cause of Allah' because Allah loves the charitable (7). This sense of obligation towards his neighbour is felt as strongly among the Pakistanis as among any other Muslim group.

Much of the Muslim way of life is misrepresented in people's minds because of their own prejudices and antipathies which they bring to any consideration of it. For example, there is nothing odd about the fact of food tabus in eastern societies, for such tabus exist in all societies including our own. We are not particularly partial to snakes, frogs, horse-flesh or lizard soup, but there are some societies where these 'delicacies' are enjoyed. Similarly, a large number of people in our society consume bacon for breakfast or ham for lunch, but many societies, including both Jewish and Muslim, forbid the consumption of swine's flesh in any shape or form. The Koran says:

'Eat of the good lawful things which Allah has bestowed on you and give thanks for His favours if you truly serve Him. He has forbidden you the flesh of beasts that die a natural death, blood, and pig's meat; also any flesh consecrated in the name of any but Allah. But whoever is constrained to eat of it without intending to be a rebel or transgressor, will find Allah forgiving and merciful' (8).

An earlier *sura* makes a slight addition to this tabu by forbidding the flesh of animals which have been strangled, beaten or gored to death, killed by a fall or mangled by beasts of prey; nor are followers allowed to kill game when they are on a pilgrimage (9).

Such food tabus are obviously important to remember when inviting a Muslim Pakistani to a meal. But it is also important to note that, according to the Koran, the mere consumption of pig's flesh or meat offered to idols does not constitute for the Muslim a mortal sin: it is the inner intention that matters. The Muslim food tabu list compares very favourably with the long list presented, for example, to the orthodox Jew in the Old Testament book of Leviticus (10). There is, however, one thing that an orthodox Muslim will not drink: that is any liquor containing alcohol (11); this tabu is observed by most Muslims in Pakistan, particularly those untouched by city life or uninfluenced by western ways. The staple diet of East Pakistanis consists of fish, rice and vegetables, whilst that of West Pakistanis is mainly wheat, maize and milk. When eating, all Muslims use the right hand only since the left hand is used for the less dignified necessities of life.

Most of the Pakistanis with whom we are concerned in the context of immigration are involved in some form of agriculture. They are labourers who, in the main, come from small villages in the areas already mentioned; some of them work as joint farmers on the larger farms, or as small peasant proprietors, or simply as labourers on farms belonging to others. They have very little in the way of industry, except some traditional cottage weaving and handicrafts, and their general economy is extremely weak. There is a very wide gulf between the educated Pakistanis, who are almost English in tradition after having studied at schools and universities based on the English model, and the uneducated Pakistani workers, who know no English and who are insulated from all western concepts by their orthodox Islamic upbringing. The life of the latter centres upon the Koran, the mosque, daily prayers, the giving (or receiving) of alms, and the month-long fast of Ramadan.

The general poverty and low standard of living of the areas from which the Pakistani immigrants come has led in the past to a fair amount of mobility, particularly on the part of the Mirpuris and Sylhetis. There is a long-standing tradition among these peoples of sending their younger sons to India and overseas, both east and west, in order to earn money to send back home and help to raise the living standard of their families, at least above the famine level (12). Thus, emigration is by no means a new experience for these areas; it is simply one that has become intensified since the problems and difficulties which have arisen from the Partition in 1947 and its after-effects.

B THE EXTENDED FAMILY

The Muslim way of life involves also, of course, the whole structure of family life, and in Pakistan this structure is very similar to that found among the Hindus of India. The family is of the extended type, comprising the nuclear element of husband, wife and children and, in addition, all the male descendants in the father's line, including their families. This can obviously mean a very large community or kin-group; but it also means a solid economic unit in which all the working members are contributing to the life necessities of the group. Such a situation has obvious advantages in that, despite the fact that those who earn more have to share with those who earn less, there is a modicum of security within the unit against the incidence of sickness and unemployment. The solidarity of the extended family, or kin-group, is more than an insurance against death, disease and old age – although of course it is that – it is a spiritual and social bond which provides a sense of identity for a particular group of people in the face of all problems, oppositions, successes or failures.

There is a prevalent misconception among people in the west that all Muslim peoples are polygamous. The fact is, however, that a steadily decreasing number of males from Islamic countries marry, or can afford to marry, more than one woman. Although the Koran certainly permits a man to have up to four wives at any one time, there are certain admonitions about the capacity of the husband to look after them all properly, with a sense of fairness and the maintenance of equality among them (13). Yet Muhammad, who had nine wives, apart from slave-girls, realized fully the human problem of treating all wives in the same way, and he suggested that it would make it easier for a man to avoid injustice if he married only one. Indeed, he adds with not a little pathos, 'Try as you may, you cannot treat all your wives impartially' (14). This may not be divine revelation, but at least it sounds like very accurate human experience. As far as the citizens of Pakistan are concerned, a man may marry a second wife only with the approval of his first wife, and with the express permission of a court.

Farrukh Hashmi has suggested that polygamy

'is designed to keep society morally healthy in abnormal conditions, such as prolonged wars, to prevent prostitution when there is a shortage of men or perhaps to prevent children being registered as illegitimate' (15).

This appears to be, however, something of a retrospective rationalization of the situation. The *limitation* upon polygamy imposed by Muhammad was undoubtedly an attempt, and a reasonable attempt, by the prophet to make more women of marriageable age available to young men who, in the seventh century AD in Arabia, were finding it very difficult to procure mates. The reason for this was that the rich sheiks had actually cornered the 'woman' market, not merely for wives and concubines to fill their harems, but also for traffic in slave-girls to fill the harems of others. The fact is that women were regarded as things, as chattels, as a form of capital and currency. No amount of justification of polygamy on other grounds can obliterate the view of womanhood that both gave it birth and kept it alive.

The history of polygamy, or more accurately here 'polygyny', is very much older than the time of Muhammad and the development of Islam, and appears to derive basically from a variety of causes: man's great anxiety to obtain a male heir, the imbalance between the numbers of men and women, man's natural concupiscence, and his need to find an attractive and universal form of currency. There are other causes, but we are not here concerned to detail them all – merely to point out that polygamy was not a rational, artificially designed institution created to solve certain social evils.

From very ancient times when the first wife was unsuccessful in the production of a male heir, or any children at all, another woman might be chosen to take her place in the role of child-bearing. When Sarah, for example, failed to provide an heir for Abraham he took her servant girl, Hagar the Egyptian, as a second wife and she gave birth to Ishmael (16). Certainly there is little evidence that polygamy was 'designed to keep society morally healthy in abnormal conditions'. In fact, in Islam itself it has always existed in normal conditions, and as the equal rights of women are more and more accepted so polygamy will have less and less excuse for existing.

Max Weber has taken a somewhat extreme view of Islam in relation to slavery and polygamy, although no doubt his position can still be defended in some areas where Islam is, or has been, supreme. He states that

'Islam displays other characteristics of a distinctively feudal spirit: the obviously unquestioned acceptance of slavery, serfdom, and polygamy; the disesteem for and subjection of women. . . .' (17).

Certainly the Government of Pakistan does not accept unquestioningly slavery and serfdom, and even the institution of polygamy is becoming less acceptable than it was. Moreover, the Government's demand for 'a break-through in women's education' is a clear recognition that the former 'disesteem for and subjection of women' is no longer tolerable (18).

It has sometimes been suggested that divorce is easily obtained in the Muslim world, and that a man has only to say three times to his wife, 'I divorce you,' in front of witnesses and it is a *fait accompli*. But this is not quite true, and certainly does not work out like this in practice. In the Koran there are three *suras* which speak explicitly of divorce: *sura* 2 entitled 'The Cow', *sura* 4 on 'Women', and *sura* 65 which is headed 'Divorce'. Islam is anxious by every means possible to retain a marriage intact, and to this end, if there is any danger of a break-up, the Koran states:

'If you fear a breach between a man and his wife, appoint an arbiter from his people and another from hers. If they wish to be reconciled Allah will bring them together again' (19).

The 'arbiter' here is acting as a sort of marriage guidance counsellor, and the above-quoted *sura* appears to put the emphasis where it inevitably resides in such issues, namely upon the desire of the two parties involved for reconciliation.

If, however, no reconciliation seems possible, or desired, the husband may go through the process of pronouncing divorce twice. This is revocable divorce, and according to the Koran after the renunciation there must be a waiting period of four months, during which time husband and wife will keep themselves apart. At the end of this time, if they change their mind, they may cohabit once more. If, however, the husband wishes to go through with the divorce he must now pronounce, for the third time, and in front of witnesses, 'I divorce you' (20). Once a man has divorced his wife he cannot take her back until after she has remarried and been divorced by her second husband. According to the Koran a woman cannot sue for divorce on any grounds (21); but in this respect matters have not stood still in Islam any more than in other religions or in societies with religious sanctions. According to Dr Farrukh Hashmi,

'Divorce is permitted in Islam on the grounds of adultery, incompatibility, impotence or wilfully neglecting to maintain one's wife and family. . . . In such an eventuality the children according to Moslem jurisprudence belong to the mother until the age of seven, although the father pays for their maintenance and the maintenance of the mother until she has remarried. After the child is seven the father has the right to claim his child and bring him up the way he wishes, provided that he does not deny the mother the right to visit at reasonable intervals' (22).

Thus, wilful neglect on the part of the husband may be a sound reason for a woman's suing for divorce. Adultery is a somewhat more problematic ground since it requires at least four eye-witnesses of the act, and the guilty parties must literally be caught *in flagrante delicto*.

Women are enjoined, both in the Koran and by common Islamic consent, to be modest in public and remain segregated as far as possible in the home. Here again, as with so many other Koranic injunctions, one accepts that the original intention was a sound one during a period of extreme licentiousness, when no woman alone in the company of a man was safe from sexual assault; and when any woman who displayed her charms in public was considered to be offering herself to any male bidder. *Purdah*, which means literally a 'curtain', was instituted in order to protect women against the lasciviousness of men. In fact, where the Koran refers to believers who visit the Prophet's home, it specifically enjoins them:

'If you ask his wives for anything, speak to them from behind a curtain. This is more chaste for your hearts and their hearts' (23).

In public, the pursuance of *purdah* takes the form of covering the female figure so that no flesh is showing; and a veil, or *yashmak*, is worn over most of the face (24). E. G. Parrinder comments that

'The status of women is one of the most important aspects of the Muslim way of life. Veiling is not prescribed in the Qur'an and is not practised in all Islamic countries, though some form of it exists in most of them. Most women in Pakistan still wear veils, though some of the younger ones wear very fetching nylon veils which reveal more than conceal' (25).

Reference 24 indicates that there is some mention of veiling in *sura* 33 of the Koran, where the Prophet is commanded to enjoin his wives and daughters and the wives of true believers 'to draw their veils close round them'. There are Muslim commentators who have, during the present century, suggested that the whole system of *purdah* and veiling was never intended by Muhammad to be more than a temporary measure, and there are clearly a number of Muslim societies which agree with this view.

In many Pakistani homes, however, the general principle of *purdah* still applies, and its only limitation is the actual accommodation available. Women are kept separate from the men, with their own living quarters and their own washing facilities. In many of the simpler homes *purdah* may quite literally be 'a curtain' concealing the women from the men. Women do not normally engage in leisure activities with their men-folk, but they gather their female relations and friends around them and discuss their family and personal problems. Men and women, even husbands and wives, are not expected to display affection in public, since this is regarded as offensive to public decency.

In the extended family the males are responsible for making provision for all its members; in practice, they will pool all their monetary resources and share any natural products of the land. A married woman becomes a member of her husband's kin-group or extended family, and is in all things subordinate to both her husband and, in particular, her husband's mother. Her role is realistically expressed by John Goodall in the following terms:

'In effect she becomes a contractual servant to her husband, satisfying his sexual desires, bearing and rearing his children, preparing his food, and arranging a good marriage partner for his children' (26).

The children are mainly the concern of the women, although the boys become more involved with the adult males after about the age of six or seven; whilst the girls will begin their involvement in *purdah* at about the same age and will mingle less with male members in the home. Young boys undergo the ritual of circumcision; and after a very rigorous study and learning of the Koran they will, during the years of puberty, go through a sort of *rite de passage* in which they will be expected to satisfy a Muslim teacher that they know the essential elements of Islamic faith.

Most Pakistani parents are anxious that their children should have a good education, but there is, at the same time, something ambivalent about their attitude. Boys are encouraged to help in the work in the fields when they are about eight years of age, so that there will inevitably be times when work is more important than school. The important event in a girl's life is marriage, which may take place at any time after she is about fifteen or sixteen. Until that time she may well be encouraged to go to school unless her mother desperately needs her help at home; but she will not receive much encouragement to become involved in higher education, unless there is the likelihood of her entering the teaching or the medical profession.

There is considerable concern among the Muslim Pakistanis to preserve the virginity of their daughters before their time of marriage. Should a girl prove not to be a virgin the marriage may become void. Once the marriage has been agreed upon between the parents concerned, and a 'dowry' fixed, the actual marriage ceremony is simple and soon completed. A magistrate will have carefully listed the bride's essential features before the wedding takes place in order to ensure that the bridegroom is getting the wife who was the subject of the contract. At the wedding the man who is betrothed will be asked 'Do you love her?', and the bride, 'Do you love him?'. If these questions are answered in the affirmative the marriage will have been completed. The 'dowry' is a sum of money which is provided by the bridegroom, or his family, as 'security money' for the bride, so that if the marriage breaks down she can claim it to help support her.

In the extended family there is considerable concern for the older members who are looked after by the younger ones. The Koran admonishes all the faithful to look after their elders:

'Show kindness to your parents, to your kinsfolk, to the orphans, and to the destitute. Exhort men to righteousness. Attend to your prayers and pay the alms-tax' (27).

The alms-tax is a form of welfare for the poor and needy and is represented by one-fortieth of an individual's income, which may be distributed in money or in kind. When an individual dies his property is divided among his heirs in a precise proportion, instructions concerning which are laid

208 / *The Background of Immigrant Children*

down in the Koran (28). Whilst Koranic law recognizes the rights of all dependants, male and female, it once more emphasizes male superiority: 'A male shall inherit twice as much as a female.' Although at first sight this may seem straightforward enough, there follows in *sura* 4 a more detailed description of individual forms of inheritance which is too long to reproduce here. There is, however, one telling paragraph in the middle of the inheritance laws:

'You may wonder whether your parents or your children are more beneficial to you. But this is the law of Allah; He is wise and all-knowing' (29).

Parents are beneficial in death in the sense that their children inherit; children are beneficial in life in the sense that they are an insurance for their parents against poverty and loneliness in old age. The village, tribal institution of the extended family provides in Pakistan a consciousness of unity and identity through many generations in both time and space. There may be, as Max Weber has suggested, 'characteristics of a distinctively feudal spirit' displayed by Islam; there may also, at the same time, be certain basically human elements in it which a fully technological society cannot hope to replace.

REFERENCES

1 Hashmi, F., *The Pakistani Family in Britain* (Community Relations Commission, 4th impression 1969), p. 7.
2 The Koran, *sura* 2.
3 Ibid., *sura* 4.
4 Ibid., *sura* 4.
5 *Vide* Ephesians 5, verses 22–4.
6 The Koran, *sura* 4.
7 Ibid., *sura* 2.
8 Ibid., *sura* 16.
9 Ibid., *sura* 5.
10 *Vide* Leviticus 11; cf. Deuteronomy 14.
11 The Koran, *sura* 5.
12 *Vide* Hashmi, F., op. cit., p. 5.
13 The Koran, *sura* 4.
14 Ibid., *sura* 4.
15 Hashmi, F., op. cit., p. 8.
16 *Vide* Genesis 16.
17 Weber, Max, *The Sociology of Religion* (Methuen, 1966), p. 264.
18 Ministry of Education and Scientific Research, *Proposals for a New Educational Policy* (Government of Pakistan, Islamabad, July 1969), p. 42, paras. 1–3.
19 The Koran, *sura* 4.
20 Ibid., *sura* 2.
21 *Vide* Guillaume, A., *Islam* (Penguin, 2nd revised edition 1956), p. 71.

22 Hashmi, F., op. cit., p. 7.
23 The Koran, *sura* 33.
24 *Vide* ibid., *sura* 33. 'Prophet, enjoin your wives, your daughters, and the wives of true believers to draw their veils close round them. That is more proper, so that they may be recognized and not molested.'
25 See the article by Parrinder, E. G., 'The Ethics and Customs of the Main Immigrant Peoples' in Hinnells, J. R. (ed.), *Comparative Religion in Education* (Oriel Press, 1970), p. 89.
26 Goodall, J., 'The Pakistani Background' in Oakley, R. (ed.), *New Backgrounds* (O.U.P., 1968), p. 78.
27 The Koran, *sura* 2.
28 Ibid., *sura* 4.
29 Ibid., *sura* 4.

BIBLIOGRAPHY

Davis, K., *The Population of India and Pakistan* (Princeton Univ. Press, 1950).
Eglar, Z., *A Punjabi Village in Pakistan* (Columbia Univ. Press, 1960).
Faridi, Begum Tazeen, *The Changing Role of Women in Pakistan* (Ferozesons Ltd, Karachi, 1962).
Gaudefroy-Demombynes, M., *Muslim Institutions* (Allen & Unwin, translated by John Macgregor, 1950).
Hashmi, F., *The Pakistani Family in Britain* (Community Relations Commission, 1969).
Hussain, A., *Pakistan, Its Ideology and Foreign Policy* (Cass, 1966).
Johnson, B. L. C., *How People Live in E. Pakistan* (Educational Supply Association, 1961).
Khan, A. M. *et al.*, *Young Pakistan* (O.U.P., 1951).
Levy, R., *The Social Structure of Islam* (C.U.P., 1957).
Oakley, R. (ed.), *New Backgrounds* (O.U.P., 1968), Chapter IV by John Goodall.
Qureshi, I. H., *The Pakistani Way of Life* (Heinemann, 1956).
Rushbrook Williams, L. F., *The State of Pakistan* (Faber, revised edition 1962).
Spain, J. W., *The Pathan Borderland* (Mouton, The Hague, 1963).
Spate, O. H. K., *India and Pakistan: A General and Regional Geography* (Methuen, 2nd edition 1957).
Stephens, I., *Pakistan: Old Country, New Nation* (Penguin, 1964).
Tinker, H., *India and Pakistan: A Short Political Guide* (Pall Mall Press, 1962).
Ward, Barbara (ed.), *Women in the New Asia* (UNESCO, 1963).
Weeks, R. V., *Pakistan: Birth and Growth of a Muslim Nation* (Van Nostrand, 1964).
Wilber, D. N., *Pakistan Yesterday and Today* (Holt, Rinehart & Winston, 1964).
Wilber, D. N., *Pakistan: Its People, Its Society and Its Culture* (H.R.A.F. Press, New Haven, 1964).

o

Chapter 14

Education of
the Pakistanis

A THE PRESENT SITUATION

'Pakistan ranks among the countries which accord the lowest priority to education' (1). Such is the official view of the Ministry of Education and Scientific Research of Pakistan, and this is borne out by the fact that only 1·8 per cent of their gross national product is devoted to education. This certainly compares very unfavourably with UNESCO'S recommendation that developing countries should devote 4 per cent of their gross national product to the expansion of their educational programmes.

But it would be very unfair to judge the Pakistani Government's present attitude by the expenditure figure of 1969, or its general educational philosophy by the First Five-Year Plan of 1955–60. It was formerly quite true to say, as John Goodall suggested in 1968 (2), that the élitist view of education still persisted in Pakistan, but between the *National Education Commission Report* of 1959 and the Ministry's *Proposals for a New Educational Policy* of 1969 some very hard thinking had been going on. A society, of course, does not change overnight and in those ten years there must have been some very tough battles fought in order to turn an élitist view on its head.

Before considering the future possibilities of education in Pakistan we will look at the situation up to the time of the ministerial proposals of July 1969. Broadly speaking, there have been two educational systems at work which the Pakistanis themselves refer to as the 'modern' system and the 'classical' system. These terms are not, in themselves, particularly appropriate since the 'modern' system of British imperialist rule developed in the early nineteenth century, whilst the 'classical' system of the Muslims did not really get under way in its present form until the turn of the century. But this usage has official Pakistani sanction and so we shall continue to adopt it here.

The modern system was introduced by the British during their occupation of India in order, according to the Pakistani Ministry of Education, 'to create a class of persons, Indian in blood and colour, but English in taste, in opinions, in morals and in intellect' (3). The main object of this system of education was to produce suitable individuals for service with the East India Company, and then later with the British Government; and it resulted in the production of clerical cadres and pools of trained personnel who were generally competent and servile assistants. The system has been self-perpetuating, and since the independence of Pakistan in 1947 it has remained almost unchanged.

The classical system developed because the Muslims disliked the ideas, customs and values which were being introduced into the Indian sub-continent by the British. The cultural values of Islam, in fact Islam itself, were felt by its leaders to be in grave danger of being submerged by Western customs and concepts. In consequence they established a number of *madrassahs*, or Muslim colleges, in order to provide a sort of inoculation against alien indoctrination. Their object was to preserve intact their religion and their social system, and their educational methods have remained virtually unchanged over the years.

These two very distinct systems of education in fact have a great deal in common in method, if not in aim and content. Both are authoritarian, and both emphasize the absorption of material and learning of facts by rote. But neither system has made any really great impression upon the vast mass of ignorance, superstition and illiteracy that exists in all areas of Pakistan. Since the beginning of the First Five-Year Plan in 1955 comparatively little money has been spent on primary education; and, moreover, the *National Education Commission Report* of 1959 emphasized the importance of secondary and higher education at the expense of primary education. This has meant, certainly up to the time of the commencement of the Fourth Five-Year Plan in 1970, that primary schools have been deprived of even the basic amenities for the teaching of young children.

School conditions vary as much in Pakistan as elsewhere, but although most villages will have a primary school of some sort there are some areas where schools are few and far between. This applies in particular to the border areas, such as Sylhet in East Pakistan and Mirpur in West Pakistan, both of which are areas of major emigration to Britain. There are altogether about twenty million children in the age group between five and ten years; of these only nine million, or 45 per cent, are enrolled in elementary or primary schools. Of those in the secondary age-group only 12 or 13 per cent are in attendance in a secondary school. Secondary schools in general have been regarded as training centres for admission to colleges, and so their curricula have been tailored to the necessary paper qualifications, such as the matriculation examination. Only recently have these schools been regarded as a terminal form of education for all who do not go on to higher education.

The Pakistani Government has accepted, quite realistically, the assertion that 'academic standards are poor and have been steadily deteriorating over the years' (4), but it has refused to take any superficial view of the problem. The reasons for the deterioration of standards certainly cannot be summarized in the one word 'partition', or simply lack of adequate finances. The total structure and organization of education need revision and rethinking in terms of a new nation which has not yet emerged as a unity.

Pakistan has one of the lowest literacy rates in the whole of Asia; in fact in 1969 the overall literacy in the country was no more than 20 per cent. John Goodall gives the figure for 1961 as 19 per cent (5), which means that in eight years the overall literacy of those over the age of five years increased by only 1 per cent. This is certainly not a very impressive record, and it has become clear that some really drastic policies are required for the future.

Teachers have been regarded for a long time as little more than glorified clerks who, in the villages, write for everyone who needs any writing done and are regarded as authorities mainly in the transmission of factual information, because they are among the élite who can read. In the towns and cities they find not only that they are denied any real intellectual freedom, but that they are also subordinated to a bureaucracy which exercises complete control over them. The members of this bureaucracy exercise full rights of appointment, promotion, transfer or dismissal. Teachers themselves are at present classified (Class I, II, III, etc.), so that there is considerable distinction in the required qualifications for each class. The pay throughout the teaching profession is poor, and there is literally nothing in salary, status or amenities of service which would attract talented or highly-qualified young people into teaching.

B THE PROBLEMS OF THE SITUATION

It is obvious, after three Five-Year Plans between 1955 and 1970, that both the modern and classical systems have failed to achieve any solid improvement in the quality of education or in the number of the educated. Systems tend to become hardened and habitual; the modern system is mainly secular in nature, although non-technical in content; the classical system purveyed by the *madrassahs* emphasizes Arabic teaching. The modern system 'cannot be considered a suitable system of education for an independent developing nation' (6), if only because it fails to promote any sort of national cohesion. Before a new country can really begin to develop it must create a norm of coherence in which people find an identity of cultural and social values. When it has achieved this, or rather whilst it is achieving it, the developing society also urgently requires the impartation of technical skill and know-how. The modern system has made no attempt to do this.

On the other hand, the classical schools have failed, in an ever-widening technological world, to impart a sense of unity for development. In their anxiety to preserve Muslim culture they have failed to realize that no society can live entirely on its past; it needs to promote positive analytical and critical approaches to both its learning and its social and economic aims. The *madrassahs* have existed simply to mediate the culture of the past. Thus neither the modern nor the classical modes of education have been orientated to social, economic or political needs, and they are considered by the Pakistani Ministry of Education and Scientific Research to have failed.

Education, up to 1970, has clearly failed to promote anything approaching a national consensus in Pakistan. The physical problems of division between West and East Pakistan by about 1,000 miles of land is difficult enough in terms of unity, but internal divisions and differences of outlook, language and even religion make consensus very difficult. The educational system has failed dismally to open up those channels of communication so urgently required if a national consensus is to develop. There are broad distinctions in society between the very poor and those who are comfortably well off, and who in consequence can ensure for their children the sort of education that will guarantee, eventually at least, a position of some responsibility. More will be said later of this barrier of privilege when we consider the educational policies for the Fourth Five-Year Plan (1970–75).

Another element which militates against a national consensus is the language problem. One of the legacies of the British government of the sub-continent of India has been that English remains the language of administration, whilst the masses speak a variety of languages according to whether they originate from West or East Pakistan, from the village or the town, and so forth. This is obviously a dangerous situation when the large majority of the people could, if government saw fit, be kept in almost total ignorance of the affairs of state. And this is not difficult in a society where 80 per cent are illiterate in their own language anyway. The great gulf between those who rule and those who are ruled is maintained by the system in which the medium of instruction at both college and university level is English.

The Government does not intend that this situation shall continue, and as long ago as 1954 it had decided to introduce the national languages into official use by 1974. Urdu is the national language of West Pakistan, and Bengali of East Pakistan. Because of this language barrier between the English-speaking élite and the rest there has been a considerable waste of the resources enshrined in human ability; but the process of conversion to an administration using national languages has been slow. Some have undoubtedly considered that the prestige-value of English-speaking administrators outweighed the value of Urdu- and Bengali-speaking nationalists. Consensus, however, is reached ultimately through thought-forms, speech-forms, symbols and formulas which are common to and understood by all. Hence the conversion to national languages by the administration is considered a matter of some priority.

Pakistan is, not unnaturally, having a very close look at the present time at those foreign influences and institutions which appear to have created barriers within her society. There has been a lack of communication between those elements of society trained by British methods for secular office, and those taught by 'orthodox' Muslim methods to prevent them from losing touch with their cultural heritage. The official government reports refer to this lack of communication as a 'religious' barrier. This does not necessarily mean a difference of religions between the two products; many trained by British methods have retained a nominal and attenuated Muslim faith; others have lost all religious belief; the remainder will have a veneer of Christendom rather than a conversion to Christianity. And just as Roger Ascham bewailed the 'Italianate Englishman' in the sixteenth century as a devil incarnate (7), so many orthodox Muslims regard their British-trained, secularized administrators as foreign-contaminated apostates.

The Government sees the solution to this particular problem in the establishment of equivalence between the various stages of the *madrassah* form of education and those of the modern form. Pakistan must

'aim at ideological unity and not ideological vacuum. It must aim at providing a uniform and integrated system of education which seeks to impart a common set of cultural values based on the precepts of Islam' (8).

Only in this way can the students of the *madrassahs* obtain all those appointments which are at present available only to the products of the modern method. There is already in existence in East Pakistan a Madrassah Education Board, which regulates by law the studies and curricula of these colleges, and which has some control of the maintenance and inspection of their standards.

It is felt that the situation is further complicated, and the religious barriers aggravated, by the existence of a large number of educational institutions (including both primary and secondary schools) as well as teachers' training-colleges run by foreign missionaries. The authorities are in no doubt about the considerable contribution which these institutions have made towards the educational product of their society; nor are they in doubt about its quality at the moment. The missionaries have, in fact, provided a better education than that afforded by the state, and so they have, in the view of the Government, helped to maintain and even increase the privilege barrier. It is an interesting reflection that the Government's proposal to nationalize these schools comes at a time when the public schools, in our own society, are under the threat of absorption in our comprehensive system. The reasons given are very much the same.

Thus it is argued that the educational system to date has not opened up the channels of communication between the rich and the poor, the English-speaking and those who speak only their national languages or dialects, and the Muslim *madrassah*-trained and the modern as well as missionary-trained. Another cause of dissatisfaction in regard to the educational system is the fact that education has failed to fulfil its proper role in relation to national development. The *Proposals for a New Educational Policy* emphasizes throughout that education is a necessary investment in man. Without education any real changes in society of an economic nature are difficult; it is held that roughly 40 per cent adult literacy is necessary in any population before industrialization can occur (9). And Pakistan hopes that, by eradicating illiteracy as far as possible in her society, new social attitudes will be developed and that those attitudes which prevent economic progress, such as unthinking submissiveness to authority and contempt for manual work, will disappear. The Government has gone so far as to say that

'for national development purposes, the first priority of education should be to create a literate society' (10).

The wastage of human resources is no more clearly seen than in the fact that there is a very high rate of unemployment among the educated youth of the country, namely, more than 200,000. This is undoubtedly the result of the élitist view of education which has existed down to the present day. The system has been geared to the production of particular types of government service, but when the latter cannot absorb the product the inevitable result in Pakistan is that the trained youths are unprepared to work at anything else. It is government service or nothing, for nothing else is good enough. It has been estimated that at the secondary level of education there are no more than 4 per cent of the total school population engaged in vocational and technical courses. The whole end in view is entry into college rather than into life; and college can no longer promise or guarantee a job. The whole economy is suffering from a loss of manpower because of the present college cul-de-sac in which a form of education that has been prestigious is largely unproductive in terms of the national economy.

On the whole the Pakistan Government has been quite frank about the poor and deteriorating standards of education down to 1969 and the beginning of the Fourth Five-Year Plan. Much of this has been due to the inadequate share which education has received of the gross national product. There has been a lack of adequate finances for capital equipment, buildings and playgrounds, furniture, teaching aids, texts, writing materials and teachers' salaries. The Government also blames the fact that the administration is far too bureaucratic and highly centralized (11). This means that students, teachers and research workers in the field of education are all frustrated in any efforts to display initiative and to develop their capacities and talents to the full. Another reason given for weak academic standards is the poor control which the Government has exercised over private educational institutions. Perhaps it is true of Pakistan, as in other countries, that private enterprise tends to provide both the best and the worst in education – but at least it provides something where otherwise nothing might be offered. It is responsible, partly, for the perpetuation of the privilege barrier because it furnishes better education, and so discrimination within the social structure (12); but also, of course, some institutions financed by private enterprise are simply money-spinners and they give poor service for money spent.

C FUTURE AIMS AND POLICIES
Pakistani aims in education are bound up with a total view of life, and a political and social ideology. This can best be described by the word 'Islamiat'. Islamiat involves the whole ethos of Islamic or Muslim culture, religion, philosophy and way of life; it is a thorough study of, and involvement in, Koranic truth and Arab civilization. It is not, however, an obscurantist view of social life, behaviour and development. Islamiat is the basis of consensus and should, according to the Government, be a compulsory subject of study up to the age of fifteen years, and optional after that age; it should also have high priority in university research. Only in this way can the Pakistani society be provided with a common set of cultural values which are based upon a truly indigenous view of life. The Ministry of Education and Scientific Research stresses that 'colonial traditions and Islamic values are not consistent with each other' (13); and therefore the colonial traditions, like any other barriers to national identity, must be eradicated, since Pakistan's unified system of education should be an Islamic one.

In this attempt at a more uniform system of education, the Government has clearly seen that the *madrassahs* can act as a conserving force since this is already their function. But it has anticipated their possibly restrictive and stultifying influence by arguing that they should be integrated into the normal school system. The latter, in turn, must be brought more in line with the new ideological demands of the Pakistani society. The foreign missionary institutions are regarded officially as 'highly anachronistic' in a free, independent Islamic republic (14). The doctrines of religion and culture which they promulgate are considered to be alien to Islamic values and concepts of life. It is the future policy of the Ministry to nationalize these institutions; but it hastens to add that this does not apply to educational institutions run by Pakistani non-Muslim communities. So far the ideological unity of the new state seeks to exclude foreign missionary educational institutions but not indigenous non-Muslim minorities.

The Ministry aims to create a literate society. There is a very strong, one might even suggest almost naïve, belief that the spread of literacy will answer most of the social and economic problems of the Pakistani society. In a more sophisticated and literate society such as our own we might be forgiven for a somewhat cynical reflection upon the official views on literacy and social attitudes. Literacy, according to the Ministry's *Proposals*, will eventually help to overcome ignorance, superstition, low levels of work discipline, unpunctuality, disorderliness, irrationality, lack of alertness, low aptitude for co-operation, low standards of personal hygiene, unwillingness to understand the importance of family planning, and submissiveness to authority and exploitation. The Report goes on to say that

'By teaching a man to read and write, it should be possible to mount an attack on the social attitudes which it is desired to change. Dissemination of knowledge through printed material is only possible in a literate society. And without such dissemination social change is difficult to induce' (15).

Literacy can certainly do a lot, and without a high percentage of literacy in a society there can be no industrial or technological development. But whether literacy has in itself the power to change character and social attitudes in the way suggested is more open to debate. Certainly literacy facilitates the acquisition of the skills requisite for economic and technical progress in any particular society. To this end Pakistan is entering upon a crash literacy programme during its Fourth and Fifth Five-Year Plans, that is from 1970 to 1980. The basic target is to impart literacy to 68 million adults by 1980; and this programme will involve a 'functional' literacy for those employed in the urban manufacturing sector, for those living in the vicinity of large project areas involving dams, factories, or nuclear power plants, and for the drop-outs from primary schools, particularly in the rural areas.

Of the existing 80 per cent illiterates the majority live in the hill areas. This means that any crash programme has to envisage both static and peripatetic units in order that even the apparently most inaccessible areas may be serviced. One of the great problems in advancing education in Pakistan has always been the uneven geographic coverage, the fact that educational opportunities have not been equally available to all people throughout the country, whether in the large towns, in the hill tracts or the frontier regions.

The Ministry envisages the conscription of a National Literacy Corps modelled on the Iranian Literacy Corps. This scheme involves the conscription of all young men who pass intermediate examinations, and all young women who pass matriculation examinations, between the ages of eighteen and twenty-two years. It was visualized that the first year's intake, in 1970, would be in the region of 28,000 recruits, and that by the end of 1975 the annual intake will be 72,000 recruits. The intake will be stabilized at that figure until the end of 1980, when it is hoped that the target of 68 million adult literates will be reached. The recruits are to be drilled and disciplined by army personnel for a period of three months, after which they will be given a three months' course of teacher training.

This course must, of necessity, be a highly condensed one embracing the essential techniques for the teaching of reading, writing and arithmetic. Conscripts will serve in the N.L.C. for a total of two years during which they will be paid a small amount of pocket money, supplied with a uniform, and will become members of village or hill communities who will provide them with simple food and shelter. At the end of the two years' national service every member of the N.L.C. will be entitled to sit the examinations for the B.Ed. degree of one of the Pakistani universities.

One of the proposals of the Ministry is that a large proportion of the educated unemployed should be absorbed into the teaching profession and the N.L.C. And it is obvious that, with the pressures of conscription between the ages of eighteen and twenty-two, many of the 200,000 educated unemployed youths would seize the opportunity of becoming teachers. It is argued, of course, that people pressurized into teaching do not make the best teachers. This is a familiar argument in all areas of conscription, but experience has rarely supported the belief. Teaching may of course be the exception, and really reluctant teachers can do a great deal of damage. But if we are honest we must admit that in our own society many youths have chosen teaching as a second best, or even as a last resort; and many of them have not only learned to enjoy teaching but also to be highly successful at it. In Pakistan, as in Iran, this is a matter of great urgency; and such situations demand extraordinary measures. If Pakistan reaches anything like its target of 68 million adult literates by 1980, the whole experiment will have been well worth while.

Another aim of the new educational policy is to attach a high priority to the development of technical and analytical skills. This will mean a virtual revolution in secondary education in which up to the present all the weight has been placed upon arts subjects with the almost exclusive purpose of gaining entry into college and university. Secondary education will be reorganized in order to incorporate a massive shift towards technical and vocational training. In rural areas this would mean an agricultural orientation, and in the urban areas less emphasis upon academic learning and more upon such commercial subjects as typing, shorthand, book-keeping and accountancy. At college and university level there would be the introduction of an increasing number of degrees and diplomas concerning engineering technology, printing, plumbing, tailoring and so on. Courses would lead to such qualifications as Matric (Tech.), Inter (Tech.) and B.Sc. (Tech.). The object of this shift is to 'add to the dignity of labour', and to provide a pool of skilled and semi-skilled technicians.

'It should be realized that such a class of trained technicians would generate its own employment potential and would not necessarily be job seekers' (16).

The Government is now seeking to attract some of the finest talent of the country into the teaching profession. It is fully cognizant of the fact that the teacher's status has to be improved and that its rewards must be made higher. His status can be improved by granting that intellectual and academic freedom which at present is totally denied him. It is also agreed that 'the teaching profession should be made classless', and that the practice of placing teachers into grades or classes, 'like ordinary Government Servants is both unnecessary and undignified' (17). It is recognized that methods of training must be improved and that there must be considerable development of educational technology and of the availability of film strips, feature films, audio-visual aids, charts, diagrams, models, radio and television programmes.

In its decision to use education as a force of national unification the Government also decided that the best chance of achieving this was to decentralize the educational administration. The whole of Pakistan was to be divided up into District School Authorities somewhat like our L.E.A.s, and the Inspectorate of Schools would cease to exercise any control over the schools. The proposed plans for the reconstruction of the educational system would absorb up to 3·6 per cent of the gross national product by 1980; which, even if it does not (as the Ministry says) 'compare favourably' with the recommendations of UNESCO, is not far short of the 4 per cent that it suggested as the allocation for the educational sector in a developing country (18). The Government regards the total educational expenditure as an investment in man himself, whether that investment should take the form of the building of a school or the salary of a teacher.

The proposals contained in the Report of the Pakistani Government, under discussion in this chapter, will involve the education of the following by 1980 (19):

(a) 68 million adults to the stage of literacy.
(b) 30 million students to the primary stage.
(c) 12 million students to the middle stage.
(d) 700,000 students to Matric (Tech.) in agricultural technology.
(e) 500,000 students to Matric (Tech.) in industrial technology.
(f) 400,000 students to Inter (Tech.) and B.Sc. (Tech.) in agricultural technology.

(g) 200,000 students to Inter (Tech.) and B.Sc. (Tech.) in industrial technology.

(h) 500,000 university graduates.

(i) 41,000 professional graduates.

This output is in addition to those who will be in the educational system. This is a massive educational programme and implies the development of popular education as a priority. The view of the Government is that the success of popular education will make available a broader base from which talent can be selected for further and higher education. Moreover, popular education has the advantage that it effects social change within the whole of society, as distinct from the 'islands' of the élite. Finally, within the sphere of economic development, which is one of the concerns of education, a marginal improvement in productivity over the entire population is more meaningful than a marked improvement over a very small and select part (20).

The Government is agreed that, whilst having a general policy of popular education, it would not be desirable to eliminate either the *madrassahs* or the 'cadet' colleges, some of which are government run and some privately operated. At the moment both types of school perpetuate barriers, whether of religion and culture or of privilege. It is felt that the best way to combat these particular problems is not to close these schools, but rather to make them more open, and to ensure that admission is on the basis of merit and that students are subsidized by an adequate scholarship and grant system. The modernization of the *madrassahs* by the introduction into the curricula of mathematics and the sciences, and by the training of their teachers to teach modern subjects, would give them an increasingly popular appeal and would, eventually, remove their distinctive religious bias.

The main language barriers will, it is hoped, be overcome within the next decade, although there is obviously a great deal of work to be done here. The present 'caste' distinction between the English-speaking government officials and the Urdu- and Bengali-speaking masses will be eliminated by a change at the top. Urdu will become the official language of West Pakistan and Bengali of East Pakistan by 1974, and both will be in use by the Central Government by 1975. The medium of instruction at all levels of education in East Pakistan will be Bengali, and in West Pakistan it will be Urdu. In the secondary stages of education Bengali will be introduced as a compulsory subject in the West, and Urdu in the East; English will be taught as an option. English, thus, becomes a third language instead of a first. Viewed in the context of future emigration to this country, these language changes should mean greater facility of communication between immigrants from any part of Pakistan, but probably no great change in their ability to communicate through English.

The general educational reconstruction envisages the integration of primary and middle schools to form elementary schools. It seems odd that, at a time when our society is reorganizing in certain L.E.A.s to produce middle schools, Pakistan is working the other way. It is not altogether clear from the Ministry's Report of 1969 why this particular proposal has been made, but it may well be – although this is not explicitly stated – that in the past a primary school education has been regarded as a terminal one for many. The creation of an 'elementary' stage, which ends only after eight years of schooling, may well encourage many more, particularly girls, to stay at school for a longer period. To date, the enrolment of girls in primary schools has represented only 20 per cent of the total enrolment at that stage (21), and it is becoming clear that there is a great need to encourage a considerable increase in the education of women. In order to accomplish this it is essential to overcome the ingrained prejudices of parents, who are inclined to think that it is a waste of time to educate a woman anyway. There are also certain religious and social tabus that make co-education problematic in Islamic societies, so that there is a need for more girls' schools.

By 1980 the Government hopes to have 67,000 elementary schools in East Pakistan with an enrolment of 15·6 million students, and 63,000 elementary schools in West Pakistan with an enrolment of 11·2 million students, a total intake of nearly 27 million students. The secondary stage is referred to in the Report as the high-school stage, and it is proposed that this should last for two years. There is great emphasis laid upon the provision of facilities for technical and vocational education for at least 60 per cent of the high-school students.

The Government does not intend to open any new government colleges during the period 1970–80, nor to allow any private college to start. Rather, the existing colleges will be expanded and consolidated by the provision of more and larger buildings, better equipment, laboratories and workshops. In 1969 there were 500 colleges in Pakistan; 225 in East Pakistan and 275 in West Pakistan, with a total enrolment of about 300,000 students (22). Of the colleges in East Pakistan some 90 per cent are private, whereas in West Pakistan about 50 per cent come within this category. It is argued that the annual rate of increase in enrolment, which has been about 15 per cent during the last decade, will be arrested in the future because opportunities will be available for students to join the technical and vocational streams of education.

There are at present in Pakistan twelve universities: seven of a general type at Karachi, Lahore, Peshawar, Hyderabad, Dacca, Chittagong and Rajshahi; two engineering universities at Dacca and Lahore; two agricultural universities at Lyallpur and Mymensingh; and the Central University at Islamabad, which is exclusively for post-graduate research.

In 1969 the total student enrolment was more than 22,000, of whom 17,000 were in general universities and the remainder in universities of agriculture and engineering. The Ministry of Education's Report states that there is a low output of scientists, a generally high failure rate and very poor research facilities. The whole university situation demonstrates the irrelevance of the educational process to the needs of the country. Whatever the output of scientists may be, the actual university input of students in science and technology is less than 12 per cent of the total student enrolment. In our own society in 1966 the total entry of students into the faculties of science and technology was about 40·5 per cent (23).

The Pakistan Report finally bewails the fact that, despite the great need which Pakistan has of professional men generally, including scientists, doctors and technologists, there is a brain drain away from Pakistan. The motivation behind this migration to other countries is largely economic, and the Government accepts that the only way to attract such professionally qualified men back again is to form a 'talent pool', which all Pakistani talent working abroad would be invited to join and to declare

'the terms and conditions of service and the opportunities of employment which they would like to accept in Pakistan before returning so that suitable openings for their talent may be found or special facilities created and arrangements made for their return to work for the national good' (24).

Pakistan is a great believer in her social and economic potential, but she understands fully the cost in terms of expenditure at all levels of education. To achieve her ambitious aims of the Fourth Five-Year Plan, Pakistan knows full well that the expenditure on education must be at least doubled to 3·6 per cent of the gross national product. She is perhaps sanguine, if not unrealistic, in thinking that by 1980 'it should be possible to bring down the annual allocation to 3·3 per cent of GNP' (25). It is obvious that her programme for achieving adult 'functional literacy' must be a costly one; but at the same time she is, in fact, hoping to achieve it very economically through the National Literacy Corps.

The future employment of many thousands of these conscripts as fully-trained, graduate teachers may well prove to be a much more expensive affair; whilst the cost of the expansion of scientific and technological education and research will increase rather than diminish as the Pakistani society becomes more industrialized. The Report recognizes this fact in its estimate of the total expenditure envisaged for the Fifth Five-Year Plan (1975–80), which is in the region of 173 per cent of the educational expenditure for the years 1970–75. Whether this will represent an adequate proportion of the gross national product it is difficult to say at this point in time. No one can adequately predict the changed educational demands and requirements of a developing society which within a decade will have developed a high level of literacy, and in which the number of schools will have been approximately doubled.

REFERENCES

1 Ministry of Education and Scientific Research, *Proposals for a New Educational Policy* (Govt. of Pakistan, Islamabad, July 1969), p. 9.
2 Goodall, J., 'The Pakistani Background' in Oakley, R. (ed.), *New Backgrounds* (O.U.P., 1968), p. 83.
3 Ministry of Education and Scientific Research, op. cit., p. 11.
4 Ibid., p. 6.
5 Goodall, J., op. cit., p. 83.
6 Ministry of Education and Scientific Research, op. cit., p. 11.
7 *Vide* Ascham, Roger, 'The Schoolmaster' in Dover Wilson, J., *Life in Shakespeare's England* (C.U.P., 2nd edition 1913), pp. 71–4.
8 Ministry of Education and Scientific Research, op. cit., p. 2.
9 *Vide* Anderson, C. A. and Bowman, J. B. (ed.), *Education and Economic Development* (Cass, London, 1966), Chapter 18 on 'Literacy and Schooling on the Development Threshold: Some Historical Cases'.
10 Ministry of Education and Scientific Research, op. cit., p. 4.
11 Ibid., p. 6.
12 Ibid., pp. 15–17.
13 Ibid., p. 12.
14 Ibid., p. 14.
15 Ibid., pp. 18–19.
16 Ibid., p. 23.
17 Ibid., p. 24.
18 Ibid., p. 46.
19 Ibid., pp. 10 and 46. On p. 46, Section 1 (d), the figure is mistakenly given as '12 million' instead of '12 lakh' (or 1,200,000).
20 Ibid., p. 20.
21 Ibid., p. 42.
22 Ibid., p. 31.
23 Council for Scientific Policy, *Enquiry into the Flow of Candidates in Science and Technology into Higher Education* (Dainton Report, Cmnd. 3541, H.M.S.O. 1968), Figure 7, p. 20.
24 Ministry of Education and Scientific Research, op. cit., p. 43.
25 Ibid., p. 9.

BIBLIOGRAPHY

Curle, A., *Planning for Education in Pakistan* (Tavistock, 1966).
Johnson, B. L. C., *How People Live in E. Pakistan* (Educational Supply Association, 1961).
Ministry of Education and Scientific Research, *Proposals for a New Educational Policy* (Government of Pakistan, Islamabad, July 1969).
Nurullah, S. and Naik, J. P., *A History of Education in India* (Macmillan, 2nd edition 1951).
Oakley, R. (ed.), *New Backgrounds* (O.U.P., 1968), Chapter IV by John Goodall.

Chapter 15
Culture Contact with the Host Society

The Muslim way of life of Pakistan is not easily transferable to another society, particularly to one such as our own which is already involved in the technological revolution. Even if all other conditions were ideal there would still occur something of that 'cultural shock' which is inevitable when the representatives of a country with an entirely alien culture come into the orbit of another society.

It is, of course, not true that there is 'no sin east of Suez'; but the *mores* and sanctions of the Pakistani society are quite different from our own. Indeed, the first contact of Pakistani immigrants with our 'permissive' society might well give them the impression that there is, in fact, 'no sin west of Suez' and that almost anything goes. But this second view would, of course, be as wrong and superficial as the first.

The Pakistani, as a follower of Islam, has an ordered and regulated existence in which there are clearly delineated codes of behaviour both within the confines of the home and in public. His moral code, food tabus, and social attitudes generally may well appear to be 'feudal' to his host society, but they are of such a kind that, once they are assimilated within his own world, he has little difficulty in pursuing them provided he can make, as it were, his own conditions for living wherever he goes. In one sense he is not unlike the ancient Israelite who took a sack of Palestinian earth with him wherever he went so that, before he spread his tent, he could always put down the earth and worship his God, Yahweh, in a foreign land. The Pakistani takes his prayer-mat and his copy of the Koran and feels that Allah is present with him.

We are so used to calling other societies 'pagan' and 'heathen' that it must come as something of a shock to some in our society that Muslims regard Christians as idolaters and polytheists. The Koran states that

'The Jews say Ezra is the son of Allah, while the Christians say the Messiah is the son of Allah. Such are their assertions, by which they imitate the infidels of old. Allah confound them! How perverse they are! They worship their rabbis and their monks, and the Messiah the son of Mary, as gods besides Allah; though they were ordered to serve one God only. There is no god but him' (1).

Thus the Koranic view is quite clear on the issue, and there is little doubt that immigrant Muslims will see in Christian belief at least a mild form of polytheism in which 'three gods' are worshipped; and Christians will be regarded *ab initio* as 'unbelievers' (2). And the concept of Mary as 'the Mother of God', however interpreted, will prove quite objectionable to most Muslims.

Nor, of course, will it be easy to explain to Muslims that Christian theology is a little more sophisticated than the expressions of it in the *suras* on 'Repentance' and 'The Table' already referred to. For the most part Pakistani immigrants will accept the Koran as the fully inspired word of Allah without any conceivable possibility of error. Moreover, their uncompromisingly monotheistic background could not envisage the idea of Allah having a 'mother' or procreating a 'son'. Similarly, of course, the Pakistani immigrant may find himself among people, whether professing Christians or not, who find it difficult to appreciate his preoccupation with frequent and ritualistic forms of prayer, accompanied by physical cleansing and Koranic repetitions, and his lengthy periods of fasting.

The virtual equality in this country between man and woman is something which the average Muslim male must find strange and insupportable when he first mingles in our society. There is no veiling of women, no *purdah*, and a decreasing sense of deference towards the 'superior status' of the male (3). The interchangeable roles of male and female within the home, with the exception of the biological role of childbearing, and the parallel functions, if not entirely identical, within the world of business, commerce and the professions, are facts which must at first startle and even offend the Muslim immigrant. The gap between the world of the fully-covered, veiled, modest and retreating Muslim woman, and the half-covered, scantily-clothed and revealing English woman, is one which surprises, but which it is not easy for the Pakistani male immediately to apprehend. It is not simply that every time he leaves his home he sees more of a woman than he has been accustomed to; it is also the mental association which he inevitably carries with him – namely, that a woman so clothed (or unclothed) must be immodest and lacking in morals. Naturally, the longer he remains the less, perhaps, he will think in these terms.

Another thing that will undoubtedly strike him about our society, in contrast to his own, is the small nuclear unit of the family system, in which for the most part the only members are the mother, father and children. The extended family of his own society is virtually non-existent in our own. He will also note that many of the functions performed by the kin-group in his own society, such as the care of the sick and the aged, are taken over by the Welfare State in the host society. The endogamous village kin-groups to which he has been accustomed in Mirpur or Sylhet he will find completely

P

missing here, where nuclear groups are highly mobile and where individuals may very quickly lose contact with even their close kin, to say nothing of their cousins and their uncles and their aunts.

Most of the Pakistani immigrants here have arrived since about 1958; and the first to arrive were in the main single men, or men who had left their wives and children in Pakistan. In 1963, 79 per cent of the Pakistanis here were men, only 8 per cent were women and 13 per cent were children (4); and the general pattern of immigration from Pakistan has been the same since. This male character of the migration has been partly due, as E. J. B. Rose has pointed out, to the strict seclusion of Muslim women to which we have already referred (5). The men arrive first and seek out a relative or friend from their home village and kin-group. This invariably means living in a communally owned house which has been turned into a sort of dormitory for as many of the family group as possible. There may be doubling up in some rooms, a bed being occupied by one man by day, and by another man at night.

This sort of overcrowding may, in fact, be a matter of choice; certain economies may be effected and larger postal orders may in consequence be sent back home each week to help improve the standard of living of the rest of the extended family. Money may also be deliberately saved in order to acquire enough to set up a separate home and to send for dependants from Pakistan.

'In his first few years every penny is saved to discharge obligations: many Pakistanis remit as much as half their earnings. It was estimated that in 1963 remittances amounted to as much as £26 million, or more than the inland revenue of East Pakistan' (6).

The dormitory house has the advantage of maintaining the norms of Pakistani life, whether it be in diet, language, religion or recreation. There are great temptations which face the young Pakistani male divorced from the sanctions of the village extended family group. Where they lack incentive to maintain their Muslim standards of behaviour, they may well begin to form alliances with white girls, usually of a temporary nature until their own womenfolk are able to come here.

Of such Pakistanis Dr Farrukh Hashmi has said:

'Many men, particularly those who have left home for the first time, tend to behave in a rather immature fashion during the settling-down period in this country. They go through a phase of realignment in their social, moral and religious attitudes and tend to take liberties with their cultural code of behaviour. It is almost as if the fact of leaving their rigid family and community set-up for the first time heralds a regression of attitudes and brings on a second adolescence, which they eventually outgrow and settle down' (7).

The settling-down period, even though it may be an extensive one, is assisted eventually by the arrival of their women, children and other dependants. The sense of solidarity, which the family provides within the context both of familial relationships and of Islamic ethico-religious ideals, is something that is kept alive by the stabilizing influence of responsibility for wife and children.

Thus, the maintenance of Pakistani culture, although difficult within an alien society, becomes a matter of challenge and pride: and in most instances the temporary submission to the permissiveness of our society is replaced by a recrudescence of Koranic conservatism. All the values and customs of the village kin-group are once more brought to life when the family situation is re-established; and there follows a vigorous endeavour to retain intact the extended family method, bridging the gulf between, for example, the Mirpuri village and a Bradford immigrant community. Nevertheless it is clear from E. J. B. Rose's *Colour and Citizenship* that the villagers from Mirpur and similar Pakistani areas are very rapidly becoming, not only city-dwellers, but also active participants in community creativity. The Report points out that in Bradford there has been an expansion of Pakistani grocers and butchers from two in 1959 to fifty-one in 1967; by the latter date there were fifty Pakistani schools of motoring and an increase in the number of cafés from three to sixteen (8). Thus, in many instances, the rural migrants have become the initiators in the process of expanding urbanization.

Whilst problems of sex and sexual relationships are inevitably different in different societies, the clash of cultures can aggravate the incidence and the complexity of such problems. Whereas in the normal Pakistani community back home sex would not be discussed in an open manner, the immigrant finds that in our society the subject is not only frankly debated but also publicly exploited. If he possesses a television set the Pakistani will additionally find that sex is brought into his living-room throughout the evening leisure hours; and the sort of frank discussion which he would not introduce into the family himself will be taking place on the television screen, frequently with physical accompaniments. He will find himself, too, in a society which theoretically upholds the sanctity of monogamous marriage, yet which practises increasingly a sort of serial polygamy whilst at the same time despising, and not infrequently envying, the so-called polygamous attitudes of Pakistani immigrants.

The fact remains, however, that polygamy is not at present accepted as a norm in our society. A male Pakistani immigrant may, nevertheless, bring into Britain two wives provided that he married them in Pakistan. As far as dependants' allowances, income tax relief and so on are concerned, the immigrant can claim on one wife only; and whilst some do bring two wives into the country, the economic difficulties of fully supporting more than one wife and of treating them with Koranic equality may in the long run deter them from practising polygamy – whether here or in their own land.

It is naturally important to get these matters in perspective in considering such a topic as culture. As Farrukh Hashmi emphasizes, whilst a number of male Pakistanis may 'kick over the traces' somewhat when they first arrive here, sexual misadventures by female members of their society will not be tolerated. Hashmi maintains that one hardly ever sees a Pakistani prostitute in this country or hears of a Pakistani unmarried mother. Whilst it is not easy to obtain statistics on matters such as these, one can accept, as Hashmi indicates, that such instances as do occur are extremely rare and are hushed up by the family as much as possible (9).

How far such a high level of chastity can be retained by Pakistani women in a 'permissive' society such as ours will depend very much upon how far such immigrants assimilate to the *mores* of their new environments. John Goodall has rightly said that 'assimilation is not a necessary condition of integration' (10); but non-assimilation to a new sense of personal choice, freedom, equality and democracy will require concerted efforts on the part of those Pakistanis who have any sort of authority with their people. There are some very definite and organized attempts being made to perpetuate Muslim religion and Islamic culture generally among Pakistanis. In Birmingham, for example, there is at least one Muslim school which is attended by children once or twice a week (usually on Saturdays or Sundays) in order that they may not lose contact with the teaching of the Koran; there is also an Islamic Institute where adults may consider in depth some of the issues raised by culture contact. John Goodall, who has researched the settlement of Pakistani immigrants in Bradford, states that the majority of Pakistani children there attend a mosque for an average of fifteen to twenty hours per week, either before or after school on weekdays, or on Saturday and Sunday mornings. During these sessions the children are taught by the *imam* (the spiritual leader and teacher in the mosque) both Arabic and Urdu, and they will learn to read the Koran and various prayers and codes of behaviour of the Islamic faith (11).

Something of the problem of cultural ambivalence is experienced in particular by Pakistani schoolgirls who traditionally are kept segregated from males and their gazes. In this country they find themselves in mixed schools in which little or no differentiation may be made between the sexes, and certainly no concessions made to female modesty. They may be sent to a school in their traditional tunic (*kemise*) and trousers (*shalwar*), which will immediately set them apart as different and belonging to an alien culture. But they may, in some schools, be subjected to stresses which are virtually insupportable because they find that they are between two cultures, each pulling in very opposed and uncompromising directions.

Some headmasters have insisted, or perhaps tried to insist, upon the wearing of a school uniform that can be regarded by the Pakistani parents only as a threat to their religious faith, their culture and their girls' modesty. When a headmaster can say, as one is reported to have said, 'No Pakistani girl is going to wear her native trousers in my school,' one can imagine the almost neurotic situation that can and does arise. In discussing some of the factors involved in social change, R. M. MacIver and C. H. Page remark that

'When the individual is subjected, especially at the formative stage of life, to the counterdemands of clashing culture patterns, he may fail to achieve an adequate *personal* accommodation. He undergoes a process of cultural denudation or, seeking vainly to reconcile in his behaviour the opposing demands, he becomes more or less schizophrenic' (12).

This process of 'cultural denudation' might well occur in our society, with a sense of 'culturelessness', without allegiance to east or west, without identity or social purpose.

It is, perhaps, in the particular area of education that young Pakistanis find one of the major problems of culture contact. In their village kin-group, and in the nuclear family unit within the host society, they are accustomed to authority and submission. But education in this country accepts much more firmly the principles of discovery, personal initiative and freedom. In consequence, many Pakistani parents get the impression that their children are not being taught properly or adequately, and that they are not learning anything worth while. Similarly, many of their children find it very difficult to adjust to a system which demands that they shall enter into a programme entailing self-discipline, personal involvement in heuristic approaches to knowledge and truth, and the opportunity to participate in creative project work. Many young Pakistanis, as well as other coloured immigrants, when faced with the problems of *active* engagement in learning processes, have suffered a temporary 'culture shock'. They find themselves quite unable to initiate thought and action after having lived under a regime of authoritarianism and submission.

Cultural ambivalence is a socio-psychological experience which is undergone by all ages among the immigrants, and at all social levels. It is obviously impossible here to enter into the minutiae of Koranic legal practice, or the Islamic view of criminal responsibility and intent involved in any action that violates Koranic law. It must be sufficient simply to say that the British and the Pakistani attitudes vary quite considerably in these areas; and that the variation is enough to make much of our criminal code strange and puzzling to the Pakistani. This is, of course, largely a matter of making the immigrant aware of his new responsibilities, and of ensuring that the Pakistani schoolchildren are properly socialized in the context of the host society.

A very high percentage of immigrant Pakistanis are, like the West Indians, involved in manual work. The figure, given by E. J. B. Rose in *Colour and Citizenship*, for Pakistani heads of households engaged in manual occupations is 86 per cent. The corresponding figures for West Indians and Indians are 86 per cent and 76 per cent respectively (13). The corresponding figure for the total population of the country in the manual category is 51·2 per cent, or 67 per cent if the 'retired and unoccupied' group is removed. The Pakistanis, however, have 5 per cent in the clerical category, whereas the West Indians have only 3 per cent, and the Indians 4 per cent; the figure for the total population of the country is 6·6 per cent actively engaged in clerical work.

It is sometimes wrongly asserted that the professional and technical occupations are virtually closed to all coloured immigrants alike, but nothing could be further from the truth. The figure for the country's total population is 6·4 per cent, whilst that for each of the coloured immigrant groups with which we are concerned is 6 per cent. It would seem, therefore, that professional and technical expertise, generally speaking, knows no barriers of race, colour, class or creed. But a predominantly white society is reluctant to use coloured peoples at the administrative and managerial level, even when there is some competence to cope with the situation. The only sort of working situation where such a status seems acceptable is where the workers who are being managed form a solid 'gang' of coloured immigrants.

There is some reluctance also to use immigrants as teachers, although many of them appear to be reasonably well qualified in their home society. About 4 per cent of the heads of households of the Indian immigrants are teachers, but less than 0·5 per cent of the Pakistani immigrants come in this category. It must be accepted that, generally, immigrant teachers are not the best people to teach immigrants and that the seeking out of such teachers 'specifically to teach immigrant children' is a dangerous notion (14). Where they are employed they often prolong the period in which native languages are used for basic communication and inquiry; but it must be underlined, in addition, that the frequently poor English accents and lack of mastery of English idiom of the immigrant teachers are conveyed to, and perpetuated in, their pupils. It is important to emphasize, once more, that the Pakistani classical Muslim methods of learning, like those of the Indian Hindus, are almost entirely rote methods in which facts are learned by heart and regurgitated, even at higher education level.

The hiatus between English and Pakistani workers is emphasized by what the writers of *Colour and Citizenship* refer to as the 'self-sealing' process developed by Pakistani immigrants (15). This process originates in the dormitory house, but is carried over into working hours particularly in the shift-working ethnic gangs. Thus, the immigrant may not meet his English opposite number at work, nor may he meet him outside working-hours because of the self-sealing process. The natural meeting-place for workers in our society is the public house, but the Pakistani's religion forbids the drinking of alcohol, and if he wishes to remain an orthodox member of his faith he may find it difficult to mix socially at all with white workers. He may not be invited to their homes, and if he eventually has womenfolk in his own home living in *purdah*, or partial *purdah*, he may well be reluctant to invite his white colleagues there.

The Pakistanis find themselves in two worlds – the world of the stable close-knit extended family with its links both in this country and in the village back home, and the world of mobile individualism within the host society. This is not a dichotomy or cultural ambivalence that can be resolved by a prescriptive policy: there are conflicts of loyalties which cause incredible and almost unbearable stresses, particularly in the case of children who came here as immigrants with their parents, and the second generation of immigrants who have never seen their land of origin. The Pakistani village with its mosque, school and *imam*; the English town with its partial re-creation of the village kin-group; the English school with its new and strange demands upon individuality; the newly-created mosque and its attempt to re-establish Muslim values, beliefs and customs; the English opportunities for permissiveness, freedom and personal choice; the Muslim demands for submission, obedience and group identity – all these symbolize the polarities of the two worlds which continue to create their stresses and their individual and peculiar problems.

But even the statement that the Pakistanis find themselves in these two somewhat discordant worlds is an over-simplification. The Pakistanis are anything but a homogeneous group. Their home loyalty is not so much to Pakistan, nor even to West or East Pakistan, as to the tribe or state to which their village kin-group belongs.

'East Pakistanis live exclusively apart from West Pakistanis, even in London where the acute housing shortage might have brought them together. In Bradford, there is no sharing between West Pakistanis from different regions – Pathan tribesmen live on their own, Campbellpuris and Mirpuris avoid one another, and there is a similar division between Punjabis and non-Punjabis. Houses are apt to be grouped according to area of origin' (16).

It is only when the religion of Islam itself is involved that a Pakistani's loyalties begin to transcend his somewhat parochial attachments. Thus the Pakistani immigrant may find himself with a whole catena of loyalties – to his village kin-group, his tribe, his nation of origin, his religion, and now his newly adopted foreign and predominantly white society.

The desire to find security with one's own kinfolk in a foreign society inevitably leads to the development of areas which seek to reproduce as far as possible home conditions. The stabilization of such communities inevitably leads to the reassertion of conservative norms, beliefs and attitudes. The buying up of old property in slum areas, and the filling of all houses to more than normally accepted capacity, will inevitably lead to accusations of unhygienic slum conditions. But invariably the slum conditions existed before the Pakistani immigrants arrived there to inherit some of the worst areas in our society, and some of the worst slum types of school.

Whatever the living conditions in our society, however, they are regarded by a large proportion of Pakistanis as at least preferable to their own equally crowded living conditions at home, with far lower standards of living. It has been estimated that the average annual per capita income of Pakistanis in Mirpur, in 1966, was in the region of £30 (17), whereas that of Pakistanis working in this country at roughly the same time was about £930 (18). Raw comparisons in monetary terms are not always helpful; but allowing for different costs of living as well as the greater variety of economic wants in our society, the Pakistani immigrant is considerably better off and has a greater sense of security.

Up to 1960 at least, of the three major groups of immigrants that we have discussed the Pakistanis were the most likely to return home after having made some money. In fact, between the years 1955 and 1960, 69 per cent of the Pakistanis re-emigrated compared with 19 per cent of the West Indians and 40 per cent of the Indians (19). But the Report on *Colour and Citizenship* indicates that very few of the Pakistani immigrants at present here are likely to return to Pakistan. They look upon Britain as a sort of 'El Dorado' where amenities are *pukka*; they are, in fact, more or less 'compelled to remain as worker bees outside the hive'; and for many migration has represented an escape from the inherited disabilities and bonds of their home society. In the new urban society there is a large proportion of Pakistanis who will find liberation from the narrowing limitations of an ancient, but parochial and stifling, hierarchical system (20).

REFERENCES

1 The Koran, *sura* 9.
2 Ibid., *sura* 5.
3 *Vide* ibid., *sura* 2.

4 Hooper, R. (ed.), *Colour in Britain* (B.B.C., 1965), p. 21.
5 Rose, E. J. B. *et al.*, *Colour and Citizenship: A Report on British Race Relations* (O.U.P., 1969), p. 441.
6 Ibid., p. 443.
7 Hashmi, F., *The Pakistani Family in Britain* (Community Relations Commission, August 1969), p. 10.
8 Rose, E. J. B., *et al.*. op. cit., p. 443.
9 *Vide* Hashmi, F., op. cit., p. 10.
10 Goodall, John, 'The Pakistani Background' in Oakley, R. (ed.), *New Backgrounds* (O.U.P., 1968), p. 91.
11 Ibid., p. 90.
12 MacIver, R. M. and Page, C. H., *Society: An Introductory Analysis* (Macmillan, 1957), p. 580.
13 *Vide* Rose, E. J. B. *et al.*, op. cit., Table 14.1, 'Occupational Status of Heads of Household', p. 183.
14 *Vide* Hawkes, N., *Immigrant Children in British Schools* (Pall Mall Press, 1966), p. 55.
15 Rose, E. J. B., *et al.*, op. cit., p. 443.
16 Ibid., p. 444. Note 54 on p. 474 states that 'Dahya lists 983 Pakistani houses in Bradford in 1964, broken down as follows: 142 East Pakistani, 190 Chacci (Campbellpuri), 24 Pathan, 3 Gujarati Muslim, 135 Punjabi, 489 Mirpuri'.
17 Ibid., p. 59. This figure was given by President Ayub Khan in an address to the Royal Institute of International Affairs, 1966.
18 Ibid., p. 185. This figure is based upon the stated 'take home pay' of the respondents in the Birmingham survey, carried out in 1966–7. The reader should, however, read the whole of Chapter 14 of this Report in order to see the full implications of these figures.
19 *Vide* Hooper, R. (ed.), op. cit., p. 20. Cf. also Patterson, Sheila, *Immigration and Race Relations in Britain: 1960–1967* (O.U.P., 1969), p. 7, note 1, which reads: 'Statistics of re-migration or return migration were not available until the Commonwealth Immigrants Act of 1962 came into operation, and indeed, the statistics kept since then of numbers leaving Britain do not permit of precise distinction between returning migrants, visitors, and others. In general, however, it has been estimated that the West Indians are the most settled of the three major groups, the Pakistanis by far the least settled and the Indians somewhere in between. . . .'
20 *Vide* Rose, E. J. B., *et al.*, op. cit., pp. 451–2.

BIBLIOGRAPHY

Banton, M., *The Coloured Quarter* (Jonathan Cape, 1955).
Bethmann, E., *Bridge to Islam* (Allen & Unwin, 1953).
Burgin, T. and Edson, P., *Spring Grove* (O.U.P., 1967).
Collins, S., *Coloured Minorities in Britain* (Lutterworth Press, 1967).
Coulson, N., *A History of Islamic Law* (Edinburgh Univ. Press, 1969).
Davison, R. B., *Commonwealth Immigrants* (O.U.P., 1964).
Hashmi, F., *The Pakistani Family in Britain* (Community Relations Commission, 1969).
Hooper, R. (ed.), *Colour in Britain* (B.B.C., 1965).

Hunter, Kathleen, *History of Pakistanis in Britain* (The author, 33 Tavistock Square, W.C.1, 1962).

Oakley, R. (ed.), *New Backgrounds* (O.U.P., 1968), Chapter IV by John Goodall.

Patterson, Sheila, *Immigration and Race Relations in Britain: 1960–1967* (O.U.P., 1969).

Rex, J. and Moore, R., *Race, Community and Conflict: A Study of Sparkbrook* (O.U.P., 1967).

Rose, E. J. B. (ed.), *Colour and Citizenship: A Report on British Race Relations* (O.U.P., 1969).

Conclusion

The development of a multi-cultural society is something that demands constant thought, vigilance and awareness of the considerable variety of problems involved. It is certainly not a question which should be left to the doctrinaire declamations of politicians or the sometimes hysterical demonstrations of insistent egalitarians. Any consideration of the future evolution of our society will, it is true, inevitably involve politics and sociology; but it will equally involve education, and it is with education that we are here mainly concerned.

At the present time our educational system tends to treat the whole immigrant question as if it were a somewhat localized one which gives rise to some difficult and awkward problems in specific, not to say 'deprived', areas. In fact, immigration is regarded almost as if it were a special case of deprivation. The Plowden Report, for example, devoted five out of about 550 pages to 'Children of Immigrants', but in that brief space it made the very valid point that

'Special measures inevitably identify children as "different" and their duration should be as brief as possible' (1).

Of course, immigrant children are deprived in the sense that they lack the linguistic and cultural equipment to cope with the new situation in which they find themselves. But the development of a harmonious multi-cultural society is not just a question of teaching English as a second language (E2L) to foreigners, although this is certainly very important, or of showing them how to use our toilets, or of teaching them our various customs. It involves a personal and collective vision of what an integrated cultural society could and should be like.

So far we have avoided as far as possible the use of the term 'multi-racial society' because this already has certain rather unpleasant associations with societies where black or coloured members may be segregated as a deliberate policy; and where, despite all protestations to the contrary, non-whites always appear to be treated at a level lower than that of the whites. The concept of racial segregation, or *apartheid*, is one which most people in this country oppose, at least in theory, and it will certainly find no support in this chapter. But because of the prejudices that attach to, and are aroused by, theories of race the term 'multi-racial' will be avoided as much as possible, even though in one sense it may be an accurate anthropological description of a society. This is not a question of hiding one's head in the sand, it is a question of recognizing that, for example, the English are one of the most mixed groups, racially speaking, that the world has produced; but to seek to compare 'the English' with 'the Indians', or with 'the Pakistanis' from a racial point of view, and with certain stereotypes in mind, is to court trouble. In the words of E. J. B. Rose,

'To say of an individual that he belongs to a certain racial group has no uniquely predictive value: we cannot determine whether that person is taller or shorter, darker or lighter, more or less intelligent, than an individual belonging to some other "race"' (2).

There is a sense in which perhaps most of us are *ethnocentric*; that is, we have a tendency to regard our own characteristics and qualities as superior to those of other groups. And because of this tendency towards ethnocentrism we inevitably select our best virtues and the worst features of other races or groups for comparison. Any objective analysis of ourselves and others, whether as individuals or groups, is fraught with the complexities of self-esteem, colour consciousness, prejudicial attitudes resulting from life experiences, and a whole host of unconscious associations which in themselves may be quite irrational.

But the creation of a really multi-cultural society is not a one-sided affair; and, although we should recognize our own tendencies towards xenophobia and fear of the unaccustomed, we should also be wary of that extreme view which would seem to suggest that all the work in integration of immigrants is upon our own shoulders. If, as Dipak Nandy so rightly suggests, we should no longer think in terms of an 'immigrant problem' (3), it is equally true that we should not regard it all simply as a 'host problem'. The full and vigorous development of a multi-cultural society implies that each separate culture has something to learn from all others, and not merely incidentally either. There must be a conscious two-way traffic and it is here that education has a very large part to play. Eric Irons makes this very point when he discusses 'The immigrants' own contribution' in *Colour in Britain*. He suggests that

'Integration does not mean that the Muslim has to eat pork, the Sikh cut his hair, or the West Indian stop having parties. But it does mean that the Muslims and Sikhs should try to learn English and the West Indian should think more about his next-door neighbours' (4).

There is, throughout, a balance of responsibility which can be inculcated only by a conscious and deliberate consideration of what the real problems are. Words which appear on the surface to be merely attempts to clarify actual sociological processes develop pejorative connotations, and a word that is used with one connotation by a particular individual or group may be strongly objected to by others who are employing an entirely different connotation. The word *accommodation*, for example, has been defined as 'the achieving of a *modus vivendi* between newcomers and the receiving society' (5). But to John Dollard the principle of accommodation involves something virtually deleterious, namely, the renunciation of protest or aggression against undesirable conditions of life, and the organization of the character of the individual or group so that eventually not only does protest not appear, but acceptance does. Gradually, through this process, what was originally feared and resented is finally accepted and even loved (6). But Dollard appears to have taken the concept of 'accommodation' a stage further to something nearer 'assimilation'.

If the immigrant is to feel 'at home' in his host society, he must make certain accommodations to begin with in order to fit in. His accommodation will be selective according to his own culture and background, but it will be basically a question of knowing sufficient about the customs and habits of the new environment so that he does not run completely counter to acceptable levels of behaviour in the host society. This phase of accommodation, occurring early in the culture contact experience, provides a breathing space as it were during which the newcomers are able to assess the main areas in which their differences from the host community lie, and during which they may also consolidate those elements in their own culture which they feel are essential if they are to continue to exist as a cultural entity.

The stage of complete *assimilation* is reached when any immigrant group has ultimately relinquished its separate culture and identity. This process will, of course, take a considerable time and will inevitably involve inter-marriage between the immigrant group and members of the host society. In this country such assimilation or absorption has occurred in the past in the case of the Huguenots. Such assimilation in our own society is obviously easier with white, European groups than with coloured ones; moreover, of course, assimilation will occur only where there is a complete willingness on the part of the minority group to become absorbed by the majority (7).

But it is quite clear that many coloured immigrant groups do not wish to become completely assimilated to a white culture nor to become identified with its religion or its general way of life. The 'cultural islands' that are developing in our society, whether we like to use the term 'ghetto' or not, represent the anxiety of many of these groups to provide for themselves a sort of defence or security against the mainstream culture. Culture-conflict, culture-shock and culture-ambivalence are painful experiences socially and psychologically, and one of the ways of minimizing their effect is to provide a means of escape from their fullest impact. The re-creation of the home culture in as many details as possible will provide for the immigrant a more accustomed environment.

The alternative to assimilation, however, is not necessarily segregation, whether voluntary or enforced. Philip Mason, in an article on 'What is meant by Integration', has made it clear that there are, broadly speaking, two scales of reference: one is the *adaptation* scale which relates to the extent to which the minority group is prepared to adapt to customs and values of the host society; the other is the *acceptance* scale which is a measure of the extent to which the host society accepts the minority group. In the developing multi-cultural society the objective must be

'a steady increase in the two processes of adaptation and acceptance, until a stage is reached in mutual accommodation which could be called *inclusion*. This would be integration, but not assimilation' (8).

The use of the word 'inclusion' here is a very happy one in the context of integration, and in the context of the educational processes required to effect it. Inclusion, as Martin Buber has expressed it, implies a dialogical relation; and if ever there were need for dialogue between differentiated groups it is within such a society as our own where there is an ever-increasing variety of minority groups (9).

Integration, then, implies the inclusion of minority groups within the total, multi-cultural society, without the complete loss of their individual religious beliefs, social structures, family patterns, or even of native tongue as a first or second language. In her study of West Indians in London, Sheila Patterson has referred to the phase of group absorption as *pluralistic integration*, or cultural pluralism, involving the co-existence of a number of cultures within a society and their mutual acceptance and tolerance. This is a stage in which the immigrant group manages to adapt itself, by means of its organizations, to a full and permanent membership of the host society in some of the major spheres of association, such as civic and economic life (10).

In the evolution of a cultural pluralism of this order it is clear that the processes of education must take a principal part. But it is somewhat dis-couraging to discover that immigrant children receive, on the whole, a poorer education than other average children (11). As Eric Butterworth points out, the majority of schools in the central areas of cities and towns, where most immigrants are being educated, are understaffed. The schools themselves, like the living conditions of their pupils, are poor and thoroughly inadequate and certainly not on the surface calculated to bring about equality of education. On the contrary, the prevailing conditions are more likely to establish firmly authoritarian methods in teaching and class control.

In January 1968 the total number of immigrant pupils in maintained primary and secondary schools in England and Wales was 200,742 or 2·7 per cent of all full-time pupils in these schools. The term 'immigrant pupils' here refers to children born outside the British Isles who have come to this country with, or to join, parents or guardians whose countries of origin were abroad; and also children born in the United Kingdom to parents whose countries of origin were abroad and who came to the United Kingdom on or after January 1, 1958. The three coloured groups with which we have been concerned in this book comprised 74·4 per cent of all immigrant pupils on January 1, 1968; Indians numbered 42,440 or 21·1 per cent of the total; Pakistanis numbered 16,963 or 8·5 per cent; and West Indians (including Guyanese) numbered 89,988 or 44·8 per cent (12). By January 1969 the total of immigrant pupils had risen to nearly 250,000, or 3·2 per cent of all full-time pupils in maintained primary and secondary schools (13).

No one can pretend that 3·2 per cent of the school population is merely a small minority deprived in a special or peculiar sort of way. It is a steadily increasing minority (about 1·8 per cent in January 1966; 2·5 per cent in January 1967; 2·7 per cent in January 1968; and 3·2 per cent in January 1969). On the other hand, it is certainly not our purpose here to make any rash predictions about its size at the turn of the century; the important thing is that the immigrant minority is, and will be, a very vital element in our pluralistic society, and we must adopt a really positive policy towards it. Clearly more than a 'remedial' mentality is required in dealing with the situation. We are concerned in our educational programme for 'cultural pluralism' not with the remedial or compensatory education of a handful of immigrants, but with a total programme of education for a new type of society.

Such a programme demands an entirely fresh approach to cultural problems through an integral philosophy of society. It is no longer a question of minority groups accommodating, adjusting or assimilating; it is a question of mutual understanding, of learning from one another, of absorbing one another's culture at all levels, and of finding something of the best in them all. The problems of prejudice, for example, have to be tackled at their very source; and since 'the prejudiced personality has to be developed and its development starts in early childhood' (14), it is in early childhood that positive approaches towards the concept of pluralism must be developed.

We fear what is strange, what we do not know, and what we do not understand; and the only way to eliminate fear is to eradicate ignorance. An obvious starting-point is with the teachers of the future, a large number of whom enter colleges of education direct from school. It is a short-sighted policy to imagine that it is sufficient to give a small percentage of these students, who are likely to teach in 'contact areas', a minimal sort of preparation in remedial English or in English taught as a second language. All teachers convey their attitudes and their prejudices, as well as their knowledge (or ignorance), to their pupils – and all are living or growing up in a multi-cultural society. Our teachers in training must be prepared for this sort of society of the future, and for the children of the future who must develop views of society and living together which transcend all varieties of cultural patterns.

It is not without significance that sociology and the social sciences generally have found considerable favour in our time, despite the suspicion that is still shown towards the study of society in some quarters. 'Immigration' is a part of the changing and mobile social scene; but, as Dipak Nandy insists, we are not primarily concerned with a 'problem' of immigrants but with the education of the whole society – and not least with the host element with its assumptions of superiority. Nandy, with not a little justification, underlines the somewhat patronizing way in which we make reference to the contributions which immigrants are able to make to our society:

'When we talk of the contribution immigrants can make we often drown ourselves in a sea of platitudes: we talk of hospitals and public transport, or, on another level, of Indian curries and saris, of calypsos and of Caribbean spontaneity. But these are not the central things – and we know it. The contribution immigrants have to make to this society has something to do with the quality of life, with the way in which they perceive human relationships and its demands' (15).

If we can only see that the variety of cultures within our midst has something to contribute to the quality of life and enrichment of our society, we shall make a double effort to learn about those cultures and to comprehend them at greater depth. Teachers in training need courses which, above all, will release them from that 'cultural encapsulation' (16) which bedevils such a large proportion of our society. The excellent work of the Community Relations Commission in devising and analysing suitable syllabuses for teacher-training, in their monograph on 'Syllabuses', should be examined by the reader (17). This monograph considers the two major categories involved in race relations, namely, the education of immigrant communities and the promotion of a multi-cultural society. This is a firm recognition that both immigrant children and adults must be assisted in the initial process of adaptation through the development of basic technical and social skills; but that in addition to this preliminary work educationalists are striving, through both immigrants and the host community, to develop and promote a 'cohesive society, in which group and personal tensions are held in a dynamic, harmonious balance' (18).

It is, of course, important to inculcate in potential teachers attitudes of tolerance, understanding and involvement in a developing multi-cultural society. But schools must also develop, *pari passu*, curricula in which there are positive approaches for their children towards questions of race, stereotypes, prejudice, colour and cultural variations. All these elements require careful planning, whether in terms of particular subject areas, topics, combined curriculum or integrated studies, or some form of inter-disciplinary enquiry (I.D.E.). But one must remember always that know-ledge 'about and about' things, as both Zen Buddhists and Taoists would remind us, is not the same as really apprehending and being aware in our innermost consciousness. June Derrick has emphasized the importance of the *unobservable* things which help to form the immigrant child's cultural background, and it is these intangible elements of personal and group experience that both adults and children in our society must seek to dis-cover and really to come to terms with (19).

The importance of language in the total scheme of things must certainly not be underestimated as one of the great constituents and potential barriers in a multi-cultural society. But this is simply an extension of the general recognition today of the psychological and sociological implications of language in the personal, social and educational development of the individual. Such writers and researchers as L. S. Vygotski, A. R. Luria, J. Piaget, B. L. Whorf and B. Bernstein have forced upon us a realization of the interaction of the factors of intelligence, environment and language, and it is clear that we cannot afford to neglect their findings in the educa-tion of teachers for the fullest understanding and development of their pupils. Certainly no superficial study of language will suffice if the teacher is really to be of assistance to his pupils, whatever their country of origin. P. K. C. Millins, Principal of Edge Hill College of Education, has empha-sized this fact in no uncertain terms:

'All students should leave their institutions with a firm grasp of the under-lying principles of modern linguistic theory and practice, and they should be able to adopt a carefully planned oral approach to teaching geared to the intellectual and emotional needs of children and adolescents. Sound language teaching should be closely linked with an understanding of the social and cultural factors as they affect individual children' (20).

It is not our purpose here to go into detail regarding the language problems of immigrants, but perhaps one example will illustrate some of the difficulties. June Derrick makes the point that, at first blush, many un-tutored teachers will imagine that West Indian immigrants have fewer linguistic problems than, for example, Indians or Pakistanis. But Creole English can, in fact, interfere more with the learning of 'Standard British English' than Urdu or Bengali might, if only because it is a related language with its own peculiar grammar, syntax, idiom and vocabulary (21). One thing is clear: the teaching of English to immigrants as a second language requires a different approach from that of teaching English as a native language, and those who teach it require a special sort of training.

The absorption of immigrants into our society is not something that should be tackled piecemeal with a patchwork of 'remedial' exercises, whether in the realm of housing, health or education. It requires a total policy – in fact, a philosophy – for an integrated and pluralistic society, in which all of its members are part and parcel of the integrative process.

It is not a question of 'How can the West Indians (or any other immigrant group) integrate with our society?'. It is a question of how we and the West Indians may best integrate in order to develop a richer, fuller and more viable society. Tolerance is important; and, according to the various polls in the years between 1958 and 1968, the percentage of those who were tolerant and tolerant-inclined increased from 50·6 per cent to 73 per cent (22). But tolerance is not enough. One can tolerate and yet not actively include the other. Nothing short of total inclusion can form a sound philosophy for a multi-cultural society.

Such a policy will require a common cultural programme for all children in our society, to the extent that each at least knows, understands, and can cultivate some sympathy with the customs, beliefs, hopes and aspirations of the other. Integration is not one-sided, nor to use the words of the Rt Hon. Roy Jenkins, M.P. is it to be regarded as

'a flattening process of assimilation but as equal opportunity accompanied by cultural diversity, in an atmosphere of mutual tolerance' (23).

This may be an ideal, but one thing is certain – it cannot be attained without a total programme of inter-cultural education.

REFERENCES

1 D.E.S., *Children and their Primary Schools* (Plowden Report) (H.M.S.O., 1967), p. 73, para. 198.
2 Rose, E. J. B. *et al.*, *Colour and Citizenship: A Report on British Race Relations* (O.U.P., 1969), p. 36.
3 Nandy, D., 'Towards a Multi-Racial Society' in N.C.C.I., *Towards a Multi-Racial Society* (National Committee for Commonwealth Immigrants, 1966), p. 32.
4 Irons, E., 'The immigrants' own contribution' in Hooper, R. (ed.), *Colour in Britain* (B.B.C., 1965), p. 200.

5 Patterson, Sheila, *Dark Strangers* (Penguin, 1965), p. 24.
6 Dollard, J., *Caste and Class in a Southern Town* (Harper, 2nd edition 1949), p. 255.
7 Rose, E. J. B. *et al.*, op. cit., p. 23.
8 Mason, P., 'What is meant by Integration' in N.C.C.I., *Towards a Multi-Racial Society*, p. 7.
9 *Vide* Buber, M., *Between Man and Man* (Collins, The Fontana Library, 1961), pp. 125–31.
10 Patterson, Sheila, op. cit., pp. 21–4. See also E. J. B. Rose *et al.*, op. cit., pp. 23–5 ('A Glossary').
11 Butterworth, E., 'The School and the Community' in N.C.C.I., *Towards a Multi-Racial Society*, pp. 17–21.
12 *Vide* D. E. S., *Statistics of Education, 1968, Volume I: Schools* (H.M.S.O., 1969), para. 31, p. xvii and Table 39, p. 73.
13 D. E. S., *Education and Science in 1969* (H.M.S.O., 1970), para. 38, p. 36.
14 Hashmi, F., 'The Psychology of Prejudice' in N.C.C.I., *Towards a Multi-Racial Society*, p. 8.
15 Nandy, D., op. cit., in note 3, p. 32.
16 See the excellent article by Millins, P. K. C., 'The Preparation of Teachers' in N.C.C.I., *Towards a Multi-Racial Society*, pp. 13–16.
17 *Vide* Community Relations Commission, *Education for a Multi-Cultural Society, 1: Syllabuses* (C.R.C., January 1970).
18 Ibid., p. 1.
19 Derrick, June, 'School – The Meeting Point' in Oakley, R. (ed.), *New Backgrounds* (O.U.P., 1968), Chapter VI, p. 120.
20 Millins, P. K. C., op. cit., in note 16, p. 14.
21 Derrick, June, op. cit., p. 125.
22 Rose, E. J. B., *et al.*, op. cit., p. 593.
23 Quoted by Patterson, Sheila, *Immigration and Race Relations in Britain 1960–1967* (O.U.P., 1969), p. 113. This was from the address of the Rt Hon. Roy Jenkins, M.P., which he gave to a meeting of Voluntary Liaison Committees on May 23, 1966.

GENERAL BIBLIOGRAPHY ON RACE
AND IMMIGRANT PROBLEMS

Adorno, T. W. *et al.*, *The Authoritarian Personality* (Harper, 1950).
Allport, G. W., *The Nature of Prejudice* (Addison-Wesley, 1954).
Banton, M., *White and Coloured* (Jonathan Cape, 1959).
Banton, M., *Race Relations* (Tavistock, 1967).
Barnett, A., *The Human Species* (Penguin, revised edition 1961).
Berger, M., *Race, Equality and the Law* (UNESCO, Paris, 1954).
Bettelheim, B. and Janowitz, M., *Social Change and Prejudice, including Dynamics of Prejudice* (Free Press of Glencoe, 1950).
Bibby, C., *Race, Prejudice and Education* (Heinemann, 1959).
Borrie, W. D. (ed.), *The Cultural Integration of Immigrants* (UNESCO, Paris, 1959).
Bowker, G., *Education of Coloured Immigrants* (Longmans, 1968).
Clarke, R., *The Diversity of Man* (Phœnix House, 1964).
Cmnd. 2379, *Immigration from the Commonwealth* (H.M.S.O., 1965).
Collins, S., *Coloured Minorities in Britain* (Lutterworth Press, 1957).
Community Relations Commission, *Education for a Multi-Cultural Society: 1 Syllabuses* (C.R.C., January 1970).
Community Relations Commission, *The Young Englanders* (C.R.C., 1967).
Daniel, W. W., *Racial Discrimination in England* (Penguin, 1968).
Davison, R. B., *Black British* (O.U.P., 1966).
Deakin, N. (ed.), *Colour and the British Electorate 1964* (Pall Mall Press, 1965).
Derrick, June, *Teaching English to Immigrants* (Longmans, 1966).
D.E.S., *The Commonwealth in Education* (Pamphlet No. 51, H.M.S.O., 1966).
D.E.S., *Children and their Primary Schools* (Plowden Report) (H.M.S.O., 1967), Chapter 6.
D.E.S., *Statistics of Education, 1968, Volume I: Schools* (H.M.S.O., 1969).
D.E.S., *Education and Science in 1969* (H.M.S.O., 1970).
Eisenstadt, S. N., *The Absorption of Immigrants* (Routledge, 1954).
Foot, P., *Immigration and Race in British Politics* (Penguin, 1965).
Goldman, R., *Research and the Teaching of Immigrant Children* (C.R.C., 1967).
Goodman, M. E., *Race Awareness in Young Children* (Collier Books, 1964).
Gorer, G., *Exploring English Character* (Cresset Press, 1955).
Hashmi, F., *Psychology of Racial Prejudice* (National Committee for Commonwealth Immigrants, June 1968).
Hawkes, N., *Immigrant Children in British Schools* (Pall Mall Press, 1966).
Hepple, B., *Race, Jobs and the Law* (Allen Lane, The Penguin Press, 1968).
Hill, C. S. and Matthew, D. (eds.), *Race: A Christian Symposium* (V. Gollancz, 1968).
Hooper, R. (ed.), *Colour in Britain* (B.B.C., 1965).
Hooton, E. A., *Up from the Ape* (Macmillan, 1958).

Hughes, E. C. and H. M., *Where Peoples Meet: Racial and Ethnic Frontiers* (Free Press of Glencoe, 1952).

Klineberg, O., *Race Differences* (Harper, 1935).

Klineberg, O., 'Race and Psychology' (A–129: The Bobbs-Merrill Reprint Series in the Social Sciences, 1951).

Lester, A. and Deakin, N. (eds.), *Policies for Racial Equality* (Fabian Society, 1967).

Lewis, M., *Race and Culture* (UNESCO, Paris, 1952).

Little, K. L., *Race and Society* (UNESCO, Paris, 1952).

Mason, P., *Commonsense About Race* (V. Gollancz, 1961).

Mather, K., *Human Diversity* (Oliver & Boyd, 1964).

Ministry of Education, *English for Immigrants* (Pamphlet No. 43, H.M.S.O., 1963).

National Committee for Commonwealth Immigrants, *Practical Suggestions for Teachers of Immigrant Children* (N.C.C.I., 2nd edition 1968).

National Committee for Commonwealth Immigrants, *Towards a Multi-Racial Society* (N.C.C.I., 1966).

Oakley, R. (ed.), *New Backgrounds* (O.U.P.), Chapters V and VI.

Patterson, Sheila, *Dark Strangers* (Penguin, 1965), Chapters 1, 18 and 19.

Patterson, Sheila, *Immigration and Race Relations in Britain 1960–1967* (O.U.P., 1969), especially Chapters 4 and 7.

Persons, S. (ed.), *Evolutionary Thought in America* (Yale Univ. Press, 1950), Chapter III by Dobzhansky, T. on 'The Genetic Nature of Differences Among Men'.

Political and Economic Planning and Research Services Ltd, *Racial Discrimination in Britain* (P.E.P., 1967).

Richmond, A. H., *Colour and Prejudice in Britain* (Routledge, 1954).

Richmond, A. H., *The Colour Problem* (Penguin, revised edition 1961), Chapters 5, 6 and Postscript.

Rose, A., *The Roots of Prejudice* (UNESCO, Paris, 1951).

Rose, E. J. B. *et al.*, *Colour and Citizenship: A Report on British Race Relations* (O.U.P., 1969), especially Chapters 1, 4, 23, 28 and 33.

Schools Council, *English for the Children of Immigrants* (Working Paper No. 13, H.M.S.O., 1967).

Simpson, G. W. and Yinger, J. M., *Racial and Cultural Minorities: An Analysis of Prejudice and Discrimination* (Harper, 3rd edition 1965).

Stafford-Clark, D., *Prejudice in the Community* (National Committee for Commonwealth Immigrants, new edition 1967).

Stember, C. H., *Education and Attitude Change* (Institute of Human Relations, N.Y., 1961).

Wickenden, J., *Colour in Britain* (O.U.P., 1958).

Yudkin, S., *The Health and Welfare of the Immigrant Child* (National Committee for Commonwealth Immigrants, 1965).

NAME INDEX

NOTE: This index is confined to the names of authors mentioned in the body of the text and in the References, and to historical personages. It does not include the authors of books mentioned in the Bibliographies. The names of geographical locations, peoples, mythological and semi-legendary or fictitious characters are all to be found in the Subject Index.

SUBJECT INDEX

Doaba, 161
Doabs, 169
Dolichocephalic type, 100
Dome of the Rock, 190
Dominica, 21, 26
Dominican Republic, 28
Dravidian, 147, 173
Drinking, 64
Drought, 41
Drugs, 46, 98
Druzes, 195
Dualism, 112
Dukkha, 123
Dungle (Dung-Hill), 47
Duppies, 41, 45, 49, 64
Dutch, 28, 102
Dutch West Indies, 26
Earth Mother, 41
East Africa, 195
East India Company, 102, 193, 210
East Indian Association, 61
East Indian Progressive Society, 39
East Indians, 39, 57–61
Ecstasy, 49
Education, 60, 62, 69–82, 145–57, 210–23
Egalitarians, 133, 235
Egypt, 113
Eightfold Path, 124–6
Élan vital, 42
Elect, 44, 128
Emancipation, 27, 36–7, 61, 69, 70, 124
Emancipation of Slaves Act (1833), 27, 36, 37
Endogamy, 134, 140, 225
Engineering, 152
Enlightenment, 122
Equality, 102, 225
Ernadans, 135
Esoteric rites, 64
Ethiopia, 46–8
Ethnocentrism, 236
Eunomia, 75
Ewe, 81
Extended family, 63, 139–43, 202–8
Extra-marital intercourse, 163
Extra-residential mating, 52
Facial traits, 100
Faithful concubinage, 53–7
Fakirs, 16
Familial structure, 52–7
Family, 52–7, 139–43, 202–8, 238
Family planning, 95, 141–3
Fertility, 33, 41, 57
Flagellation, 43
Florida, 25
Folk stories, 65
Fornication, 200
Four Noble Truths, 123–4
France, 193
Fraternity, 102
Freedom, 27, 36–7, 43, 47, 70, 103
French, 28, 58, 102
Fruits, 24–5
Fundamentalism, 35, 49
Gabriel, 182, 185
Gambling, 34
Ganga, 47
Genesis, 40
Geography, 74

Geometry, 74
Georgetown (Guyana), 60–2
Germany, 43
Ghatikas, 146
Ghazni, 175
Ghettos, 15, 87–8, 237
Glossolalia, 46
Gold, 25, 98
Govinda, 114
Grandmother family, 55
Great Awakening, 43
Greater Antilles, 32, 58
Greece, 40, 113
Grenada, 21
Gross National Product (GNP), 115, 210, 221
Guianas, 26
Gujarat, 98, 149, 152, 158
Gujaratis, 148–9, 159, 160, 164
Gurdwaras, 17, 129, 163–4
Gurmukhi script, 163
Gurus, 116, 124, 128–9
Guyana, 23, 28, 31, 33, 52, 57–63, 71, 80, 86, 239
Habiru, 179
Hair, 58–9, 99
Haiti, 28, 34, 46
Harappa, 16, 100, 101, 116, 145
Harems, 203
Harijan days, 138
Harijans, 109, 136
Harijan weeks, 138
Hashishis, 195
Hatha Yoga, 116
Head formation, 100
Healing, 44
Hebrews, 179
Hejaz, 184
Herrenvolk theory, 133–4
High gods, 40
Hijra (Hegira), 184
Himalayas, 95, 121
Himsa, 119
Hindi, 81, 147–50
Hindsa, 101
Hindu culture, 61, 71, 139, 158–9
Hinduism, 37–9, 99–101, 106–17, 129
Hindus, 61, 71, 106–17, 139, 146, 161–2, 176, 203
Hindustan, 95
Hindustani, 147
Iberian colonists, 69
Iblis, 182
Ibo, 41
Identity, 16
Idolatry, 180–1, 224
Illegitimacy, 52, 57, 64
Illiteracy, 142, 145–6, 213
Illusion, 112, 115
Imam, 188, 194, 231
Immaculate conception, 121
Immanence, 42
Incarnation, 114
Incas, 25
Inclusion, 238
Indecency, 200
Indentured labour, 28, 37–9
India, 28, 93–166, 193
Indian Mutiny, 102, 193

252

Metalwork, 76
Methodists, 32, 44, 70
Methodology, 72, 154
Mica, 98
Mico College, 72
Middle Way, 123
Migration, 83–90, 174, 226 *et passim*
Millet, 98, 171
Minerals, 24, 98
Mirpur, 174, 199, 211, 225, 232
Mirpuris, 202, 227
Missionaries, 35–6, 43, 62, 70, 217
Mmotia, 41
Modus vivendi, 237
Mogul (Mughal), 101
Moguls, 176, 193
Mohenjo-Daro, 16, 100, 106
Moksha, 112, 115, 118–20
Mona (Kingston), 78
Monism, 112
Mon-Khmer, 147
Monophysites, 180
Monotheism, 112, 129, 186
Monsoon, 97
Montserrat, 21
Moors, 37
Morant Bay, 37, 43
Moravians, 35, 37, 70, 73
Mores, 15, 26, 56, 224, 228
Mosque, 146, 231
Mother-substitute, 64
Mt Everest, 95
Muezzin, 189
Muhajirs, 177
'Muhammadan', 185
Mukti, 120
Mulatto, 58
Multi-cultural society, 49, 71, 90, 243, 236, 238, 242
Multi-racial society, 15–18, 49, 71, 73, 90
Mushrik, 184
Music, 65, 74
Muslim culture, 71, 158
Muslim League, 176
Muslims (Moslems), 37–9, 101, 127, 146, 148, 179–209, 224–32, 239
Mustee, 58
Musteffino, 58
Myal, 45
Mysticism, 17, 127, 195
Myths, 32, 40, 106, 109
Nagaland, 152
Nag Hammadi, 113
Nam, 129
National Literacy Corps, 217, 222
Native Baptist Movement, 35
Nayadis, 135
Negritos, 100
Negritude, 90
Negroids, 100
Nepal, 95
Nestorians, 180
Neti, neti, 112, 115
Nigeria, 26
Nihilism, 118
Nint Night, 65–6
Nirvana, 115, 125
Noble Eightfold Path, 124–6
Nomad, 179

Non-duality, 115
Nordics, 106
Ntikuma, 51
Nuclear family, 55, 139, 229
Obeah, 42–9, 64
Obscenity, 64–5
Official Languages (Amendment) Act (1967), 149
Oil, 24, 98
Oil-seeds, 171
Outcasts, 108–9
Pacifists, 120
Paganism, 16
Pahul, 129
Pakistan, 23, 95, 127, 148, 150, 175–7, 194
Pakistanis, 102, 162, 164, 167–234
Palestine, 193
Pali, 145
Panchayat, 103
Panchayati raj, 103
Panentheism, 112
Panontism, 112
Pantheism, 112
Papayas, 25
Paper-making, 98–9
Papua, 35
Paradise, 187
Paranormal activity, 42
Pariahs, 108, 136
Parsees, 101
Partiality, 17
Participation mystique, 42
Partition, 169, 175–7, 202, 212
Pathans, 173, 199, 231
Patois, 62
Patriarchate, 53
Peanuts, 25, 98
Pentecostalists, 32, 49, 50
People's National Party, 48
Perennial philosophy, 16, 130
Persia, 101, 181, 192–3
Personality, 123
Peshawar, 221
Petroleum, 24, 98
Phallicism, 40
Pharmaceuticals, 98
Pidgin, 85
Pig, 201–2, 236
Pigmentation, 99
Pilgrimage (*hajj*), 188
Pirateers, 34
Pitch, 24
Planters, 24, 34–7, 43, 53, 76
Plowden Report, 234
Pluralism, 90, 238–9
Pluralistic integration, 238
Pocomania, 32, 42–6, 49
Pogroms, 43
Poitiers, 193
Pollution, 110, 135–6
Polygamy, 44, 52, 56, 190, 203, 227
Polygyny, 204
Polytechnics, 154
Polytheism, 49, 112, 180–1, 184, 224
Population density, 95, 141–2
Portland (Jamaica), 24
Portugal, 43
'Portugals', 43
Portuguese, 26, 28, 58, 60, 102